# Pro Microservices in .NET 6

## With Examples Using ASP.NET Core 6, MassTransit, and Kubernetes

Sean Whitesell
Rob Richardson
Matthew D. Groves

*Foreword by Scott Hunter*
*VP Director, Azure Developer Experience*
*Microsoft*

Apress®

*Pro Microservices in .NET 6: With Examples Using ASP.NET Core 6, MassTransit, and Kubernetes*

Sean Whitesell
KIEFER, OK, USA

Rob Richardson
Gilbert, AZ, USA

Matthew D. Groves
Grove City, OH, USA

ISBN-13 (pbk): 978-1-4842-7832-1
https://doi.org/10.1007/978-1-4842-7833-8

ISBN-13 (electronic): 978-1-4842-7833-8

Managing Director, Apress Media LLC: Welmoed Spahr
Acquisitions Editor: Joan Murray
Development Editor: Laura Berendson
Coordinating Editor: Jill Balzano

Cover designed by eStudioCalamar

Cover image designed by Freepik (www.freepik.com)

Distributed to the book trade worldwide by Springer Science+Business Media LLC, 1 New York Plaza, Suite 4600, New York, NY 10004. Phone 1-800-SPRINGER, fax (201) 348-4505, e-mail orders-ny@springer-sbm. com, or visit www.springeronline.com. Apress Media, LLC is a California LLC and the sole member (owner) is Springer Science + Business Media Finance Inc (SSBM Finance Inc). SSBM Finance Inc is a **Delaware** corporation.

For information on translations, please e-mail booktranslations@springernature.com; for reprint, paperback, or audio rights, please e-mail bookpermissions@springernature.com.

Apress titles may be purchased in bulk for academic, corporate, or promotional use. eBook versions and licenses are also available for most titles. For more information, reference our Print and eBook Bulk Sales web page at http://www.apress.com/bulk-sales.

Any source code or other supplementary material referenced by the author in this book is available to readers on GitHub via the book's product page, located at www.apress.com/9781484278321. For more detailed information, please visit http://www.apress.com/source-code.

Printed on acid-free paper

*This book is dedicated to you, the reader. Writing good software is hard enough. Learning and conquering the development of microservices is an even greater challenge. I hope this book serves you well in your journey to developing great solutions for your users.*

# Table of Contents

# About the Authors

**Sean Whitesell** is a Microsoft MVP and cloud architect at TokenEx, where he designs cloud-based architectural solutions for hosting internal services for TokenEx. He serves as President of the Tulsa Developers Association. He regularly presents in the community at developer events, conferences, and local meetups.

**Rob Richardson** is a software craftsman, building web properties in ASP.NET and Node, React, and Vue. He is a Microsoft MVP; published author; frequent speaker at conferences, user groups, and community events; and a diligent teacher and student of high-quality software development. You can find his recent work at robrich.org/presentations.

**Matthew D. Groves** is a Microsoft MVP who loves to code. From C# to jQuery, or PHP, he will submit pull requests for anything. He got his start writing a QuickBASIC point-of-sale app for his parents' pizza shop back in the 1990s. Currently a Product Marketing Manager for Couchbase, he is the author of the book *AOP in .NET* and created the video "Creating and Managing Your First Couchbase Cluster."

# About the Technical Reviewer

**Mike Benkovich** A developer, business owner, consultant, cloud architect, Microsoft Azure MVP, and an online instructor, **Mike Benkovich** is an alumni of Microsoft from 2004 to 2012 where he helped build developer communities across the United States, through work on Microsoft Across America, MSDN Events, MSDN Webcasts, DPE, and Channel 9. He's helped to create and grow developer conferences and user groups in various cities across the United States. While at Microsoft he helped create the Azure Boot Camp events that were run in cities across the United States and at PDC and TechEd before it was transferred to the community.

In his spare time he helped start a Toastmaster club for Geeks called TechMasters in Minneapolis where we grow speakers for conferences. He's a LinkedIn Learning Instructor for Azure, having developed many online courses. Mike actively works in Azure Cloud Governance, Application Architecture, and Software Delivery consulting.

# About the Technical Reviewer

# Acknowledgments

There are challenges, and there are life goals. Writing this book has certainly been an accomplishment of a life goal. I could not have done this alone. There are people in my life that have given phenomenal support, and I'm eternally grateful.

To the Lord for helping me through challenging times, especially the ones I get myself into.

To my wife and biggest cheerleader, Barb, thank you for your unceasing support. It is so much more than I deserve. You have been so understanding of my goals and the challenges that come along with them. To my daughter McKayla, you are my gem and are the reason I fight hard to be a good dad. Remember, the best goals are worth fighting for.

To Michael Perry, I can't thank you enough. Your willingness to help me is amazing. I appreciate our discussions, where I get to learn so much from you. I'm thankful I got to learn from your book *The Art of Immutable Architecture*. Details in your book really helped this book and me as an architect.

To Floyd May, thank you so much for your friendship and our time on the whiteboard discussing microservices. I really appreciate your guidance.

To Phil Japikse, thank you so much for helping me get started with this book project. I appreciate your guidance throughout this book.

To Josh Brown, thank you so much brother for helping to spur ideas and the great discussions about databases.

To Rob Richardson and Matt Groves, thank you for helping me get this book done. I appreciate being able to lean on your expertise.

—Sean Whitesell

I would like to thank the Lord whose inspiration I rely on daily. His help has been instrumental in accomplishing this work.

—Rob Richardson

I'd like to acknowledge my patient wife Ali, Kevin and Mary Groves, and all of my Twitch audience that helped me to learn this microservices stuff.

—Matt Groves

# Foreword

Software development is in the middle of a revolution. Moving away from monolithic application development with a team working on a large project that ships on a slow cadence to microservice based development where the application is broken into smaller pieces, which version independently, are built by smaller teams and ship on a fast cadence. .NET 6 is part of the revolution of .NET that makes it the perfect framework for building these microservice based applications.

.NET was re-imagined starting in 2016 to be the highest performance full stack development framework running across Linux, macOS and Windows on x86, x64, Arm32, Arm64 and M1 architectures. It includes support for cross platform RPC with gRPC, support for API's with Web API and Minimal API's and support for services with Worker Template.

Sean, Rob, and Matt have been building microservices in .NET and speaking on this form of development for many years. This book will help you learn how to build modern applications with microservices using the latest version of .NET.

I'm excited to see what you will build!

Scott Hunter

VP Director, Azure Developer Experience

Microsoft

# Introduction

The microservice architecture breaks software into smaller pieces that can be independently deployed, scaled, and replaced. There are many benefits to this modern architecture, but there are more moving pieces.

In the olden days, we compiled the entire software product into one piece and deployed it infrequently. Deployment was hard, so we opted not to do it very often. With the advent of containers, deployment has become much easier. We can now break our application into lots of little pieces – microservices. When one microservice needs more horsepower, we can scale up only this portion of the web property. If a feature needs to work differently, we can deploy only this microservice, avoiding the churn with the entire system.

With this power come some additional layers of complexity. In the legacy monolithic software applications, we merely made a function call if we wanted to call into another part of the system. Our internal methods now have IP addresses, multiple instances, maybe load balancers distributing the load, and many more moving pieces.

How do we discover the address of the microservice? How do we scale to just the right level of availability without wasted cost? This is the magic of microservices, and this is the purpose of this book. You'll learn how to design, architect, scale, monitor, and containerize applications to build robust and scalable microservices.

## Who Should Read This Book

In some respect, anyone involved with software projects related to distributed architecture should read this book. Even if a software project is not a distributed architecture but may become one, this book will shed some light on understanding existing business processes that may need to be handled by microservices.

From development managers to product owners to developers will find this book useful in understanding many complexities of a microservices architecture. Application architects and developers will gain quick insight with the hands-on code samples. The step-by-step coding approach covers examples with direct microservice calls as well as by messaging communication.

# Book Organization

The microservices architecture is multifaceted and complex. Chapter 1 covers many of the subjects involved in this architecture style. Chapter 2 covers the advancements of .NET 6. In Chapter 3, we use a fictional story to help convey the purpose of breaking apart a monolithic application to a microservices architecture. We cover using Event Storming and Domain-Driven Design tenants to help understand existing business processes to determine where and why to create a microservice.

In Chapter 4, we cover direct communication with microservices. This chapter is also where you begin creating microservices using Visual Studio 2022 with .NET 6. Chapter 5 covers the messaging communication style. Also, you will create more microservices that communicate using MassTransit for messaging.

Chapter 6 covers breaking apart data from a centralized data store to distributed data stores. We also cover Saga patterns for handling transactions across multiple systems.

In Chapter 7, we cover testing the microservices using direct communication. We also cover testing the microservices that communicate using messaging. You will create the test projects for both communication styles.

Chapter 8 covers hosting microservices in Docker containers as well as using Kubernetes. By understanding containerization options, you understand how to handle the scaling of microservices.

In Chapter 9, we cover health concerns for microservices. The microservices developed in earlier chapters only have business logic. This chapter covers logging concerns, gathering metrics, tracing, and points for debugging.

# CHAPTER 1

# Introducing Microservices

Twitter, PayPal, and Netflix had serious problems. Problems like scaling, quality, and downtime became common and increasing issues. Each had a large, single-code base application known as a "monolith." And each hit different frustration points where a fundamental architecture change had to occur. Development and deployment cycles were long and tedious, causing delays in feature delivery. Each deployment meant downtime or expensive infrastructure to switch from one set of servers to another. As the code base grew, so did the coupling between modules. With coupled modules, code changes are more problematic, harder to test, and lower overall application quality.

For Twitter, scaling servers was a huge factor that caused downtime and upset users. All too often, users would see an error page stating Twitter is overcapacity. Many users would see the "Fail Whale" while the system administrators would reboot servers and deal with the demand. As the number of users increased, so did the need for architecture changes. From the data stores, code, and server topology, the monolithic architecture hit its limit.

For PayPal, their user base increased the need for guaranteed transactions. They scaled up servers and network infrastructure. But, with the growing number of services, the performance hit a tipping point, and latency was the result. They continuously increased the number of virtual machines to process the growing number of users and transactions. This added tremendous pressure on the network, thereby causing latency issues.

Netflix encountered problems with scaling, availability, and speed of development. Their business required 24 × 7 access to their video streams. They were in a position where they could not build data centers fast enough to accommodate the demand. Their user base was increasing, and so were the networking speeds at homes and on devices. The monolithic application was so complex and fragile that a single semicolon took down the website for several hours.

1

© Sean Whitesell, Rob Richardson, Matthew D. Groves 2022
S. Whitesell et al., *Pro Microservices in .NET 6*, https://doi.org/10.1007/978-1-4842-7833-8_1

In and of themselves, there is nothing wrong with a monolith. Monoliths serve their purpose, and when they need more server resources, it is usually cheap enough to add more servers. With good coding practices, a monolith can sustain itself very well. However, as they grow and complexity increases, they can reach a point that feature requests take longer and longer to implement. They turn into "monolith hell." It takes longer to get features to production, the number of bugs increases, and frustration grows with the users. Monolith hell is a condition the monolith has when it suffers from decreased stability, difficulty scaling, and nearly impossible to leverage new technologies.

Applications can grow into a burden over time. With changes in developers, skillsets, business priorities, etc., those applications can easily turn into a "spaghetti code" mess. As the demands of those applications change, so do the expectations with speed of development, testing, and deployment. By pulling functionality away from monolithic applications, development teams can narrow their focus on functionality and respective deployment schedule. This allows a faster pace of development and deployment of business functionality.

In this chapter, you will learn about the benefits of using a microservices architecture and the challenges of architecture changes. You will then learn about the differences between a monolithic architecture and a microservices architecture. Next, we will begin looking at microservices patterns, messaging, and testing. Finally, we will cover deploying microservices and examine the architectured infrastructure with cross-cutting concerns.

# Benefits

For large applications suffering from "monolith hell," there are several reasons they may benefit by converting to a microservice architecture. Development teams can be more focused on business processes, code quality, and deployment schedules. Microservices scale separately, allowing efficient usage of resources on infrastructure. As communication issues and other faults occur, isolation helps keep a system highly available. Lastly, with architectural boundaries defined and maintained, the system can adapt to changes with greater ease. The details of each benefit are defined in the following.

# Team Autonomy

One of the biggest benefits of using a microservice architecture is team autonomy. Companies constantly need to deliver more features in production in the fastest way possible. By separating areas of concern in the architecture, development teams can have autonomy from other teams. This autonomy allows teams to develop and deploy at a pace different than others. Time to market is essential for most companies. The sooner features are in production, the sooner they may have a competitive edge over competitors.

It also allows for but does not require different teams to leverage different programming languages. Monoliths typically require the whole code base to be in the same language. Because microservices are distinctly different applications, they open the door to using different languages, allowing flexibility in fitting the tool to the task at hand.

With data analytics, for example, Python is the most common programming language used and works well in microservice architectures. Mobile and front-end web developers can leverage languages best suited for those requirements, while C# is used with back-end business transaction logic.

With teams dedicated to one or more microservices, they only hold the responsibility for their services. They only focus on their code without the need to know details of code in other areas. Communication will need to be done regarding the API endpoints of the microservices. Clients need to know how to call these services with details such as HTTP verb and payload model, as well as the return data model. There is an API specification available to help guide the structure of your API. Consider the OpenAPI Initiative (https://www.openapis.org/) for more information.

# Service Autonomy

As team autonomy focuses on the development teams and their responsibilities, service autonomy is about separating concerns at the service layer. The "Single Responsibility Principle" applies here as well. No microservice should have more than one reason to change. For example, an Order Management microservice should not also consist of business logic for Account Management. By having a microservice dedicated to specific business processes, the services can evolve independently.

Not all microservices exist alone with the processing of business logic. It is common to have microservices call others based on the data to process. The coupling is still loose and maintains the flexibility of code evolution.

With loose coupling between microservices, you receive the same benefits as when applied at the code level. Upgrading microservices is easier and has less impact on other services. This also allows for features and business processes to evolve at different paces.

The autonomy between microservices allows for individual resiliency and availability needs. For example, the microservice handling credit card payment has a higher availability requirement than handling account management. Clients can use retry and error handling policies with different parameters based on the services they are using.

Deployment of microservices is also a benefit of service autonomy. As the services evolve, they release separately using "Continuous Integration/Continuous Deployment" (CI/CD) tools like Azure DevOps, Jenkins, and CircleCI. Individual deployment allows frequent releases with minimal, if any, impact on other services. It also allows separate deployment frequency and complexity than with monolithic applications. This supports the requirement of zero downtime. You can configure a deployment strategy to bring up an updated version before taking down existing services.

## Scalability

The benefit of scalability allows for the number of instances of services to differentiate between other services and a monolithic application. Generally, monolithic applications require larger servers than those needed for microservices. Having microservices lets multiple instances reside on the same server or across multiple servers, which aids in fault isolation. Figure 1-1 shows a relationship between the number of code instances and the size of the code.

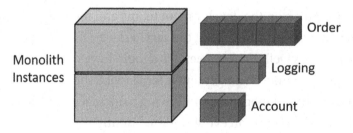

*Figure 1-1.* *Example of instance and size of code*

By utilizing a microservice architecture, the applications can leverage servers of diverse sizes. One microservice may need more CPU than RAM, while others require more in-memory processing capabilities. Other microservices may only need enough CPU and RAM to handle heavy I/O needs.

Another benefit of having microservices on different servers than the monolith is the diversity of programming languages. For example, assuming the monolith runs .NET Framework, you can write microservices in other programming languages. If these languages can run on Linux, then you have the potential of saving money due to the operating system license cost.

# Fault Isolation

Fault isolation is about handling failures without them taking down an entire system. When a monolith instance goes down, all services in that instance also go down. There is no isolation of services when failures occur. Several things can cause failure:

- Coding or data issues

- Extreme CPU and RAM utilization

- Network

- Server hardware

- Downstream systems

With a microservice architecture, services with any of the preceding conditions will not take down other parts of the system. Think of this as a logical grouping. In one group are services and dependent systems that pertain to a business function. The functionality is separate from those in another group. If a failure occurs in one group, the effects do not spread to another group. Figure 1-2 is an oversimplification of services dependent on other services and a dependency on a data store.

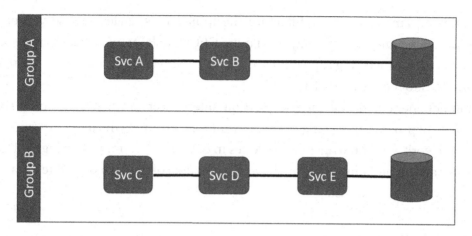

***Figure 1-2.*** *Depiction of fault isolation*

As with any application that relies on remote processing, opportunities for failures are always present. When microservices either restart or are upgraded, any existing connections will be cut. Always consider microservices ephemeral. They will die and need to be restarted at some point. This may be from prolonged CPU or RAM usage exceeding a threshold. Orchestrators like Kubernetes will "evict" a pod that contains an instance of the microservice in those conditions. This is a self-preservation mechanism, so a runaway condition does not take down the server/node.

An unreasonable goal is to have a microservice with an uptime of 100% or 99.999% of the time. If a monolithic application or another microservice is calling a microservice, then retry policies must be in place to handle the absence or disappearance of the microservice. This is no different than having a monolithic application connecting with a SQL Server. It is the responsibility of the calling code to handle the various associated exceptions and react accordingly.

Retry policies in a circuit breaker pattern help tremendously in handling issues when calling microservices. Libraries such as Polly (http://www.thepollyproject.org) provide the ability to use a circuit breaker, retry policy, and others. This allows calling code to react to connection issues by retrying with progressive wait periods, then using an alternative code path if calls to the microservice fail X number of times.

## Data Autonomy

So far, there have been many reasons presented for using a microservice architecture. But they focus on the business processes. The data is just as important, if not more so. Monolithic applications with the symptoms described earlier most certainly rely on a data store. Data integrity is crucial to the business. Without data integrity, no company will stay in business for long. Can you imagine a bank that "guesses" your account balance?

Microservices incorporate loose coupling, so changes deploy independently. Most often, these changes also contain schema changes to the data. New features may require new columns or a change to an existing column, as well as for tables. The real issue occurs when the schema change from one team impacts others. This, in turn, requires the changes to be backward compatible. Additionally, the other team affected may not be ready to deploy at the same time.

Having data isolated per microservice allows independent changes to occur with minimal impact on others. This isolation is another factor that encourages quicker time to production for the business. Starting a new feature with a new microservice with new data is great. Of course, that is easy to implement.

With separate databases, you also get the benefit of using differing data store technologies. Having separate databases provides an opportunity for some data to be in a relational database like SQL Server, while others are in non-relational databases like MongoDB, Azure Cosmos DB, and Azure Table Storage. Having a choice of different databases is another example of using the right tool for the job.

## Challenges to Consider

Migrating to a microservice architecture is not pain-free and is more complex than monoliths. You will need to give yourself room to fail. Even with a small microservice, it may take several iterations to get to exactly what you need. And you may need to complete many rounds of refactoring on the monolith before you can support relocating functionality to a microservice. Developing microservices requires a new way of thinking about the existing architecture, such as the cost of development time and infrastructure changes to networks and servers.

If coming from a monolith, you will need to make code changes to communicate with the new microservice instead of just a simple method call. Communicating with microservices requires calls over a network and, most often, using a messaging broker. You will learn more about messaging later in this chapter.

The size of the monolithic applications and team sizes are also factors. Small applications, or large applications with small teams, may not see the benefits. The benefits of a microservice architecture appear when the overwhelming problems of "monolith hell" are conquered by separating areas.

Many companies are not ready to take on the challenges and simply host monolithic applications on additional servers and govern what business logic they process. Servers are relatively cheap, so spreading the processing load is usually the easiest "quick" solution. That is until they end up with the same issues as PayPal, Twitter, and others.

Developers may push back on the idea of microservice development. There is a large learning curve for the intricate details that need to be understood. And many developers will remain responsible for various parts of the monolithic applications, so it may feel like working on two projects simultaneously. There will be the ongoing question of quality vs. just getting something to production. Cutting corners will only add code fragility and technical debt and may prolong a successful completion.

A challenge every team will face is code competency. Developers must take the initiative to be strong with the programming language chosen and embrace distributed system design. Design patterns and best practices are great as they relate to the code in monoliths and inside the microservices. But new patterns must also be learned with how microservices communicate, handling failures, dependencies, and data consistency.

Another challenge for teams developing microservices is that there is more than code to consider. In the later section on "Cross-Cutting Concerns," items are described that affect every microservice, therefore every developer. Everyone should be involved in understanding (if not also creating) the items that help you understand the health of the architectural system. User stories or whatever task-based system you use will need additional time and tasks. This includes helping with testing the system and not just the microservices.

# Microservice Beginning

With a primary system needing to work with other systems, there arose an issue of the primary system being required to know all the communication details of each connected system. The primary system, in this case, is your main application. Since each connected system had its own way of storing information, services it provided, and communication method, the primary system had to know all these details. This is a "tightly coupled" architecture. Suppose one of the connected systems changes to another system, a tremendous amount of change was required. Service-Oriented Architecture (SOA) aimed to eliminate the hassle and confusion. By using a standard communication method, each system could interact with less coupling.

The Enterprise Service Bus (ESB), introduced in 2002, was used to communicate messages to the various systems. An ESB provides a way for a "Publish/Subscribe" model in which each system could work with or ignore the message as they were broadcasted. Security, routing, and guaranteed message delivery are also aspects of an ESB.

When needing to scale a service, the whole infrastructure had to scale as well. With microservices, each service can scale independently. By shifting from ESB to protocols like HTTP, the endpoints become more intelligent about what and how to communicate. The messaging platform is no longer required to know the message payload, only the endpoint to give it to. "Smart Endpoints, Dumb Pipes" is how Martin Fowler succinctly stated.

So why now, in the last few years, have microservices gained attention? With the cost of supportive infrastructure, it is cheaper to build code and test to see if one or more microservices are the right way to go. Network and CPU have tremendously increased in power and are far more cost-effective today than yesteryear. Today, we can crunch through substantial amounts of data using mathematical models with data analytics and are gaining knowledge at a faster rate. For only $35, a Raspberry Pi can be bought and utilized to host microservices!

Cost is a huge factor, but so are the programming languages and platforms. Today, more than a handful of languages like C#, Python, and Node are great for microservices. Platforms like Kubernetes, Service Fabric, and others are vastly capable of maintaining microservices running in Docker containers. There are also far more programmers in the industry that can quickly take advantage of architectural patterns like SOA and microservices.

With the ever-increasing demand for software programmers, there also exists the demand for quality. It is way too easy for programmers to solve simple problems and believe they are "done." In reality, quality software is highly demanding of our time, talents, and patience. Just because microservices are cheaper and, in some cases, easier to create, they are by no means easy.

# Architecture Comparison

Since most microservices stem from a monolithic application, we will compare the two architectures. Monoliths are the easiest to create, so it is no surprise this architecture is the de facto standard when creating applications. Companies need new features quickly for a competitive edge over others. The better and quicker the feature is in production, the sooner anticipated profits are obtained. So, as nearly all applications do, they grow. The code base grows in size, complexity, and fragility. In Figure 1-3, a monolith is depicted that contains a user interface layer, a business logic layer with multiple services, and a persistence layer.

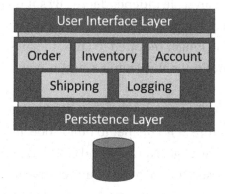

***Figure 1-3.*** *Depiction of three-tier architecture*

A monolith, in the simplest term, is a single executable containing business logic. This includes all the supportive DLLs. When a monolith deploys, functionality stops and is replaced. Each service (or component) in a monolith runs "in process." This means that each instance of the monolith has the entire code base ready for instantiation.

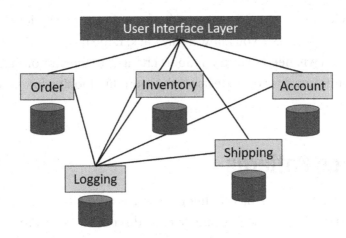

**Figure 1-4.** *Example of microservice architecture*

With the microservice architecture, shown in Figure 1-4, business logic is separated out into out-of-process executables. This allows them to have many instances of each running on different servers. As mentioned earlier, fault isolation is gained with this separation. If, for example, shipping was unavailable for a while, orders would still be able to be taken.

What is most realistic is the hybrid architecture, shown in Figure 1-5. Few companies fully transition to a microservice architecture completely. Many companies will take a sliver of functionality and partially migrate to a microservice solution.

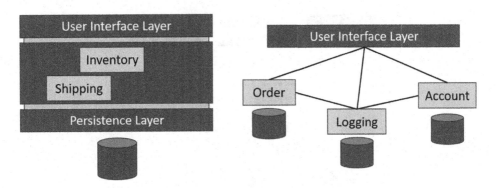

**Figure 1-5.** *Depiction of hybrid architecture*

When migrating from a monolithic to a microservice architecture, there is a huge danger when too much business functionality is in one microservice. For example, if the order microservice has tight coupling in the code with inventory management, and all of that logic was brought over, then you end up with a distributed monolith. You have gained some separation benefits while retaining many of the burdens the monolith has.

When you decide to venture down the path of creating microservices, start small. By starting with a small code base, you allow a way back. If the microservice is beyond time, cost, or patience, you will need to undo or abort changes to the monolith. While making these changes, continuously execute tests on the monolith looking for breaking code you did not expect.

# Microservice Patterns

Every microservice architecture has challenges such as accessibility, obtaining configuration information, messaging, and service discovery. There are common solutions to these challenges called patterns. Various patterns exist to help solve these challenges and make the architecture solid.

## API Gateway/BFF

The API Gateway pattern provides a single endpoint for client applications to the microservices assigned to it. Figure 1-6 shows a single API Gateway as an access point for multiple microservices. API Gateways provide functionality such as routing to microservices, authentication, and load balancing.

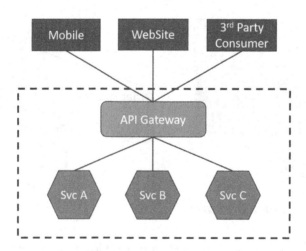

*Figure 1-6.* *Single API Gateway access point*

Depending on the scale of the architecture and business needs, a single API Gateway may cause another problem. The number of client applications may increase. The demands from those client applications may grow. At some point, separation should be done to split client applications apart by using multiple API Gateways. Design pattern Backends for Frontends (BFF), helps with this segregation. There are multiple endpoints, but they are designated based on the types of clients being served.

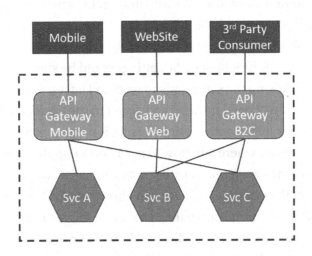

***Figure 1-7.***  *Designated API Gateway endpoints*

In this example, depicted in Figure 1-7, one application calling the microservices could be an MVC web application, whereas another client could be a mobile application. Also depicted is for connections from 3rd party consumers.

Mobile clients usually do not get/need all the content compared to a full website. Using the BFF pattern with API Gateways allows for that separation of handling the differences.

Consider the end user may be responsible for data usage charges. If the mobile application does not need that much information "ready" compared to the full website version, then the separation of end-user view management calls for the BFF pattern.

There are precautions when using an API Gateway pattern. There is a coupling of microservices to the API Gateway. As microservices evolve, so does the infrastructure. API Gateways must be maintained so there is not too much coupling. An API Gateway should not be more responsible than necessary. There may be a point at which multiple API Gateways are created, and microservices split between them. This would help with another precaution where the API Gateway can be a bottleneck and may add to any latency issues.

# External Configuration Store

Nearly all microservices will need configuration information, just like monoliths. With the ability to have many microservices instances, it would be impractical for each instance to have its own configuration files. Updating information across all running instances would be overwhelming. Instead, using the External Configuration Store pattern provides a common area to store configuration information. This means there is one source of the configuration values.

The configuration information could be stored in a data store such as SQL Server or Azure Cosmos DB. Environment-specific settings could be stored in different Configuration Stores allowing the same code to work in Dev vs. Staging or Production. Of course, each instance will need to know how to get to the Configuration Store. This information is in the local configuration files. This means there is just enough information in these files on where and how to get all other application settings.

The information in the Configuration Store may change at any time. A challenge here is knowing when to get the settings. The code can either get all the settings at startup or as needed. If only retrieving at startup, then the behavior of the microservice will not change until restarted. With some settings, this is fine, such as retrieving the environment it is running in. This may be useful with logging. If the microservice is running in Dev, then the verbosity of logging is much higher. If not Dev, then only log the additional information in certain conditions like error handling. That setting is not likely to change. Some settings do change and should be checked often. Settings like an HTTP timeout value or a maximum number of retries in a business function may change and affect the behavior.

# Messaging

As microservices are designed to fit various business needs, their communication methods must also be considered. With monolithic applications, methods simply call other methods without the need to worry about where that method resides. With distributed computing, those methods are on other servers. Interprocess communication (IPC) mechanisms are used to communicate with microservices since they are over a network.

There are three main aspects of communication with microservices. Business processes and use cases help determine the layout of messaging needs. These determine the "why" there is communication with microservices. The "what" is the data format.

Not all contents in the messages are the same, and they will vary based on purpose. Lastly, transport mechanisms are used to transfer message content between processes. This covers the "how" messages are sent to endpoints.

# Business Process Communication

There are multiple ways of communicating between business processes in a microservices architecture. The simplest but least versatile method is using synchronous calls. The three other ways are asynchronous and provide various message delivery methods.

## RPC

The synchronous, "direct" way is for when a request needs an immediate response. For example, a microservice has a financial algorithm and responds with data based on the values passed into the request. The client (monolith client or another microservice) supplies the parameter values, sends the request, and waits for the response. The business process does not continue until it has received an answer or an error. This type of call is a Remote Procedure Call (RPC) as it is direct and synchronous, from the client to the service. Using RPC should be limited in use. These have a high potential of adding unnecessary latency for the client and should only be used when the processing inside the microservice is small.

## Fire-and-Forget

The first type of asynchronous call is a "fire-and-forget" style. The client does not care if the microservice can complete the request. An example of this style is logging. A business process may need specific information to be logged, but the need to continue processing outweighs the need to verify the microservice completed successfully.

## Callback

Another style of asynchronous call is when the microservice calls back to the client, notifying when it is done processing. The business process continues after sending the request. The request contains information for how the microservice is to send the response. This requires the client to open ports to receive the calls and passing the address and port number in the request. With many calls occurring, there is a need to match the response to the request. When passing a correlation ID in the request message and the microservice persisting that information to the response, the client can use the response for further processing.

Consider the example of a barista. You place your order for a latte. The barista takes down the type of drink and your name. Then two parallel processes occur. One is the process of creating the drink. The other is processing payment. Only after the drink is ready and payment succeeds are you called. "Sean, your latte is ready." Notice there are two pieces of information used as a correlation ID. The customer's name and the drink name were taken at the time of the order and used to tell the customer the order has completed.

This example also shows a synchronous business process. I did not start waiting for the drink until after the order was taken. Then two asynchronous processes occurred: one to create the drink and the other to take payment. After those two processes were completed, another asynchronous process was initiated. I was notified the drink is ready and where to pick it up. During the time the latte is being made, I could read a newspaper or even cancel the order. This notification is called a "domain event."

# Pub/Sub

This leads to another asynchronous call style, Publish/Subscribe (Pub/Sub). This is a way of listening on a message bus for messages about work to process. The sender publishes a message for all the listeners to react on their own based on the message. A comparison of the Pub/Sub model is a newspaper company. It publishes a single issue daily to multiple subscribers. Each subscriber has the opportunity to read and react independently to the same content as all other subscribers.

A persistent-based Pub/Sub model is where only one instance of a listener works on the message. Building on the "fire-and-forget" model mentioned earlier is the logging example. As an event that requires logging occurs, a message is created containing content to be written. Without persistence, each subscriber would log the message and cause duplicate records. Using the persistence model, one subscriber locks the message for processing. Other listeners may pick up the next message, but only one message is processed. Now, only one log entry is created for each event. If the subscriber fails to complete their task, then the message is aborted, and another subscriber can pick it up for processing.

# Message Format

The format of the data in the messages allows your communication to be cross language and technology independent. There are simply two main formats for messages: text and binary. The human-readable text-based messages are the simplest to create but have their burdens. These formats allow for the transportation to include metadata. With small to medium size messages, JSON and XML are the most used formats. But, as the message size increases, the extra information can increase latency.

Utilizing a format such as Google's Protocol Buffers (`https://developers.google.com/protocol-buffers/`) or Avro by Apache (`https://avro.apache.org/`), the messages are sent as a binary stream. These are efficient with medium to large messages because there is a CPU cost to convert content to binary. Smaller messages may see some latency.

Out of the box, ASP.NET Core can use JSON or XML as the payload format. For all the references with ASP.NET Core and microservices, JSON is the chosen format. In the call to and from the services, the data is serialized and deserialized using JSON. Most of the time, using JSON is fine given the size of the payloads.

# Transport

Transportation mechanisms are responsible for the delivery of messages to/from the client and microservices. There are multiple protocols available such as HTTP, TCP, gRPC, and Advanced Message Queuing Protocol (AMQP). As you read earlier, there are direct and indirect ways of sending messages. These are direct calls to a microservice with sockets opened waiting for a caller. Port 80 is the standard port HTTP traffic, and port 443 for Transport Layer Security (TLS) encrypted HTTP traffic.

Generally, HTTP is used, but using TCP web sockets is an alternative. The drawback with synchronous messaging is there is a tighter coupling between the client and services. The client may know about details it should not need to care about, such as how many services are listening and their address. Or the client must do a DNS lookup to get an address for a service.

Representational State Transfer (REST) is an architectural style that is quite common today when creating Web APIs and microservices. For example, to retrieve data, the call uses the HTTP verb GET. To insert, modify, or delete data, the HTTP verbs POST, PUT, UPDATE, and DELETE are used. The specific verb is declared in the code of the service endpoints.

As a microservice architecture develops, there may be microservices calling other microservices. There is an inherent risk of latency as data is serialized and deserialized at each hop. An RPC technology called "gRPC Remote Procedure Call" (gRPC) is better suited for the interprocess communication. gRPC is a format created by Google using, by default, protocol buffers. Where JSON is a string of serialized information, gRPC is a binary stream and is smaller in size and, therefore, helps cut down latency. This is also useful when the payload is large, and there is a noticeable latency with JSON.

For asynchronous calls, messages are sent using a message broker such as RabbitMQ, Redis, Azure Service Bus, Kafka, and others. AMQP is the primary protocol used with these message brokers. AMQP defines publishers and consumers. Message brokers ensure the delivery of the messages from the producers to the consumers. With a message broker, applications send messages to the broker for it to forward to the receiving applications. This provides a store-and-forward mechanism and allows for the messages to be received at a later time, such as when an application comes online.

# Testing

Testing is just as crucial to product development as coding. A huge problem is when code performs incorrectly. We can make the most elaborate software that performs at amazing speed and return invalid answers. It does not matter how fast your code runs to a wrong answer.

Just like code, tests are multifaceted. From simple code handling a small amount of business logic to classes with many dependencies, targeted tests are needed to ensure the accuracy and reliability of our products.

## Test Pyramid

The test pyramid is a visual representation of testing levels. Figure 1-8 is based on Mike Cohn's concept in his book *Succeeding with Agile.* It represents the number of tests compared to each level, speed, and reliability. The unit tests should be small and cover basic units of business logic. Service tests are for individual microservices. And end-to-end tests are the slowest and most unreliable as they generally depend on manual effort and the least amount of automation.

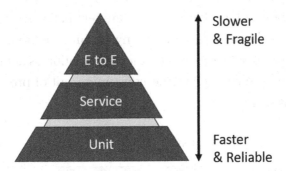

*Figure 1-8.* *Testing pyramid*

# E to E

End-to-end tests, sometimes referred to as system tests, are about testing the system's interactions that use microservices and their interaction with other services. These tests may include UI level tests using manual effort or automated tests using products like Selenium. System tests verify subsequent calls retrieve and update data.

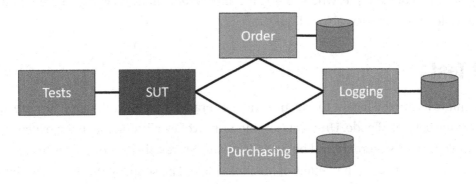

*Figure 1-9.* *Depiction of end-to-end testing*

Figure 1-9 shows a block of tests executing against a System Under Test (SUT), which calls multiple microservices. Testing at this level is very slow and fragile compared to unit tests.

# Service

Component tests are for testing a microservice apart from other services like other microservices or data stores. You use a mock or a stub to test microservices that depend on a data store or other microservices. Mocks and stubs are configured to return predetermined responses to the System Under Test (SUT).

19

A stub returns responses based on how they are set up. For example, in Figure 1-10, a stub could stand in for a data store or other long-running method. When called for saving a new order, it returns the order and other information as if it was just saved. This helps the speed of testing since it skips time-consuming, out-of-process logic and only returns however it was set up.

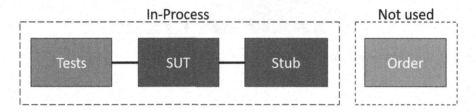

*Figure 1-10. Using stub for testing*

Mocks help verify dependencies are invoked. Mocks also require a setup of predetermined responses. They are used to help test behavior, whereas a stub helps with testing of state. For example, when calling a `createOrder` method, verify that the method to create a log message was also called.

## Unit Tests

Good unit tests are the fastest to execute and, generally, the most reliable. They are at the most basic level of code. Unit tests should not invoke calls outside of the executing process. This means there should be no calls to data stores, files, or other services. These tests are for testing the details of business logic. The scope of these tests varies in opinion. Some say the test should only cover code within a single method. Others say the test can go across many methods and even into other classes. To keep them fast, reliable, and maintainable, keep the scope small.

## Automation

Using a Continuous Integration/Continuous Deployment (CI/CD) pipeline should be considered a must-have. They help with the automation of testing and deployment. It is highly recommended to use a build step in your CI/CD pipeline that is performing the unit tests. Integration tests are generally much longer in execution time, so many companies do not add them to the CI/CD pipeline. A better recommendation is to have them executed nightly, at least, or on some other schedule.

# Deploying Microservices

Microservices are independent applications. Although their code and business functionality may have come from a monolith, they now have a life of their own. Part of that independence is deployment. As discussed earlier, one of the benefits is deployment apart from a monolith and other microservices. This section discusses factors on versioning tactics, wrapping in containers, hosting in orchestrators, and deployment pipelines.

## Versioning

As newer releases of microservices are deployed, versioning takes consideration. Leveraging a versioning semantic from SemVer (`https://www.semver.org`), there are three number segments that are used:

- Major – version when you make incompatible API changes

- Minor – version when you add functionality in a backward-compatible manner

- Patch – version when you make backward-compatible bug fixes

Using Semantic Versioning applies to your APIs as well as any NuGet packages you create. With your API, if using REST, you can add a version in the URL, for example, "api/v1/account."

As you build multiple microservices, there will be common functionality that each service will use. You will quickly build a framework that may include logging, monitoring, and alerting. In this framework, you can use NuGet packaging for each piece. With these packages, you can use Semantic Versioning if using NuGet 4.3.0 or above and Visual Studio 2017 version 15.3 or above.

## Containers

Containers allow for executables, their dependencies, and configuration files to be packaged together. Although there are a few container brands available, Docker is the most well known. You will learn more details on using containers in Chapter 8.

Deploying microservices can be done straight to servers or more likely virtual machines. However, you will see more benefits from running containers. By using containers, you can constrain resources like CPU and RAM, so processes that consume too much CPU or have memory leaks do not kill the server they reside on. They are easier to manage. Controlling the number of container instances, running on certain servers, and handling upgrade/rollback and failures can all be handled by using an orchestrator. Orchestrators like Docker Swarm, Service Fabric, Kubernetes, and others manage containers with all the features just mentioned but also include features like network and security. You will learn more details about Kubernetes in Chapter 8.

# Pipelines

With development processes like Continuous Integration and Continuous Deployment (CI/CD), you can leverage tools that help automate testing and staged releases. Tools like CircleCI, Jenkins, Travis, and Azure DevOps, to name a few, can be set up to perform various tasks. You can set them up to be either manually executed or triggered when code is checked into a repository.

Using Azure DevOps, for example, you can set up Builds that are triggered when code is checked in. Executing tasks pull code from the assigned repository, run unit tests and/or integration tests, build a container image, push the image to a container registry, like Azure Container Registry (ACR), and notify an orchestrator of the new image. In this example, you can have code checked in trigger a build and within a short time is running in a development or staging cluster. You can also set up Builds and Releases on a time-based schedule so, for example, hourly or nightly environments are updated.

Also, "Azure DevOps" have automatic or manually triggered Releases. An automated Release is triggered with a completed Build. Manually triggering a Release provides the option to specify a current or previous build version. With Release tasks, you can have more thorough tests performed, and if passing, the container images can feed a production cluster.

Microservices should be considered as their own independent application with their own deployment pipelines. They have the autonomy to evolve independently of monoliths and other microservices. As such, they should also have their own repository. Having separate repositories aids in the autonomy to evolve.

# Cross-Cutting Concerns

There are aspects that are not specific to microservices but do apply to the infrastructure. These are just as important as microservices. If a microservice became unavailable at 2 am, how would you know? When would you know? Who should know? These cross-cutting concerns (CCC) help you understand the system's health as a whole, and they are a part of it. Understanding the health of a system helps with capacity planning and troubleshooting. If the system is showing signs of resource starvation, you may need more containers or servers. Troubleshooting is also important to help identify bugs, code fixes, and infrastructure-related items like network bandwidth.

# Monitoring

To say that your microservice is running well means nothing if you cannot prove it and help with capacity planning, fault diagnosing, and cost justification.

Evaluate good monitoring solutions. Prometheus (`https://prometheus.io`) is a great option, but it is not the only good one available. And, although Prometheus is great, it has a steep learning curve. Whatever you find, make sure you build in time to learn how to use it well. After data is captured, you will need something to display that information. Tools like Grafana (`https://grafana.com`) are for displaying captured metrics via Prometheus and other sources.

Using Prometheus and Grafana helps you know if a server or Node (if using Kubernetes) is starving for resources like CPU and RAM. You can also use monitored information like call volumes and response times, as well, to know if you need to add servers to the cluster. This tremendously helps with capacity planning. Although not having enough servers is a huge issue, having too many will also hurt costs.

Implementing a form of health check provides you access to information in various ways. One of which is knowing the microservice is not dead and responds to requests. This is a "liveness probe." The other is in what information goes back to the client. Consider adding an entry point that uses HTTP GET, for example, `HTTP://{service endpoint}/health`. Have the liveness probe return details about the microservice and list the health of various service-specific details:

- Can connect to data store

- Can connect to next microservice hop, if there is one

- – Consider returning necessary data for troubleshooting and incident reporting

- – Consider returning a version that can be used to verify latest version has been deployed

The liveness probe may return an HTTP code of 200, signifying the microservices are alive. The response contents contain the health status. Each microservice will have different data to respond with that you define to fit your architectural needs. The returned data can then feed monitoring resources. You may need to add custom adapters to feed systems like Grafana. There are .NET libraries for Prometheus that capture data and are customizable.

# Logging

Logging information from microservices is as vital as monitoring, if not more so. Monitoring metrics are great, but when diagnosing fault events, exceptions, and even messages of properly working calls, logging information is an absolute must. First, decide what information you need to keep. Then decide how to keep and retrieve that information.

A centralized logging system provides a great way to accept information that may come from multiple systems. This is known as "Log Aggregation." Services like Splunk are 3rd party tools for log management. Microservices log information to stdout or stderr. This information is captured and sent to Splunk, where it can be correlated and viewed.

Consider the information you need to keep, for example, messages that include the application name, machine name, timestamp in UTC, and brief description. Another option may include a serialized Exception type and stack trace. If you do capture the Exception, I recommend looping through Inner Exceptions to capture all bubbled events. The main piece of information may be wrapped in Exception layers, and you do not want to miss the details. The stack trace will certainly help with identifying code lines, class, and additional information needed for further research.

As with any logging mechanism, there will be costs associated. First, you will need some way of capturing the log information and, second, storing it. Loggly (`https://www.loggly.com`) is a logging system with many connectors for a variety of systems. The monolith and all microservices can use the libraries and have all logs stored in a central storage location.

# Alerting

With data monitored and captured, development teams need to know when their microservices have issues. Alerting is the process of reacting to various performance metrics. It is common for CPU utilization to hit 100% momentarily. The issue is when the process exceeds a CPU threshold far too long and risks resource starvation or impacting other processes. Setting alerts based on situations like high CPU utilization or RAM starvation is simple. The following is a list of example metrics you should create alerts for:

- High network bandwidth usage

- CPU usage over a threshold for a certain amount of time

- RAM utilization

- Number of inbound and outbound simultaneous calls

- Errors (exceptions, HTTP errors, etc.)

- Number of messages in a service broker's Dead Letter Queue (DLQ)

Tools like Grafana, Azure Log Analytics, and RabbitMQ have their alerting features. Grafana can alert on most of the items in the preceding list. You will need to set up alerts in multiple systems. If your choice of service broker does not contain alerts, you may need to consider writing a custom metrics handler or see if an open source option is available.

An additional option is using webhooks to send information to a Slack channel. This way, there is a message that multiple people can see. With alerts that are severe enough to warrant paging someone in the middle of the night, there are tools like PagerDuty. This is configurable with an escalation policy to page one or more people depending on the types of alerts.

# Testing the Architecture

A previous section covered code and service testing. This section is about testing the cross-cutting concerns of the infrastructure. With monitoring, logging, and alerting in place, are they set up correctly? As your microservice architecture evolves, so should these items. The tools for these items also need upgrades and modifications as the architecture changes.

In a non-production environment, intentionally cause a failure. Consider the following questions as a starting list of items to evaluate. As you go through the list, add to it. Find the details that are specific to your case and add them to your checklist. Quickly, you will gain a trust level in the tooling, your settings, the microservices, and the team's ability to respond.

- [ ] Was the failure logged?

- [ ] Do the log entries reflect enough detail to identify the server, microservice, etc.?

- [ ] Is the failure due to code, network, 3rd party call, or data store? Something else?

- [ ] Does the failure appear on the monitoring tool?

- [ ] Was an alert generated?

- [ ] Did the alert go to the development team responsible?

- [ ] Did the alert contain enough information to start troubleshooting properly?

- [ ] Are there multiple failures noticed? Should there be one or multiple?

- [ ] Did the code retry using a "retry policy"? Should it? Was the retry adequate?

- [ ] After resolving the failure, did the alert stop? Does logging show correct activity?

- [ ] Are you able to produce a report of the failure that includes information from the monitoring tool, correlated log entries, alerts, and from those who responded?

Now consider systematically causing more failures. With each one, go through your checklist. Refine the checklist and, more importantly, fix the items discovered during this testing.

# Summary

We just went over a lot of information with a large, broad stroke. The topics mentioned are just the tip of the knowledge iceberg compared to the depth of knowledge encompassing microservice architecture. Adopting a microservice architecture is not easy nor cheap. With all the challenges, it does take allowance to fail, teamwork, and time to do it right. For many companies, the benefits easily outweighed the challenges. They saw the benefits of autonomy with teams, services, and data. They can scale their services and make the best use of their servers.

There are many patterns available for microservices. It would take another book to cover them all. But the API Gateway, BFF, and External Configuration Store will quickly serve you well. They apply to even the smallest microservice architecture.

The communication with microservices may change in your architecture. The easiest is to use synchronous RPC. But you may find yourself changing to use the asynchronous methods with a message broker since it is more extendable.

Always consider testing throughout the development cycles. Unit testing will provide confidence in the accuracy of the understanding of the business logic for the minute code. With microservices, there is an added layer of testing complexity. Testing the service layer is possible and made easier to automate with mocks and stubs. Then, when nearly ready for production, the system tests to verify that the system is operational and functional.

When developing microservices, consider automating builds using CI/CD automation tools like Jenkins and Azure DevOps. The pipelines handle so many of the mundane processes and free up developers for more coding. Also, include in the build pipelines test execution for more stable releases to various environments.

The cross-cutting concerns are for the environments hosting microservices. You should be able to monitor the health of each service and hosting server. Set up alerts to notify the right people to jump to action if/when issues occur. When they happen, logging will be crucial for troubleshooting and debugging.

Lastly, manually test the architecture. Cause issues to occur so that you know your monitoring shows enough information, logging has recorded vital clues, and alerts are notifying correct response team members. The microservice architecture will evolve just like the microservices. The infrastructure will need the same attention as the code receives.

# CHAPTER 2

# ASP.NET Core Overview

In this chapter, we'll discuss the history and features of .NET, the runtime, and ASP.NET Core, the web server. We'll also walk through installing various components you need to begin working with, the example monolithic application and microservices. Finally, we'll tour through the types of programming paradigms you can choose as you build an ASP.NET project. If you are already versed with .NET, ASP.NET Core, and MVC, you can quickly skim this chapter and jump straight into building microservices. However, if you have not yet started with those items, then this chapter is a good place to start.

## A Brief History of .NET

Microsoft introduced the .NET Framework in 2000. .NET was a great way to move away from manual memory management and into the modern, web-based world. In time, .NET Framework grew to version 4.8, and it was buckling under its legacy weight. Microsoft ported the paradigms of .NET to an open source, cross-platform version named .NET Core. With .NET 5, .NET Framework is officially declared done and will only receive security updates going forward. .NET Core has become .NET: a unified platform for building great modern apps.

In the beginning, we had .NET Framework 1.0. The .NET Framework was built at a very different age. We were starting to learn about WSDL, a mechanism for making SOAP (XML) services more discoverable. Windows Forms was the new UI framework that allowed us to build applications with drag-and-drop tools as we did in VB 6, but backed by the power of C#, a C-like language.

Fast forward to today. We have chatbots, microservices, and IoT devices. XML is almost a distant memory, replaced by more modern techniques like gRPC. The .NET Framework was showing its age. If you launched a microservice on .NET Framework, it would need to load the .NET Framework. This includes Windows Forms which bundled GDI+, XML parsing (even if you're only using JSON), and libraries for looking through the registry. Clearly, this isn't a tool for building fast, modern applications.

29

© Sean Whitesell, Rob Richardson, Matthew D. Groves 2022
S. Whitesell et al., *Pro Microservices in .NET 6*, https://doi.org/10.1007/978-1-4842-7833-8_2

The ASP.NET team began rebooting ASP.NET. Originally called Project K and then ASP.NET vNext, the project was eventually expanded to encompass the entirety of .NET. A new version of .NET was born: .NET Core 1.0. This platform is completely open source and runs cross-platform on macOS, Linux, and Windows. It runs equally well on x64 and ARM processors. You can install it on a machine just as easily as embed it in a Docker container. One can bundle .NET into a single executable or leverage the .NET runtime installed on the machine. .NET is now a modern, portable, and lean environment.

With it came ASP.NET Core, Entity Framework Core, and a plethora of similarly "Core" branded services. Microsoft ported the best of the .NET Framework to this new platform. For example, in ASP.NET, the web server component, we continued with the tradition of MVC controllers and views. In fact, if you hadn't strayed far from the template, one could easily port a website from ASP.NET (on .NET Framework) to ASP.NET Core (on .NET Core) by changing some namespaces and replacing global.asax and global.asax.cs with Program.cs and Startup.cs. When the port was complete, it was not uncommon to see significant performance gains.

.NET Core 2.0 (like .NET Framework 2.0) was really where Microsoft found its stride. The JSON project files were replaced with backward-compatible XML files, the sprawl of base class library NuGet packages were consolidated into SDK packages installed with the .NET Core SDK, and more and more APIs and programming models were getting ported over.

Over the years, .NET Core grew from .NET Core 1.0 to 1.1 to 2.0 to 2.1 to 2.2, and to 3.0 and .NET Core 3.1. .NET Framework had topped out at .NET Framework 4.7.2. As the team contemplated the next version of .NET Core, it became obvious we had a naming collision. How would we explain one should upgrade from the old .NET something 4.7 to the new .NET something 4.0? This seemed preposterous. (Granted, moving from .NET Framework to .NET Core brings a plethora of benefits. But to the untrained observer, it was just ".NET" followed by some mumbling and then a number.) So how do we unify the .NET ecosystem?

It was decided the next version of .NET Core would not be called .NET Core 4.0 but rather would be called .NET 5. This one unified base class library and runtime can now power cloud properties, desktop apps, phone apps, IoT devices, machine learning applications, and console games: "One .NET."

.NET 6.0 carries on this tradition: a single unified runtime built on the very best of open source, cross-platform .NET.

# Long-Term Support

In the old .NET Framework days, .NET was baked into the bowels of Windows. Releasing a new major version of .NET Framework was a ceremony and was often tied to a release of Windows. With this cadence, .NET Framework was generally expected to be supported as long as the Windows version it shipped with.

In the new realm of .NET Core, the team has taken a faster pace, mirroring other open source projects such as Node.js. Starting with .NET Core 2.1, they designated .NET Core releases as either "LTS" (long-term support) or "Current Release":

- "Current release" versions are supported for 18 months. .NET Core 2.2 is designated as a "Current release." It was released in late 2018, so it's support has already ended.

- "Long-term support" versions are supported for 3 years from their release date. .NET Core 3.1 is designated as an LTS release. It came out in 2019, so it will be supported until 2022.

- .NET 6 is designated as an LTS release. It shipped in November 2021, so it will be supported until 2024.

For more details about .NET and .NET Core release dates and support dates, see `https://dotnet.microsoft.com/platform/support/policy/dotnet-core`.

# Presentation Frameworks

Microsoft has said they've finished porting programming paradigms to .NET Core, now .NET 6. On the web server stack, we have ASP.NET Core MVC, Web API, and SignalR. Added to this, we now have gRPC and Blazor, a web-component framework that runs in the browser on WebAssembly. On the desktop stack, we have WinForms, including a designer new in .NET Core 5 and WPF. Added to this, we have XAML-based apps built-in Xamarin for use on mobile devices, and MAUI is a new cross-platform UI toolkit previewing during the .NET 6 timeframe.

Unfortunately, WCF and WebForms have not been ported. It makes sense as these tools were already replaced by gRPC and MVC back in the .NET Framework days. But there are open source alternatives that give us much of the features we need. There's some great work that allows an old WebForms app to run on Blazor. If you're in need of WCF, CoreWCF was donated to the .NET Foundation and may meet the need.

Or if you don't need WSDL service discovery, advanced protocol bindings, or security integrations, you can parse and serialize the necessary XML by model binding to carefully crafted and named classes.

Though there are great benefits to porting apps to .NET Core, now .NET 6, the .NET Framework is built into Windows, so it retains the super-long support schedule to match Windows. (VB 6 is also built into Windows, so the dusty Visual Basic apps written before .NET also still work.) If your app is running great on .NET Framework, it may be cheaper to leave it there and build new microservices in separate code bases running on .NET 6.

# Installing Requirements

Why use ASP.NET Core 6.0? At the time of this writing, it is the latest "long-term supported" (LTS) version available by Microsoft. .NET has been around for many years and provides a stable, open source programming framework that runs cross-platform. It works very well with Windows, macOS, and Linux. Leveraging that ability to work on those operating systems makes an easy decision to use ASP.NET Core for this project.

This section is about installing the requirements for working with the monolithic application and the microservices created later in this book. If you already have .NET 6, then you may prefer to skip this section. For those that have not installed the latest version, this section will help you install the components and learn a few commands along the way.

## Installing .NET 6.0 and ASP.NET Core

By installing .NET 6.0 SDK, you get the project templates for ASP.NET Core. There are two packages to be aware of with .NET Core. The runtime package is for servers that will run applications, but it does not have the tools to build and publish applications. The SDK is the package we will use for this book. You can download both package types from `https://dotnet.microsoft.com/download`. Selecting the option "Download .NET SDK" will autodetect what system you are using and allow you to download the appropriate installer. If a different version is required, you can select the option "All .NET downloads...."

After the installation has completed, you can verify it is installed and has the version expected. After installing, open a new command prompt and enter

```
dotnet --version
```

You can see all the SDKs and runtimes installed by entering

```
dotnet --info
```

To see a list of project templates currently available, enter

```
dotnet new --list
```

To create a quick Hello World console application, create a directory named "helloworld" and go into that directory.

```
mkdir helloworld
cd helloworld
```

Executing this command will create a console application using the name of the directory.

```
dotnet new console
```

You can create the console application using a different name than the directory. Here the name myhelloworld is used instead.

```
dotnet new console --name myhelloworld
```

This is an example output of creating the console application.

```
$ dotnet new console --name myhelloworld
The template "Console Application" was created successfully.

Processing post-creation actions...
Running 'dotnet restore' on myhelloworld\myhelloworld.csproj...
  Restore completed in 195.27 ms for D:\Temp\helloworld\myhelloworld\
  myhelloworld.csproj.

Restore succeeded.
```

Running the "dotnet new" command created two files: myhelloworld.csproj and Program.cs. Take a look inside the myhelloworld.csproj file. If using Linux, replace the *type* command with *cat*.

```
$ type myhelloworld.csproj
<Project Sdk="Microsoft.NET.Sdk">
```

```
<PropertyGroup>
  <OutputType>Exe</OutputType>
  <TargetFramework>net6.0</TargetFramework>
</PropertyGroup>
```

```
</Project>
```

You see there is very little to the csproj files now. With .NET Core, the code files are not listed anymore. Being in the same directory as the csproj file, you can run the application by entering the following command. You'll see the output like Figure 2-1.

```
dotnet run
```

***Figure 2-1.*** *Result of running dotnet run command*

Now let's build an ASP.NET Core project. There's a lot more going on in this template.

```
cd ..
mkdir helloweb
cd helloweb
dotnet new mvc --name myhelloweb
```

Like the console app, this scaffolds out a new ASP.NET Core website with controllers, views, and JavaScript and CSS files. You can run the website in the same way:

```
dotnet run
```

As the website starts up, note the web address the site runs on. The HTTP port will be a random unused port between 5000 and 5300, and HTTPS will be randomly selected between 7000 and 7300. For example, the console output could list https://localhost:7000/. Copy the URL from your console, open a browser, and paste the URL. You'll see your sample website running.

Back in the terminal, type Ctrl+C to break out of the application and stop the web server.

# Installing Visual Studio

You can choose to edit your project using command-line-based tools. However, to be fast and efficient, you are probably better off using an Integrated Development Environment (IDE) such as Visual Studio or VS Code. Both are Microsoft products that vary in capabilities and purpose. Visual Studio 2022 has three editions: Community (which is free), Professional, and Enterprise. The free Community version will work great for what we are doing in this book. The Professional and Enterprise versions have more tooling. You can compare editions by going to `https://visualstudio.microsoft.com/vs/compare`.

For what we need, we will download the Visual Studio 2022 Community edition from `https://visualstudio.microsoft.com/vs`. The installer will prompt for features to install on top of the base editor functionality. There are two that you need to make sure you check. The first is for ASP.NET Core development; see Figure 2-2. The other is for cross-platform support that includes Docker; see Figure 2-3.

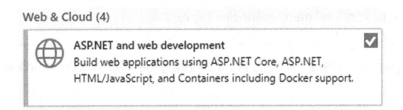

*Figure 2-2.*  *ASP.NET install component*

*Figure 2-3.*  *.NET Core cross-platform install component*

There are other features you may want to add. You can always come back to the installer to enable more features. When you are ready, select the Install button on the bottom right.

# Installing Visual Studio Code

A cross-platform editor called Visual Studio Code, also known as VS Code, or just Code, can be installed by going to https://code.visualstudio.com/download. VS Code is an editor that is not specifically for .NET development. It can be used as a simple file editor or notepad replacement. But into VS Code, you can install extensions for editing code in various programming languages. Be aware that the screenshots for the code in this book are with Visual Studio.

Code is built-in TypeScript and runs in Electron, a host for building cross-platform desktop apps. VS Code's power and elegance come in the community of extensions. Extensions can add compilers and syntax highlighting, extensions can add integrations with other tools, and extensions can add formatting, coloring, and theming adjustments. C# is not native to the editor but can be installed via a VS Code extension. This shows the power of Code in that you can install many extensions based on what types of projects you work on. In the following image, you can see extensions for Python, C#, and others. You can find extensions for Docker, Kubernetes, JavaScript, database connectors, code linters, spell checkers, and many more. See Figure 2-4.

---

**Note**   Anyone can make extensions for VS Code. Be judicious on which extensions you install.

---

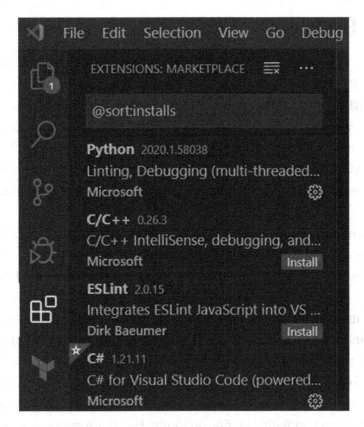

***Figure 2-4.*** *Install extensions in VS Code like the C# extension*

# .NET 6.0 at a Glance

With the base .NET runtime, you get access to console applications. One can install additional frameworks and libraries to facilitate more advanced paradigms such as WinForms and WPF desktop applications, ASP.NET websites, Android and iOS apps using Xamarin, or modern XAML-based apps using MAUI.

For example, ASP.NET Core is a set of libraries that extend the base .NET runtime. The libraries provide the code necessary for web-based communication over HTTP. With ASP.NET Core you can build applications for Internet of Things (IoT), cloud-based, mobile, and web UIs. They can run on Windows, Linux, and macOS. Also, it is possible to run .NET Core applications on ARM-based architectures like Raspberry Pi.

# MVC at a Glance

The Model-View-Controller (MVC) pattern has been around for decades. Microsoft applied it to ASP.NET about 2007 and again with ASP.NET Core as they moved to the open source .NET rewrite. The previous paradigm of web development was with ASP. NET WebForms. WebForms served to help transition a lot of developers from other stateful development methods like WinForms to stateless methodology. Now some years later the MVC pattern with ASP.NET provides a much simpler and more powerful programming model than the earlier way of using Postback and the dreaded Session State.

MVC has three main components: the Model, View, and Controller. Combined with ASP.NET there is a fourth component, Routing. ASP.NET includes these components as well as other aspects such as Convention over Configuration, Model Binding, and Anti-Forgery Token.

The MVC pattern is a wheel of steps beginning with the request and ending with the response. First, the URL is parsed into sections and flows into the router. The router looks at the URL pieces and selects the correct controller and action (class and method) to satisfy the request. The controller's action method is responsible for calling into the rest of the application to process the data, harvest the results, and pass a model (class) to the view. The view is a templating engine, mapping HTML fragments together with the data to produce an HTTP response. The action method could also choose to forgo the view for API requests, choosing instead to hand data to a serialization engine that might produce JSON, XML, or gRPC. Once the response is constructed, the HTTP headers are attached, and the data is returned to the calling browser or application.

This MVC pattern is indeed more complex than a simple URL to File path system like we had with WebForms or Classic ASP. But with this complexity comes flexibility. In the routing engine, we can choose a different controller and action based on conditions. Is the user unauthenticated? Don't send them to the class matching the URL, but instead send them to the login page. The controller's action also can make choices. Does the data requested not exist? Then let's send them to the not found page instead of the data page. Would they like JSON data instead of an HTML page? Let's forgo the view and choose a response method that serializes data instead. This flexibility to choose the next step in the chain is why the MVC pattern is so popular in .NET ecosystems as well as other languages and frameworks.

Convention over Configuration refers to how ASP.NET MVC uses naming conventions to tie URLs to controller classes and methods, controller methods to views, and URL segments and post bodies to C# classes. It is not required to have every view programmatically added to any list or association. Model binding is how data is sent to and from the browser to methods (actions) in the controllers. Data, for example, of type Customer, is deserialized into an instance of the Customer object parameter, and vice versa, as a Customer object is returned from the controller to the view.

# Routing

As a browser or service makes an HTTP connection, the URL pattern matching determines which controller and action receive the request. Using a default template, the Home controller is created and handles default requests. In the URL, the controller is defined right after the domain name, or port number if one is specified. For example, with the URL http://localhost/Home/Index, the controller class name is *Home* and the action method name is *Index*. The actions are the methods in the controller class that receive the requests, execute any business logic, and return information or just status.

The defined routes are stored in a route table. As a request comes into the web server, it is analyzed against the routes, and the first matching one is selected. This means that if custom routes are defined, then they need to be listed in the order of precedence. In the case there is not a matching route, then the default URL pattern matching rule is applied.

With ASP.NET Core, most typically the routes are configured with attributes on each class. Let's look at an example controller inside an ASP.NET Core MVC project:

```
[Route("[controller]")]
public class CustomerController : Controller
{
  [Route("get/{id}")]
  public ActionResult GetCustomer(int id)
  {
    return View();
  }
}
```

Here the Route attribute at the top specifies that if the URL starts with https://some-site/Customer, it should run methods within this class. Next, the Route attribute on the method maps to the next part of the URL. If the URL is https://some-site/Customer/get/7, then the GetCustomer() method should be called.

By convention, we can configure default rules if we'd like to avoid adding Route attributes to every class. These additional routing rules are maintained in the Startup.cs file, usually in the Configure method along with other customizations. In the following code example, a route named *default* is added to the route table. It has a defined pattern where the controller and action are specified. The id is also specified but with the question mark. This allows the field to be empty or not present in the URL. However, if a value is present, then it is applied to the id parameter of the Index action method.

```
app.UseMvc(routes =>
{
  routes.MapRoute("default", "{controller=Home}/{action=Index}/{id?}");
});
```

Beginning in ASP.NET Core 2.2, you can use endpoints instead of the route table. Endpoint mapping allows for routing rules to be defined without impacting other web frameworks, meaning that it is possible to leverage SignalR along with MVC, Razor, and others without them colliding in the middleware pipeline.

```
app.UseEndpoints(endpoints => {
  endpoints.MapControllerRoute(name: "default",
  pattern: "{controller=Home}/{action=Index}/{id?}");
});
```

Adding a Routing Attribute to the action helps control the routing logic as well. In the following example, the Index method is called with any of these URLs: /, /home/, or /home/index. The use of routing attributes also allows for method names not to match. Using the URL /home/about, in this example, will call the ShowAboutPage method.

```
[Route("")]
[Route("Home")]
[Route("Home/Index")]
public IActionResult Index()
{
    return View();
}

[Route("Home/About")]
public IActionResult ShowAboutPage()
```

```
{
  return View("About");
}
```

## Controller

The job of a controller is to map request inputs to classes, call the business classes that do the work, and provide the results to the response. They receive requests, via routing, to actions (methods), and work with model data and sending to the appropriate view. Lastly, controllers can work with validation, security, and content types to customize the response sent to the caller.

They use a naming convention, simply a name and the word "Controller," for example, CustomerController. The logic here is meant for handling requests related to customers, whereas InvoiceController is meant for invoice handling logic. This logic separation helps keep a good principle of having lightweight controllers. That is, they should have just enough logic to handle receiving and sending data. Other business logic and data access code should be in separate classes.

## View

The views are responsible for the representation of a page with or without dynamic data. The output of a view is a giant string, so they are inherently difficult to test. For this reason, the logic inside a view should be incredibly simple. If you need complex logic, move this logic into the controller's action, where it can be correctly tested. For example, a view for customers should only have enough business logic to loop through the list and display each customer. It should not have any business logic on how to retrieve that data, or logging, etc. That logic is better in controllers or other classes more central to the application.

There is a folder convention used to locate the correct view file to use. At the top level, there are folders for each Controller class. Inside the folder are Views (cshtml files) for each method in the Controller class; see Figure 2-5. In the Views folder are other folders, for example, Customers, Invoices, and of course Home. Although not required, there is an Index.cshtml file in each of the view folders in an MVC project. When accessing a URL like `http://localhost/Customers/Edit/3453` with default routing configured, we'd hit the CustomersController class, the Edit method, and find the view in the Views/Customers/Edit.cshtml file. Of course, the router could choose a different controller and action, and the action method could also choose a different view.

41

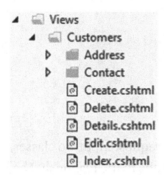

*Figure 2-5.* *Inside the Views folder, we have a folder for each controller, and a View file for each action*

# Model

Models in ASP.NET Core are classes used to represent data. Leveraged with controllers and sent to views, a model is a package holding the data the view renders. For example, when retrieving a list of customers, each customer is an instance of a customer model. It has properties for the fields of that customer. It may have a property for Name, Address, Phone Number, etc. A view's logic will loop through a collection of models and render each one.

Models may differ from other data classes in the project. For example, we may have Entities that map to tables in our database. We may also have data-transform objects, or DTOs, used to convey data between sections of an application.

When designing a class for use in a view, we could call this a view-model. This class is specifically tailored to keep the view rendering simple. Inside the controller or other business logic classes, we may map data from Entity classes into view-model classes. View-models are specific to the purpose it is being rendered. There may be a view-model for listing customers while another view-model is used for when editing customer details. You may also have a view-model that is comprised of multiple sources. That is, they should not be thought of as a one-to-one relationship with a database table.

Model binding can also use views to map request details into controller actions. In this case, we could call these request-models. For example, when saving a user's profile, we may have a request-model that includes their name, address, and phone number. This differs from the Entity class, which may also include the username and password. We definitely don't want to include these properties on the request-model, because we don't want extra data in a request to become an injection attack that might change a user's password.

# ASP.NET Core Middleware

With ASP.NET Core, nearly all functionality is bolted together using a middleware pipeline. This pipeline is a set of steps that all requests flow through. Each step in the pipeline gets to augment the request, abort the request, or do nothing. For example, we may have a middleware function that parses HTTP headers into C# classes or JSON data from the request body into a request-model. We might also have a middleware that validates the user is authenticated, returning an HTTP 401 status code if they're not. We might also have a middleware that captures and logs exceptions.

The web application can be configured on what and how to handle requests and responses. To add middleware options, open the Startup.cs file. The lower of the two methods is the Configure method. As parameters in the Configure method, we can accept any services from the IoC container. By default, we usually only take in the IApplicationBuilder and IWebHostEnvironment. The IApplicationBuilder type is the main instance the configuration uses. Leveraging IWebHostEnvironment will provide information such as if the web application is running in Development mode.

Inside the Configure method, the web application can be configured to use middleware like Routing, Authentication, and many more. In the following code example, this is configured to not only use routing for MVC but also the endpoints. This is where the default routing logic is set up. The method UseStaticFiles allows static files like JavaScript, CSS, and image files to be hosted from the wwwroot folder.

```
public void Configure(IApplicationBuilder app, IWebHostEnvironment env)
{
  if (env.IsDevelopment())
  {
    app.UseDeveloperExceptionPage();
  }
  else
  {
    app.UseExceptionHandler("/Home/Error");
  }

  app.UseHttpsRedirection();
  app.UseStaticFiles();
  app.UseRouting();
```

```
    app.UseAuthorization();

    app.UseEndpoints(endpoints =>
    {
        endpoints.MapControllerRoute(
            name: "default",
            pattern: "{controller=Home}/{action=Index}/{id?}");
    });
}
```

There are many built-in middleware options available from Microsoft. Also, there are many available from 3rd party providers via NuGet packaging. As middleware is merely functions, creating custom middleware components is a simple endeavor as well.

## ASP.NET Core Web API

Similar to the MVC project, ASP.NET Core includes a Web API template. Where the MVC template is geared toward the website, the Web API template is geared toward microservices. Both templates use the MVC pattern under the hood. In the Web API project template, Views are removed, and Controllers typically return JSON data instead. It's possible to use both MVC controllers and views and Web API controllers in the same project without incident.

Starting with ASP.NET 3.0, the Web API project includes the Swashbuckle library. Swashbuckle provides a great way to browse through and explore an API using OpenAPI (formerly Swagger). As you fire up an ASP.NET Core Web API project, browse to "/swagger/," and you can form requests and see results right from the browser, as shown in Figure 2-6.

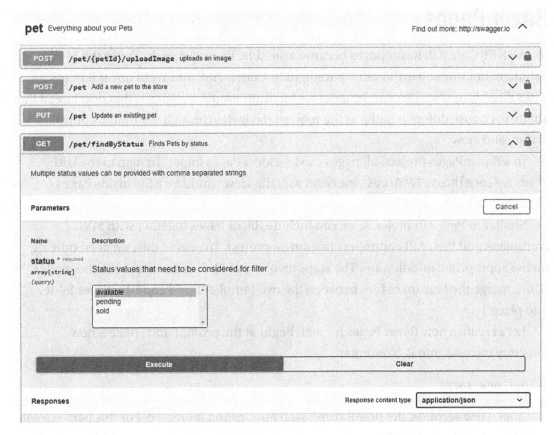

**Figure 2-6.** *A sample Swagger UI experience from the Swagger documentation at* `https://petstore.swagger.io`

Create a new Web API project by creating an empty folder in Explorer, Finder, or your shell of choice, open a new terminal in this folder, and type

```
dotnet new webapi --name mywebapi
dotnet run
```

Note the URL of the web server, and open a browser to this page. You'll likely get a 404 since, by default, nothing is listening to the home page. Add "/swagger/," and you'll get to the OpenAPI browser. For example, if the console output listed the URL as `https://localhost:7000/`, we would browse to `https://localhost:7000/swagger/`.

When you're done, hit Ctrl+C to stop the web server.

Browse through the files in this project. Notice that, unlike the MVC project, we have no Views folder. We have a Controllers folder and a Startup.cs file that rigs up the middleware pipeline.

# Razor Pages

In ASP.NET Core 2.2, Razor pages became available. Razor pages don't use the MVC paradigm but rather use the same paradigm as Classic ASP and WebForms: it maps URLs directly to files. This can be great for building simple web pages that don't need the ability to choose different paths as the request navigates through the router, controller's action, and view.

In a Razor Pages project, all pages exist inside a Pages folder. To map to the URL `https://localhost:7000/customer/detail`, the view would be a file inside `Pages/Customer/Detail.cshtml`.

Similar to Web API projects, we can include Razor Pages together with MVC controllers and Web API controllers in a single project. To enable this, we need only rig up the appropriate middleware. The steps involved are left as an exercise to the reader. (Hint: merge the Startup.cs files between the two templates and copy the Pages folder into place.)

Let's create a new Razor Pages project. Begin at the prompt and create a new directory traverse into it. Now enter

```
dotnet new razor
```

After a few seconds, the new Razor-based application is created. For this part, we will use VS Code to look at the files. At the prompt, enter the command on the following line. Notice using the dot tells VS Code to open starting at the current folder.

```
code .
```

With the application opened in VS Code, notice the Pages folder. It has some prebuilt files for errors and privacy and the main Index.cshtml file. There is also a folder called Shared. This is for shared layouts as well as a common area to leverage dependency injection. Now create a new Razor page. At the prompt, go into the Pages folder and create a new folder called Customers. Now enter

```
dotnet new page -n Index
```

This created a new Razor page called Index in the Customers folder. In VS Code, open this new file. You see there is a page tag and a model tag. In the section for code, add any HTML, for example,

```
@page
@model MyApp.Namespace.IndexModel
@{
  <p>This is the page for Customers.</p>
}
```

To run the application, enter this command at a terminal prompt:

```
dotnet run
```

After the project builds, you will see an output similar to what is shown in Figure 2-7.

```
Building...
info: Microsoft.Hosting.Lifetime[14]
      Now listening on: https://localhost:7000
info: Microsoft.Hosting.Lifetime[14]
      Now listening on: http://localhost:5245
info: Microsoft.Hosting.Lifetime[0]
      Application started. Press Ctrl+C to shut down.
info: Microsoft.Hosting.Lifetime[0]
      Hosting environment: Development
info: Microsoft.Hosting.Lifetime[0]
```

***Figure 2-7.*** *Getting port numbers*

There are two URLs listed, one for HTTP and the other for HTTPS traffic. Select the URL for HTTPS traffic, and with your browser, go to that URL and then append /Customers. For example, the URL in the console might look like https://localhost:7000/. So the full URL we'd browse to in this example is https://localhost:7000/Customers. You should see what is shown in Figure 2-8.

myfirstrazor   Home   Privacy

This is the page for Customers.

***Figure 2-8.*** *View the HTML from your new view*

# Minimal APIs

Brand new in ASP.NET Core 6.0 are minimal APIs. This uses the best of C# 10 to create less code for simple APIs. The minimal API setup is embedded in the new project templates available both in Visual Studio 2022 and the command-line templates from `dotnet new`.

Minimal API techniques can be used in MVC, Web API, and Razor Page projects. In fact, the ASP.NET developers have re-platformed these traditional methodologies on top of the minimal API. This means if your microservice is really simple, you may also see some performance gains from the minimal API approach.

In the minimal API paradigm, the Startup.cs file is folded into the Program.cs file. One could also rig up Action methods without needing to embed them in a Controller class. If you're familiar with Node.js and Express.js, you'll feel right at home with the minimal APIs.

Here's an example Hello World program using the minimal APIs:

```
var builder = WebApplication.CreateBuilder(args);
var app = builder.Build();
app.MapGet("/", () => "Hello World");
app.Run();
```

Yes, that's the whole app. Create a new folder, create a file named Program.cs, and paste the code above into it. Inside this folder, add a HelloWorld.csproj file and paste this configuration into it:

```
<Project Sdk="Microsoft.NET.Sdk.Web">
  <PropertyGroup>
    <TargetFramework>net6.0</TargetFramework>
  </PropertyGroup>
</Project>
```

Now open up a terminal in this folder and launch the app:

```
dotnet run
```

Browse to the URL specified, and you'll see the message "Hello World."

This minimal API technique can be great when you don't want all the ceremony and convention in traditional projects. Yet, the minimal API can accommodate much more powerful features such as dependency injection (DI), model binding, authentication, and more.

However, the minimal API approach isn't without its drawbacks. It's much more difficult to test a minimal API because the Program class is not public, making it difficult to reference from unit tests. Additionally, one loses the separation of concerns when one jams all the features into a single file that starts a web server.

For these reasons, this book focuses less on the new minimal APIs and instead on the traditional project templates that include Controller, View, and Models folders, together with the separated Program.cs and Startup.cs classes. With a bit of customization and a lot of debugging, you could also accomplish much of the projects in this book using minimal APIs instead.

# Summary

In this chapter, we explored .NET and ASP.NET Core, we got the necessary tools installed, and we installed two great IDEs we can use to edit C# code. We installed Visual Studio and VS Code. Both are great editors for different reasons. Although Visual Studio has a lot more development helpers available, VS Code is a solid lightweight editor.

We then went over MVC, middleware, and Razor. Both MVC and Razor provide powerful web application functionality that can also be used side by side. Understanding a bit about routing is necessary because of the way HTTP connections are connected to the correct MVC controller or Razor page. Also, when we get into microservices, you will see how adjusting routing to use protocol buffers helps with faster communication.

# CHAPTER 3

# Searching for Microservices

This chapter uses a mock scenario to understand a client's problems with an application critical for their business. You will see how a workshop-style meeting, called Event Storming, helps software developers understand the customer's business and their application in need of help. You will also learn about Domain-Driven Design (DDD) and how developers can use it to prepare for decomposing a monolithic application into microservices. To head in the right direction, we will start with a brief introduction to the customer's business. This introduction will help you understand a little about the customer's struggles, which will aid with an example of analyzing the need for microservices.

## The Business

Our hypothetical client company Hyp-Log is a shipping logistics middleman coordinator for hotshot deliveries. Hotshot deliveries are point-to-point transfers of goods or materials that require a level of expedience that may not be attainable by larger carrier firms.

Hyp-Log's value to its customers derives from its ability to source the best possible price given the type, size, and weight of a given shipment. In essence, Hyp-Log took all their rate spreadsheets and the analysis that staff were performing manually and built a "rate engine" to perform those same calculations with greater speed, higher accuracy, and better overall customer experience.

A previous employee of Hyp-Log created a custom application for them. Although the application has helped in many ways, a few business processes remain as manual effort. With growing demands, Hyp-Log decides to have a company make the programming changes necessary. Code Whiz is the hypothetical software development firm hired to make the code modifications.

© Sean Whitesell, Rob Richardson, Matthew D. Groves 2022
S. Whitesell et al., *Pro Microservices in .NET 6*, https://doi.org/10.1007/978-1-4842-7833-8_3

There are several challenges when it comes to managing shipments without automation. Let's consider an owner/operator in a carrier company. This person is not only the owner of the company, responsible for all the back-office administrative tasks, but this person is also responsible for quoting shipments and delivering said shipments. That is an awful lot of hats to wear for one individual. Here is where the monolithic carrier portal shines, and the application removes the burden of quoting each shipment. The rating engine uses carrier-provided rate sheets, fleet availability, and capabilities to generate quotes for customer shipments automatically, thus removing the burden of a quotation from the carrier.

After a few years of using spreadsheets and calling carriers for quote information, they decided to have an application made to handle their processes. An employee created an application to facilitate as much of the work as possible. That application became affectionately known as "Shipment Parcel Logistics Administration – Thing," aka "SPLAT." *Naming things is hard.*

SPLAT has three main user types: customers, carriers, and administrators. It provides a way for customers to submit load requests, pick a carrier based on a list of quotes, and provide payment. Carriers can manage their fleet and base costs per mile plus extra costs based on particular needs. Some loads require a trailer, are hazardous material, or even refrigerated.

# Domain-Driven Design

Before we can leverage Domain-Driven Design (DDD), we need to define a few things. We will go over a few tenants of DDD: Domain, Ubiquitous Language, Bounded Contexts, and Aggregates with Aggregate Roots.

# Domain

DDD is a way of developing applications with an intended focus on a domain. The domain is the realm for which you created the application. For example, if the application's primary focus is managing accounting-related functionality, the domain is accounting instead of another application primarily focused on video editing.

In the case of Hyp-Log, their domain is hotshot load management. Other domains may exist in the company, like Human Resources and Insurance, but they are not relative to why Hyp-Log exists as a company. They are ancillary domains for a company to function, but they do not help Hyp-Log stand out among competitors.

Eric Evans is the founder of DDD and author of *Domain-Driven Design: Tackling Complexity in the Heart of Software*. This chapter will leverage pieces of DDD to help understand the hotshot domain and determine when/where to create microservices. DDD was not created for the use of microservices but can be leveraged for the development of microservices. That said, this book does not explain every piece of DDD.

# Subdomains

Digging deeper into a domain are subdomains. A subdomain is a grouping of related business processes. For example, you may have a group of processes for Accounts Payable, Accounts Receivable, and Payroll in an accounting domain. The business processes related to each other for generating and processing invoices belong to the Accounts Receivable subdomain. In comparison, the business processes for managing time sheets, wages, and federal forms belong to the Payroll subdomain. At this level, we are only referring to the business processes. This grouping of focus is known as the Problem Space.

The code that provides the functionality in a subdomain should also exist in groups separate from others. The groups of code that provide functionality for their subdomain are called a bounded context. The bounded context exists in what is known as the Solution Space. We will discuss more on bounded contexts in another section. When we decide what code should become a microservice, you will see how the subdomain type weighs in.

There are three subdomain types: Core, Supportive, and Generic.

- Core – Each core subdomain in an application contains one or more bounded contexts that are critical to the company.

- Supportive – The supportive subdomains are not deemed critical but contain code that is supportive of the business.

- Generic – Lastly, generic subdomains are those that are replaceable with off-the-shelf solutions.

53

# Ubiquitous Language

One of the most important artifacts of DDD is the Ubiquitous Language (UL). The UL is a collection of phrases and terms that helps everyone involved to have a clear and concise understanding of business processes.

Some phrases like "user submit a request" are not clear to the full meaning and context to which it belongs. Rephrasing helps to build a UL that is quickly understood. For example, "the customer provides a coupon code" and "the customer issues dispute request" have entirely different contexts though both have a "user" and are "submitting a request." The clarification is crucial so that everyone involved in the project's development understands the specifics of business processes.

There are times when terms have overloaded meanings. Depending on the context, terms like "ticket" can mean various things. To say "a user submits a ticket" needs clarification to the specific context. Is this referring to a customer submitting a support ticket? Or is this referring to a driver submitting a ticket to a machine in a parking garage to pay for parking? Having a well-formed UL helps alleviate confusion between teams and can make for more concise use cases.

UL should also extend to the code. Developers tend to shy away from long class and method names. But having concise names for namespaces, classes, and methods helps the code stay in line with the UL. As time goes on and developers change roles or jobs, having code in line with the UL helps other developers come up to speed in a shorter amount of time.

# Bounded Contexts

A bounded context is a collection of codes that implements business processes in a subdomain distinctly different from other processes. For example, consider an application at a manufacturing plant. The code for inventory management of purchased parts is different than inventory management of manufactured parts. Because the business processes differed between purchased parts and manufactured parts, the code providing business functionality is also different. By using ubiquitous language here, the term "part" is distinguished to the various purposes to become "purchased part" vs. "manufactured part." Thus, there is a bounded context, determined by the language around the term "part."

Identifying bounded contexts can be done by a couple of different tactics. As mentioned, language is an indicator of a boundary, making a bounded context. Functionality that uses specific language in the namespaces, class names, and method help identify a bounded context and its purpose. Consider, too, the terms used in the functionality. For example, the term invoice is an obvious clue. But CustomerAccount may not be enough of a clue. In cases like these, look for verbs. What is acting on or with the CustomerAccount? Two possibilities of action are the creation of a customer account, while another is notification.

# Aggregates and Aggregate Roots

Not surprisingly, there can be multiple classes in a bounded context. There is a relationship between the classes based on dependency. This dependency may be due to inheritance or composition. Each group of these classes is an Aggregate and the top-level class in an Aggregate Root.

There is a rule, provided by Eric Evans, that states that classes in an aggregate may call on each other or an aggregate root of another aggregate even if it is in another bounded context. The idea is that no class in a bounded context may leverage a class in another bounded context without going through the root of an aggregate. This rule is an architectural form of encapsulation. It prevents building dependencies that quickly become fragile.

Let's consider the following example. There is an aggregate for handling Benefits in the Benefits bounded context shown in Figure 3-1. There is an aggregate root with dependent classes handling benefits such as Retirement, Health Insurance, and Short-Term Disability. In the Payroll bounded context, there is also an aggregate. It has dependent classes for handling details like time sheets, federal forms, and direct deposit. Each aggregate, in the separate bounded contexts, has its own Employee class. This duplication of the Employee class allows employee functionality to be separate and not become a God class. God classes contain functionality for multiple bounded contexts, thus blurring the lines and making them harder to evolve.

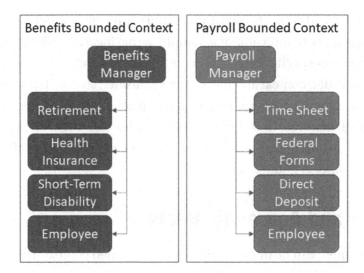

*Figure 3-1.* *Example of aggregates*

Should any class in the benefits aggregate be allowed to call the employee object in the payroll aggregate and change its state? No. Allowing any class to call any other class in a different aggregate could affect the integrity of the data in that employee's state. When changes to an employee's benefits affect their paycheck, then the code in the benefits aggregate should only make calls to the payroll aggregate root. Adhering to this rule allows for business rules to be in place to protect the integrity of the employee data and other related classes. Another example is that changes to an employee's benefits should not change their direct deposit information.

The Load Request class is related to Load and Customer classes handling new load requests in the SPLAT application. In Figure 3-2, you see the Load Request class is the aggregate root. To access load information in the request, you should not go directly to the Load class but rather through the Load Request class. Going directly to the Load Request class allows it to either provide the functionality to alter the state of a Load or Customer. In the absence of functionality, the root can protect the integrity of the state of the information.

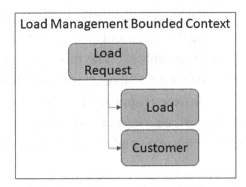

*Figure 3-2.* *Shows Load Request class as the aggregate root*

Domain-Driven Design is a large topic and takes a while to fully grasp all the details and integrate them into daily software development. The aspects I covered will help in the discussions about how the developers at Code Whiz analyze and create code that fulfills the needs for Hyp-Log. In the next section, we will cover a way of analyzing an existing code base.

# Event Storming

The team at Code Whiz decided to use a workshop-style meeting called "Event Storming" with the members at Hyp-Log. Though not the only way to help understand business processes, it is great for identifying various domains that the development team will later be modeling. Alberto Brandolini originally invented Event Storming to help identify aggregates in DDD. It is also extremely useful for companies to understand existing systems better and develop the requirements needed for a software project. Alberto has a website on Event Storming at `https://eventstorming.com`.

In Event Storming, software developers learn from subject matter experts, known as domain experts, how the industry operates, and how that company operates. The meeting is to help everyone involved gain a common understanding of how things currently work and to show processes that need to change. Event Storming meetings help new development team members come up to speed and with domain experts new to their position. A domain expert may retire, and someone without years of knowledge has to take over that role. In such cases, domain experts can also gain a complete understanding of the various pieces of a system.

Several of these meetings will take place throughout the development effort. Although it would be nice to have everything discussed and all requirements gathered before development starts, doing so will inevitably allow for misunderstandings or incorrect assumptions. It may also be more effective to have many small meetings than a few long and daunting. The relative domain experts approve the solutions created by the developers for the various problems. This approval process helps prevent a deviation between what the domain experts and development team understand about the business processes.

## Setup

Event Storming is best done on large walls using paper rolls, sticky notes, and pens. Since many people can work together, provide enough space for the sticky notes when working with multiple subdomains. It is common to use hallways to allow for enough room for people to work around each other.

Digital options are available but somewhat discouraged. Although using a site like Miro (`https://miro.com`) is a good option, it is difficult for multiple people to collaborate effectively. One advantage an online resource like Miro has over using real sticky notes is the ability to grab a group of sticky notes and move around the board quickly.

## Color Coding

To distinguish types of activities, use sticky notes of various colors. There are many suggestions on color schemes to use. Whatever color scheme you choose, make a legend like the one noted in Figure 3-3. Considering the size of the wall used during the Event Storming sessions, you may want to make copies of the legend for various areas.

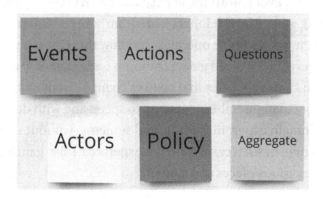

*Figure 3-3.* *Event Storming legend*

- Orange – Domain Events

- Blue – Actions/Commands

- Yellow – Actors

- Purple – Policy

- Green – Aggregate

- Red – Questions

Domain events (orange) are business processes that are noted in the past tense. They are in the past tense as they have occurred, and other items are affected by these events. Actors (yellow) either cause a domain event or are responsible for initiating an action/command. For example, the Customer actor initiated the "Order Submitted" domain event by completing an online order.

Actions/commands (blue) are artifacts that either trigger a domain event or are a process triggered by a domain event. For example, if an "Invoice Created" domain event occurred, an action could be to "Notify Customer." Notifying a customer is noted, but implementing it is beyond the scope of what problems are trying to be understood.

Policies (purple) are for noting where special business rules come into play. For example, with a domain event of "Items Purchased," note an action for a warehouse employee to pick the items. A policy may note that an item weighing over 50 pounds requires two people to lift. Another example is if an item weighs over 200 pounds, then a forklift is required. Policies are to note where such attention is needed but not meant to cover every case.

Aggregates (green) are for noting where a domain object exists. Sticking with the previous example of a domain event of "Items Purchased," an aggregate could be a "Warehouse Pick Ticket." In code, this is likely to be class objects. Another example of an aggregate could be an Invoice or Customer. Notice the aggregate is enough for showing the relationship to the business process to which it relates.

Questions (red) are when domain experts or the development team have questions but no immediate answers. They require some research but are simply flagged so the workshop can continue. Using sticky notes for noting questions, you won't forget the necessary details when it comes time for development. However, development cannot be considered complete without answers to those questions. One example could be "Who decides weight thresholds for the warehouse item policy?"

# The Meeting

The Event Storming meeting begins with only noting domain events. The domain experts start filling out orange sticky notes and applying them to the wall. They start with any domain event that comes to mind. From there, add other sticky notes as other events are remembered and thought through. Rearrange the sticky notes as discussions occur and as you discover new order of events.

It is not required to note every domain event at this stage. As the meeting progresses and other sticky notes are applied, you will add other domain events to the storyline. And there is no need to note functionality that occurs at the persistence layer (data store interactions) unless there is business-critical functionality. Hopefully, there is no business logic in the persistence layer as that would not be clean code and make for tighter coupling of dependencies.

Domain events that are not relevant to the problem space should not be on the wall. Domain events like "User Logged into System" should only be on the wall if the problem concerns users logging in. Else, the sticky notes only add confusion. Domain events regarding customers and carriers notified, in this case, should be on the wall as they directly apply to business processes in the problem space. Figure 3-4 shows examples of domain events.

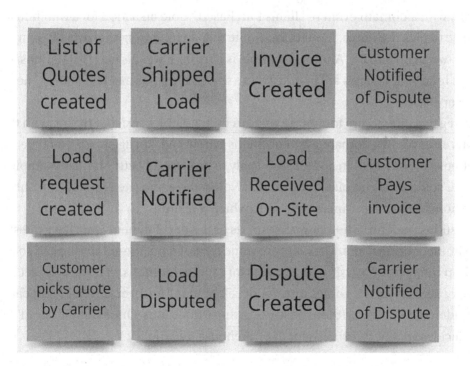

***Figure 3-4.*** *Example of domain events*

After domain events are applied, ask the group to look for duplicates that do not need to be on the board and apply the order of events. There will be cases where duplicate events should be on the wall. For example, when notifying carriers, there can be more than one time when that event occurs. However, they are context specific. That is, each domain event is relative to the contextual reason it exists.

Figure 3-5 shows a flow of events, also depicting split processes. This split process shows a decision that a load is either accepted or disputed. A parallel process shown is during the dispute handling, where the customer and the carrier are notified. They occur at the same time and are not dependent on each other.

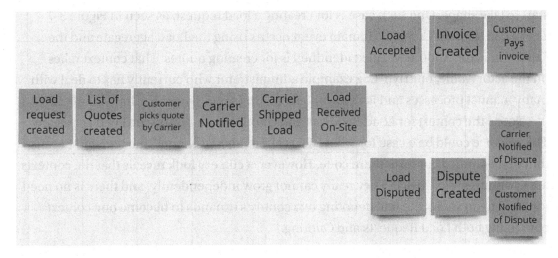

***Figure 3-5.*** *Example of split process*

Now, ask the domain experts to note the other supporting pieces of the domain events. Add the actions/commands, aggregates, actors, and policies to their relative places showing a better picture of how business processes operate. It is common to have to move many sticky notes to make room for additional supporting notes. Another possibility for duplicate sticky notes is with aggregates. In Figure 3-6, Load, Customer, Carrier, and Invoice can have copies applied to differing contexts. It is cleaner to have copies of sticky notes in cases like this than to move a sticky note.

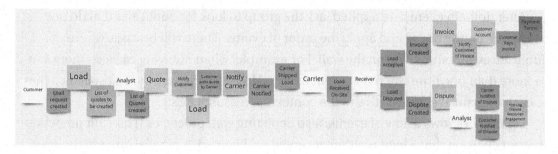

**Figure 3-6.** *Emerging contexts*

As the teams review the wall of sticky notes and discussions occur, different contexts start to take shape. One such case is for creating a load request, as seen in Figure 3-7. The "Load Request Created" domain event occurs using the Load aggregate and the Customer actor. Another context identified is for creating quotes. That context relies on the actor Annie, our Hyp-Log example administrator who currently has to deal with many manual processes and is overworked creating quotes and handling phone calls.

Notice the context for Load Requests and Quoting both rely on the Load aggregate. This reliance could be a case for what DDD calls a "Shared Kernel" relationship because different bounded contexts share code. However, a cursory look reveals that the contexts are not mutually exclusive. They really cannot grow independently, and there is no need for them to do so. So, the line denoting two contexts expands to become one context containing both Load Requests and Quoting.

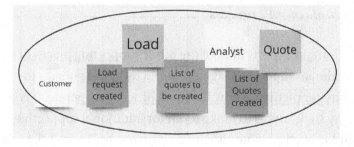

**Figure 3-7.** *Example of single context*

Other contexts are also identifiable. Depicted in Figure 3-8 are the contexts of Invoicing and Dispute Management. Since the outcome of Event Storming sessions is to reflect the current system, the contexts identified are where code exists and have differing functionality. The code for invoicing should be completely separate from the code for handling disputes. Because of this separation, the code in the various contexts is known as Bounded Contexts. Each bounded context contains business functionality that should be entirely separate from others. This separation allows for the independent evolution of the applicable code.

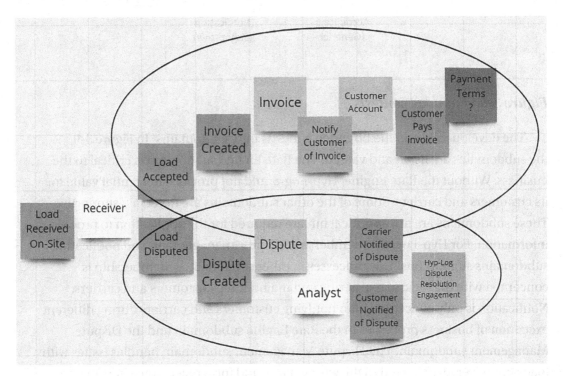

***Figure 3-8.*** *Invoice and Dispute Management contexts*

After each Event Storming meeting, both teams agree on tasks and the related priorities. This way, everyone is engaged and understands the expectations and deadlines. The development team revises and creates work items for the tasks identified. As domain experts evaluate work in progress, some work items may be revised to include rework and sometimes redesign. This rework can happen if the result of development does not meet expectations by the domain experts.

# Seeing the Domains

On the wall after Event Storming sessions, the developers can see evidence of bounded contexts. However, how should developers gauge the value of a bounded context compared to another? Another way of asking this question is, how can developers understand the worth a bounded context brings to a company?

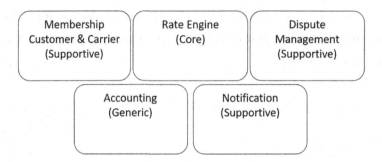

*Figure 3-9.*  *Bounded contexts*

The developers group the bounded contexts into subdomains. In Figure 3-9, the subdomains are listed and valued. The Rate Engine subdomain is critical to the business. Without the Rate Engine, Hyp-Log would not provide substantial value to its customers and carriers. Some of the other subdomains are noted as "supportive." These subdomains are not as critical but are required for the application to process information. For Hyp-Log, the membership, dispute management, and notification subdomains support business processes in other subdomains. Membership is concerned with the logic of registering and maintaining customers and carriers. Notification is only concerned with notifying customers and carriers during different execution of business processes in the Rate Engine subdomain and the Dispute Management subdomain. The Dispute Management subdomain handles issues with loads undelivered, delivered to the wrong place, and incorrect invoice information.

Understanding the value of a subdomain that a bounded context fulfills helps determine the cost of code change. Code that is in bounded contexts located in core subdomains must have more scrutiny and protection. Because of this, functionality in a core subdomain is less likely to move to a microservice and may very well be better off staying in a monolithic application.

# Domain Models

After the first Event Storming meeting with Hyp-Log, the Code Whiz developers started creating code to solve the various issues identified. A domain model is a set of codes created to solve problems in their related subdomains. The Rate Engine subdomain will have a domain model that is separate from the domain model created for handling membership registrations.

As domain models evolve, there will be times when a developer must verify domain experts agree with the new code and when changes occur to existing code. Any code written and previously approved by the domain experts should be tested repeatedly, checking for unintended breaking changes. When using Agile, the Sprint Reviews is a perfect time for verifying that existing and new changes meet the domain experts' expectations.

# Focus on Behavior

Domain models should focus on behavior instead of the state of an object. During the Event Storming sessions, pay close attention to the verbs in the UL. They are clues as to the expected behavior of the domain models. The domain models should also only contain enough code to solve the problems in their subdomain. When a model serves more functionality than needed, it adds the potential for tight coupling, bugs, and failures, making them harder to maintain.

# Domain Modelling

Further meetings with the domain experts may show the domain models need to evolve with changes. New requirements may come due to new challenges or when domain experts clarify a business process. Be prepared to throw away a domain model and start over. Although developers dislike having to start over, this is sometimes the best way to come to a more aligned model to what is needed for the business and fellow developers later.

# Decomposition

The monolith has been detailed on the wall during the Event Storming sessions. All the important domain events have been identified along with their related actors, commands, and aggregates. Now the development team needs to determine where best to modify the existing code base to fulfill the new requests by their customer.

Of the list of pain points Hyp-Log gave to Code Whiz was the issue with the Rate Engine. Also noted in the Event Storming sessions, the Hyp-Log analyst is responsible for the manual process of retrieving distance information to apply to the quotes. This process is tedious and is impacting the growth of their business. They decided it would be cheaper to apply code changes than hire more people to do this work.

The developers ask for the source code of the existing system. Someone from Hyp-Log gave them a USB flash drive while told it was the only other copy. There is no source code repository keeping the source code safe. Hyp-Log does not realize the danger they are in. With such simple problems arising, Hyp-Log could be in a far worse position.

The developers take a quick cursory look at the code files on the USB drive. They quickly confirm the code is far from clean and is, in fact, a BBoM (Big Ball of Mud) that will take a lot of time to refactor properly. Because of the amount of refactoring it would take to meet the customer's demands, the lead architect decides that retrieving distance information can be done using a microservice that calls Google's Map API and possibly others.

Using a microservice will allow the existing code to have minimal changes, keep the manual process intact, and have this feature deployed independently of other changes. Another reason for this being a microservice is that it allows other map information providers to be added without changing the monolith.

Another pain point on the list is the lack of a good invoice management system. The analyst does all the invoice handling. She must not only create the invoices but keep track of those not paid and those past due. By having a microservice handle invoices, the current system can be modified as little as possible while providing a more functional solution. But this microservice will be a bit more challenging. There is an existing database with some invoice information. Because any microservice responsible for persistent information must have its own database, the invoice data will have to move. Decentralizing data is covered in Chapter 6.

# Becoming a Microservice

Microservices should be considered independent applications free to evolve with little to no dependencies on other parts of a system. They should be maintained or owned by a single team of developers. They also require networking for connectivity for either direct RPC-based calls or messaging-based communication.

The biggest reason for Code Whiz to consider microservices for the SPLAT application is the time-to-market factor. Hyp-Log's business is growing, and the manual processes are holding them back. By making minimal changes to the monolith and adding microservices to solve their main pain points, the application will be able to scale easier over time and handle additional code projects in the future.

# Summary

We covered much ground in this chapter. Using our hypothetical company Hyp-Log, you were able to see the business processes of an existing system. You saw how Event Storming was used to understand better what the domain experts know about their system. Event Storming helps everyone be on the same page regarding what business processes exist, how they interact, and what other elements support them.

We also covered DDD at a high level. DDD helps developers by focusing on the domain, subdomains, and related behaviors. You learned about elements of DDD that help the developers leverage to make code cleaner, loosely coupled, and easier to modify for future changes. You also learned that the Ubiquitous Language is a vital piece of DDD that provides contextual support for the development team to better understand the system from domain experts. We also went over aggregates and aggregate roots and how they represent classes with a structure to support a form of encapsulation and how the aggregate roots help protect the integrity of the aggregate.

In the next chapter, we will create the first microservice. You will create a microservice to solve the issue of retrieving map information from Google. This microservice will use RPC-style communication between the monolith and the Web API endpoint.

# CHAPTER 4

# First Microservice

In the last chapter, we decided that retrieving distance information could be done by calling Google's Distance Service. The lead architect decided to make a microservice to provide this functionality. Before we start creating this microservice, we need to understand some crucial architectural details. Microservices are more about software architecture to solve problems for the business than it is about code. By understanding the business processes that require and use distance information, we can design a better solution.

For each pickup and drop-off location, Annie, the analyst for Hyp-Log, gets the distance and enters the value in the SPLAT program. For Annie, she retrieves the distance information manually. However, this is time-consuming and impacts the generation of quotes. When looking at the business process to create quotes, where does a call to a microservice make sense? Before we can answer that question, we need to look at ways microservices communicate.

## Interprocess Communication

Every application has processes where logic executes. In the logic are calls to functions that reside in memory. However, some functions are not in the same application processes in distributed systems and may not even be on the same server. The microservices architecture is an implementation of a distributed system that provides functionality over a network. The various mechanisms for communicating with a microservice are called interprocess communication (IPC). Two such mechanisms for calling a microservice are "direct" and "asynchronous messaging." You can call a microservice directly using Remote Procedure Call (RPC)-style communication. Another way is by utilizing a messaging system like MassTransit.[1] Our microservice uses the RPC

---

[1] MassTransit is an open source library for .NET applications to use messaging style communication. More information can be found at `https://masstransit-project.com`.

© Sean Whitesell, Rob Richardson, Matthew D. Groves 2022
S. Whitesell et al., *Pro Microservices in .NET 6*, https://doi.org/10.1007/978-1-4842-7833-8_4

style to retrieve distance for multiple reasons. The average time to retrieve distance information from Google's Distance API is low enough. Also, the number of calls to Google's Distance API is extremely low.

RPC is a synchronous communication method that has a request and a response. The caller is the client making a request from a function on a server. The caller sends the request and waits for a response. This waiting means that the business logic cannot continue without a specific reply. Because the call to a microservice is over a network, this allows for a separation of concerns. That is, the caller does not need to know about the internals of the microservice.

Understanding how to leverage microservices is very important as each call has a role in the business processes. Since microservices communicate over a network, there is inherent latency to the execution of a business process. If the business process cannot tolerate this additional latency in execution, then that code should not rely on a microservice.

Using RPC-style communication for microservices has another drawback. The caller must know the network address of the microservices. What happens if the microservice is no longer at that location? How do we handle scaling to several instances of a single microservice? We will start with a hard-coded IP address and then later go over the use of service discovery.

# API First Design

Microservices that receive direct requests accept these calls through an Application Programming Interface (API). As fun as it would be to just sling code for our microservice, that would be haphazard and could allow issues to occur. Instead, API first design means focusing on what functionality is exposed and expectations of requests and responses.

An API is one or more functions that are callable by code external to itself in code. These functions are public entry points that provide encapsulation of business logic. This encapsulation allows for the governance of what logic is available to external callers. These callers may be in different namespaces, classes, or even NuGet packages. When public functions in public classes expose functionality, code in another assembly can call and use that functionality. With Web API, the interfaces are only available via web-based communication protocols, usually Hypertext Transport Protocol (HTTP).

We already touched on understanding a microservice's role in business processes. But how should the microservice be called? This chapter is about RPC-style microservices. Therefore, we need to understand what to expect of this microservice that retrieves information from Google. We will build the API first. That is, we will work out what this microservice will offer functionally. What is the shape/format of the request? Does the request use JSON, XML, or a binary format? Should the request use REST or gRPC? And what about the response back to the caller?

# Transport Mechanisms

When calling any network service like a web server using HTTP, File Transfer Protocol (FTP) server, or Internet of Things (IoT) devices, there is a communication means for data sent to and from the endpoints. The means of communication among the endpoints are using a transport mechanism. There are several transport mechanisms available. In this book, we will only focus on two, REST and gRPC.

# REST

Roy Fielding created Representational State Transfer (REST) in 2000 to transfer data using stateless connections. REST provides a form of state over the stateless protocol HTTP. The development of HTTP 1.1 and Uniform Resource Identifiers (URI) standards utilized REST.

REST is best suited for text-based payloads and not binary payloads. Since most data is in memory, it must be transformed, or "serialized," to a textual representation like JSON or XML before being sent to an endpoint. Data is then deserialized back to a binary form stored in memory when received.

REST has operations called HTTP verbs. Here is a list of the most common:

- GET – used for the retrieval of data

- POST – used for the creation of data

- PUT – used for updating data

- DELETE – used for the deletion of data

The REST standard considers GET, PUT, and DELETE as idempotent. Idempotent actions mean that sending the same message multiple times has the same effect as sending once. For developers, this means we need to pay careful attention to our APIs. When receiving duplicate messages, do not allow the creation of multiple results. For example, if you have duplicate messages that each have instructions to add a charge to a bill for $5.00, the amount should only be affected by one of the messages. POST, on the other hand, is not idempotent. Making multiple calls will likely end up in duplicate records.

# gRPC

Another way for microservice communication is with "gRPC Remote Procedure Calls" (gRPC). Google created gRPC for faster communication with distributed systems by using a binary protocol called Protocol Buffers. Like REST, gRPC is language agnostic, so it can be used where the microservice and caller are using different programming languages.

Unlike REST, gRPC is type specific and uses Protocol Buffers to serialize and deserialize data. You must know the type definitions at design time for both parties to understand how to manage the data. In the section where we use gRPC, you will see how proto definition files define our data structures.

When choosing which transport mechanism to use for microservices, there are some considerations. First, gRPC uses the HTTP/2 protocol, which helps with lower latency. However, you may need to verify various pieces are compatible with HTTP/2. Another consideration is knowing when to leverage gRPC. If you know the microservices are public facing, either on the Internet or on a network deemed public, REST is the most likely chosen option. It is the most versatile and easiest to use. If the calls are from internal code such as a monolith or another microservice, you may consider gRPC. Using gRPC will help lower latency and is worth the extra time to set up. Although our microservice is internal facing only, we will start with REST for its simplicity and then show how to integrate gRPC into our project.

So far, we have learned that this microservice will use RPC-style communication with REST for the transport mechanism of data in the request and response. What should the request and response look like, JSON or XML? A brief look at the Google Distance API specification shows they are returning data with JSON. Although we could transform the data to XML for the caller of our microservice, this is just not needed. JSON is a good alternative to XML and is usually a smaller payload in transit and storage.

# File – New – Project

We are going to start writing code using the .NET Core template for Web API. As mentioned earlier about an API, a Web API is simply an API for handling web-based traffic. Calling functions in an external assembly is an example of leveraging an API. With Web API, the functions are only accessible via transport mechanisms like REST and gRPC. The setup for this Web API is very similar to the ASP.NET Core MVC pattern. It has routing, controllers, and views. Well, sort of. The views are different for Web APIs. With MVC, the view is about representing data, in the response, for human eyes. The data is formatted for the response with Web API but not for what is adorned with CSS styles. This data is to be interpreted by the caller for business logic.

In Visual Studio 2022, we are going to create the first microservice. The first step is to create a new project. Select File ➤ New ➤ Project.

Select "ASP.NET Core Web API" from the list of options, as you can see in Figure 4-1. You may need to adjust some of the project template filters to make it easier to find the template.

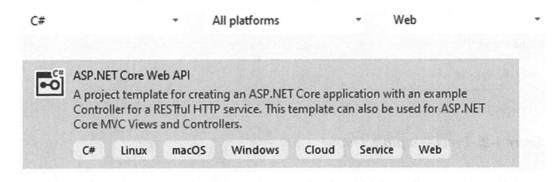

*Figure 4-1.* *Selecting project type*

After you have selected the template, select the "Next" button. Now, you will configure your new project, starting with details for name and file location. The project name and file location shown here are simply suggestions. Select the "Next" button when you have finished applying the name and file location of your choice (see Figure 4-2).

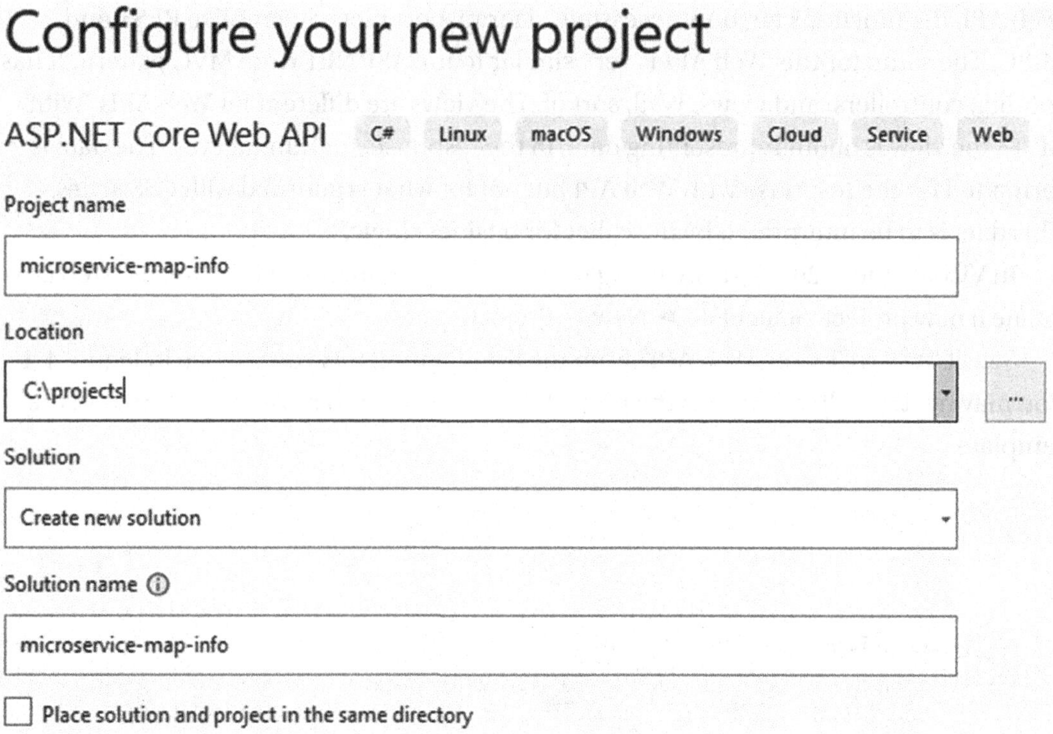

# Configure your new project

ASP.NET Core Web API   C#   Linux   macOS   Windows   Cloud   Service   Web

Project name

```
microservice-map-info
```

Location

```
C:\projects|                                                      ▼    ...
```

Solution

```
Create new solution                                                    ▼
```

Solution name ⓘ

```
microservice-map-info
```

☐ Place solution and project in the same directory

***Figure 4-2.*** *Provide a project name*

In the screen for additional information, choose .NET 6 (see Figure 4-3). For this demo, no authentication is needed. The other options are also outside the scope of this demo. After choosing the options you want, select the "Create" button.

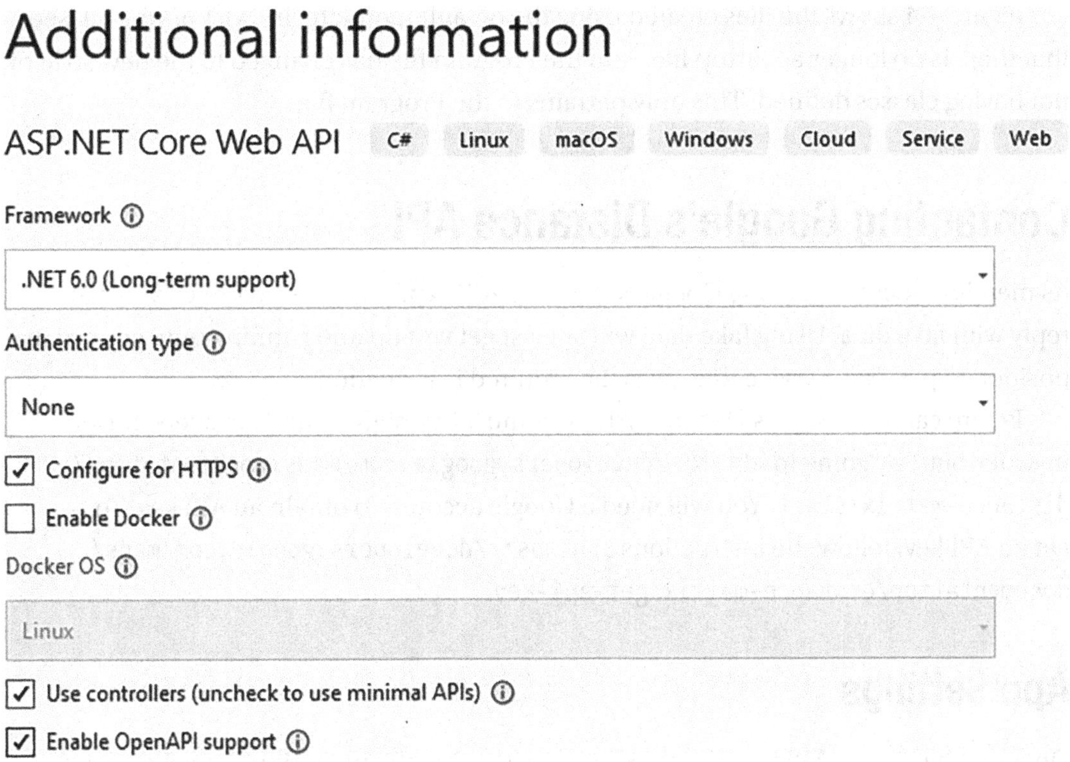

# Additional information

## ASP.NET Core Web API    C#    Linux    macOS    Windows    Cloud    Service    Web

Framework ⓘ

.NET 6.0 (Long-term support)    ▾

Authentication type ⓘ

None    ▾

☑ Configure for HTTPS ⓘ

☐ Enable Docker ⓘ

Docker OS ⓘ

Linux    ▾

☑ Use controllers (uncheck to use minimal APIs) ⓘ

☑ Enable OpenAPI support ⓘ

***Figure 4-3.*** *Setting additional project information*

After creating the project, you will see the files created from the template. It created a controller called WeatherForecastController and a class called WeatherForecast. You can build and run the project as is. You will see the example code run that presents random weather data and presents the data as JSON.

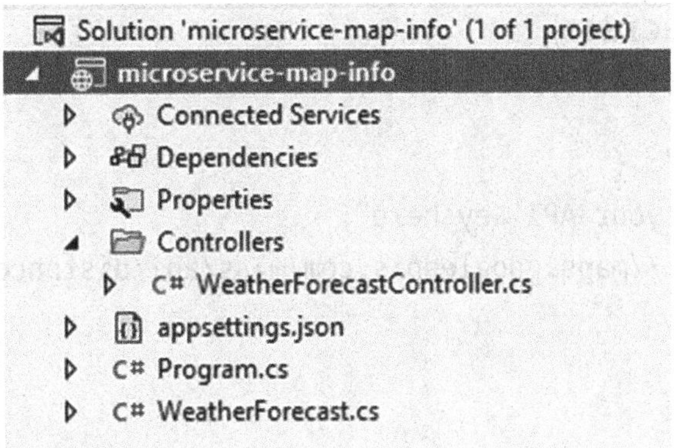

```
🗐 Solution 'microservice-map-info' (1 of 1 project)
▲  🖫 microservice-map-info
   ▷  ⊕ Connected Services
   ▷  🗗 Dependencies
   ▷  ⬚ Properties
   ▲  ▭ Controllers
      ▷  C# WeatherForecastController.cs
   ▷  🗓 appsettings.json
   ▷  C# Program.cs
   ▷  C# WeatherForecast.cs
```

***Figure 4-4.*** *Default Weather Forecast template*

Figure 4-4 shows the files created using the default template. In .NET 6, you will see that there is no longer a Startup file. And the Program file has changed to the new style of not having classes defined. This only pertains to the Program file.

# Contacting Google's Distance API

As mentioned before, calling Google's Distance API is not free. If you prefer, you can reply with fake data. Using fake data will at least get you up and running until you are in a position to pay for a service that gives the required information.

Before calling Google's Distance API, you must first sign up and get a few things in order. Start by going to `https://developers.google.com/maps/documentation/distance-matrix/start`. You will need a Google account to obtain an API key. To get an API key, follow the instructions at `https://developers.google.com/maps/documentation/distance-matrix/get-api-key`.

## App Settings

Once you have your API key, you need to store that in the appSettings.json file of your main project. In the project "microservice-map-info," open the file appSettings.json and add this block.

---

**Note**    It is best not to store any secrets or API keys in configuration files. It is very easy to deploy secrets to production accidentally. Instead, consider using the Secret Manager tool (`https://docs.microsoft.com/en-us/aspnet/core/security/app-secrets`).

---

```
"googleDistanceApi": {
  "apiKey": "Enter your API Key here",
  "apiUrl": "https://maps.googleapis.com/maps/api/distancematrix/json?"
}
```

The result will look something like this:

```
{
  "Logging": {
    "LogLevel": {
      "Default": "Information",
      "Microsoft": "Warning",
      "Microsoft.Hosting.Lifetime": "Information"
    }
  },
  "AllowedHosts": "*",
  "googleDistanceApi": {
    "apiKey": "Enter your API Key here",
    "apiUrl": "https://maps.googleapis.com/maps/api/distancematrix/json?"
  }
}
```

# New Class Library

Now, we will create a new class library project that will have the code for contacting Google's Distance information. Having this code in a separate class library allows you the option of swapping this functionality with another provider at a later time.

Right-click the solution and select Add ➤ New Project. You may need to change your filter selection to find Class Library. Select the project type for Class Library and then select the "Next" button (see Figure 4-5).

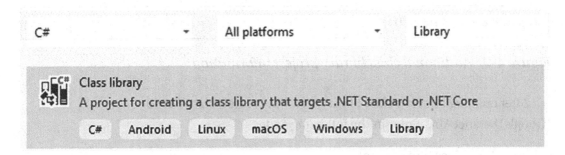

*Figure 4-5.* *Creating a new Class Library*

On this screen, shown in Figure 4-6, give your new class library project the name "GoogleMapInfo." Also, pick a folder for the project files.

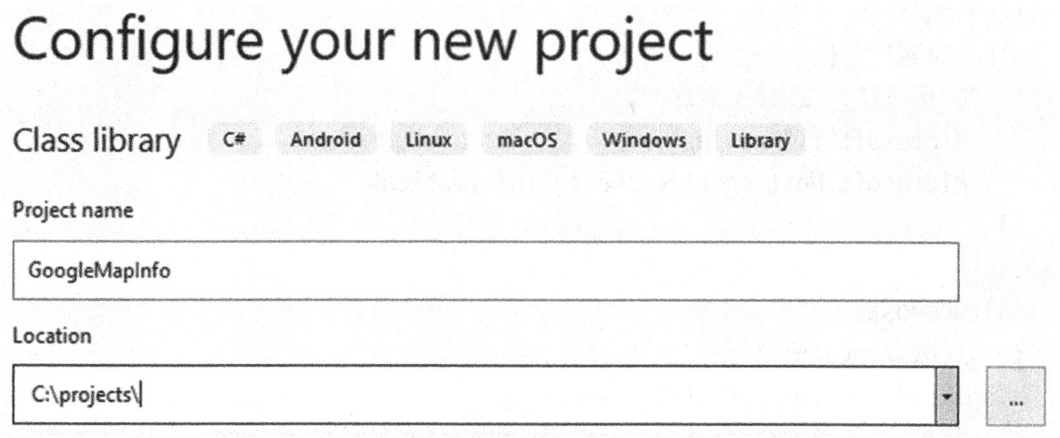

# Configure your new project

Class library    C#    Android    Linux    macOS    Windows    Library

Project name

GoogleMapInfo

Location

C:\projects\

*Figure 4-6.* *Providing project name and folder location*

Select the "Next" button, and you will see the next screen to add additional information (see Figure 4-7). Select the .NET 6 option for the framework and then select the "Create" button.

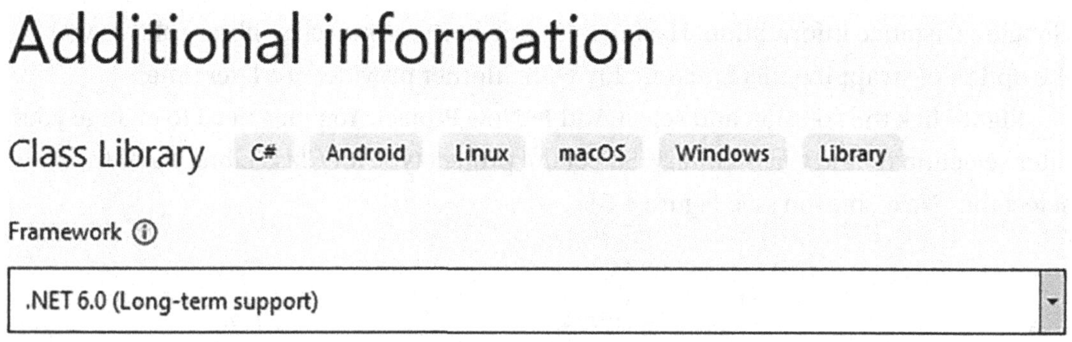

# Additional information

Class Library    C#    Android    Linux    macOS    Windows    Library

Framework ⓘ

.NET 6.0 (Long-term support)

*Figure 4-7.* *Additional class library project information*

After creating this new class library, you will create a class called "GoogleDistanceApi." Enter in the following code:

```
public class GoogleDistanceApi
{
  private readonly IConfiguration _configuration;
```

```
public GoogleDistanceApi(IConfiguration configuration)
{
  _configuration = configuration;
}

public async Task<GoogleDistanceData>
   GetMapDistance(string originCity, string destinationCity)
{
  var apiKey = _configuration["googleDistanceApi:apiKey"];
  var googleDistanceApiUrl = _configuration["googleDistanceApi:apiUrl"];
  googleDistanceApiUrl += $"units=imperial&origins={originCity}&destinati
  ons={destinationCity}&key={apiKey}";

  using var client = new HttpClient();
  var request = new
      HttpRequestMessage(HttpMethod.Get, new Uri(googleDistanceApiUrl));

  var response = await client.SendAsync(request);
  response.EnsureSuccessStatusCode();

  await using var data = await response.Content.ReadAsStreamAsync();
  var distanceInfo = await
      JsonSerializer.DeserializeAsync<GoogleDistanceData>(data);

  return distanceInfo;
  }
}
```

The call to Google's Distance API returns data in the JSON format you can deserialize
to a type. Create a new class file called "GoogleDistanceData" and enter this code:

```
public class GoogleDistanceData
{
  public string[] destination_addresses { get; set; }
  public string[] origin_addresses { get; set; }
  public Row[] rows { get; set; }
  public string status { get; set; }
}
```

```
public class Row
{
  public Element[] elements { get; set; }
}

public class Element
{
  public Distance distance { get; set; }
  public Duration duration { get; set; }
  public string status { get; set; }
}

public class Distance
{
  public string text { get; set; }
  public int value { get; set; }
}

public class Duration
{
  public string text { get; set; }
  public int value { get; set; }
}
```

With the code to call Google's Distance API in place, now you will reference this new project by the main project. On the main project, "microservice-map-info," right-click and select Add ➤ Project Reference. You will see screen listing projects you can reference (see Figure 4-8). Select the project you just created and select the "OK" button.

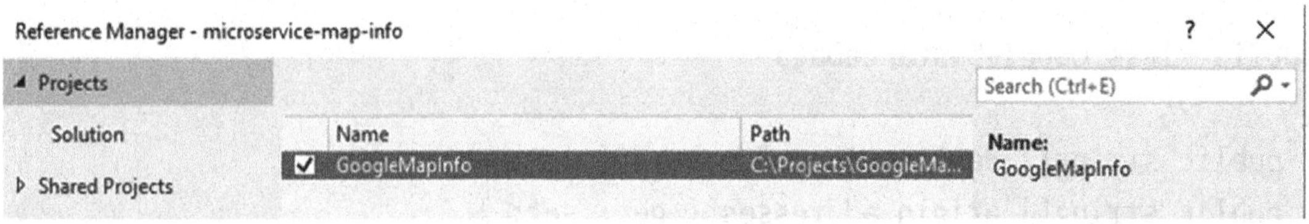

*Figure 4-8.* Setting project reference

# Map Info Controller

For the microservice to accept calls for distance information, you need to create a
controller that will process the requests. In the main project, find the Controllers folder
and right-click it. Select Add ➤ Controller. Select "API Controller – Empty" when the
screen like Figure 4-9 appears and then select the "Add" button.

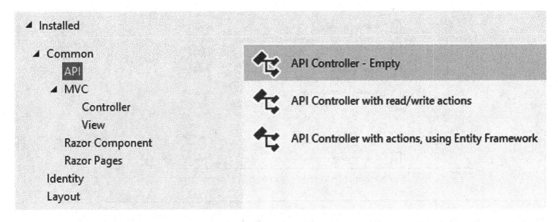

*Figure 4-9.*  *Creating a new empty API Controller*

Once the next screen appears, choose "API Controller – Empty" and apply the name
"MapInfoController.cs" (see Figure 4-10). Then, select the "Add" button.

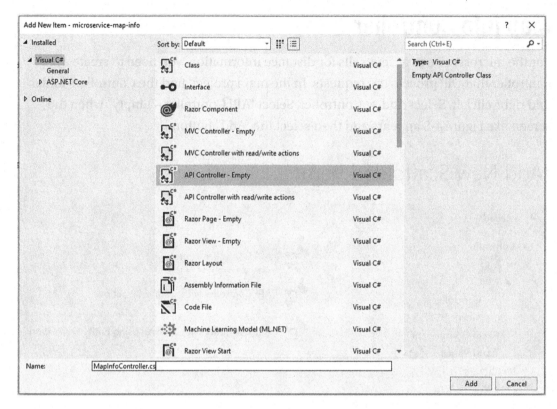

***Figure 4-10.*** *Providing a name for the new API controller*

In the new MapInfoController, modify the class to look like this code:

```
[Route("[controller]")]
[Route("[controller]/[action]")]
[ApiController]
public class MapInfoController : ControllerBase
{
  private readonly GoogleDistanceApi _googleDistanceApi;

  public MapInfoController(GoogleDistanceApi googleDistanceApi)
  {
    _googleDistanceApi = googleDistanceApi;
  }

  [HttpGet]
  public async Task<GoogleDistanceData> GetDistance(string originCity,
  string destinationCity)
```

```
  {
    return await _googleDistanceApi.GetMapDistance(originCity,
    destinationCity);
  }
}
```

We need to configure ASP.NET Core to know how to instantiate the MapInfoController to be ready for use. In the Startup.cs file, you need to add a few lines. In the method ConfigureServices, add a line above the one adding controllers. This new line registers the GoogleDistanceApi class with the built-in Inversion-of-Control (IoC) system. When the MapInfoController class is instantiated, the IoC container provides an instance of GoogleDistanceApi and gives it to the constructor of MapInfoController.

```
public void ConfigureServices(IServiceCollection services)
{
  services.AddTransient<GoogleDistanceApi>();
  services.AddControllers();
}
```

## Testing What We Have

As the project sits right now, you should be able to build and run the code. However, how will you verify it is working? There are a few ways we can do this. First, simply run that application. After several seconds a browser will open, showing the default page of this application. You will notice that it's showing the results of executing the weather forecast code instead of getting distance data from Google. The unintended result is because of the settings in the launchSettings.json file located in the Properties folder. Your file contents will look similar to the following listing but do not have to be exact:

```
{
  "$schema": "http://json.schemastore.org/launchsettings.json",
  "iisSettings": {
    "windowsAuthentication": false,
    "anonymousAuthentication": true,
    "iisExpress": {
```

```
      "applicationUrl": "http://localhost:60285",
      "sslPort": 44358
    }
  },
  "profiles": {
    "IIS Express": {
      "commandName": "IISExpress",
      "launchBrowser": true,
      "launchUrl": "weatherforecast",
      "environmentVariables": {
        "ASPNETCORE_ENVIRONMENT": "Development"
      }
    },
    "microservice_map_info": {
      "commandName": "Project",
      "launchBrowser": true,
      "launchUrl": " weatherforecast ",
      "applicationUrl": "https://localhost:6001;http://localhost:6000",
      "environmentVariables": {
        "ASPNETCORE_ENVIRONMENT": "Development"
      }
    }
  }
}
```

Notice there are two main sections, "IIS Express" and "microservices_map_info." These entries show in Visual Studio and are environments in which you can run the application. Usually shown at the top bar is the list you can pick an environment (see Figure 4-11).

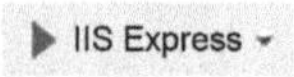

▶ IIS Express ▾

***Figure 4-11.***  *Default Visual Studio launch environment*

When you select the little arrow to the right of IIS Express, you see this drop-down list of options shown in Figure 4-12.

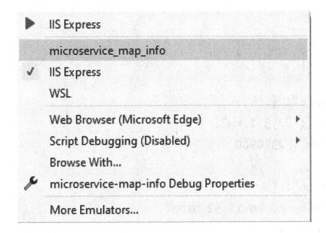

***Figure 4-12.*** *Selecting a new launch environment*

In the launchSettings.json file, notice that each section has a key of "launchUrl" and a value of "weatherforecast." This is why the weather forecast was the default page when you ran the application. The application uses the value for "applicationUrl" and concatenates the value from "launchUrl." This allows the use of HTTP URL and the HTTPS URL. Now change the value of "launchUrl" to "mapinfo." The name is that of the controller to be used by default. And it does not need the word "controller" since ASP. NET Core uses the "convention over configuration" method of identifying the controller by name. Now, in the list of environments, select the option for "microservice_map_info" and run the application again. This time it will call the "MapInfoController" class.

With the browser open showing your page, change the query string to something like this:

**https://localhost:5001/mapinfo/getdistance?originCity=Dallas,Tx&destination City=Los%20Angeles,CA**

The execution returns the result:

```
{
  "destination_addresses": [
    "Los Angeles, CA, USA"
  ],
  "origin_addresses": [
    "Dallas, TX, USA"
  ],
```

```
    "rows": [
      {
        "elements": [
          {
            "distance": {
              "text": "2,311 km",
              "value": 2310980
            },
            "duration": {
              "text": "20 hours 52 mins",
              "value": 75108
            },
            "status": "OK"
          }
        ]
      }
    ],
    "status": "OK"
}
```

At this point, you can delete the file "WeatherForecastController.cs" file and the file "WeatherForecast.cs."

## Swagger

Another way to test the application is using a tool called Swagger. Swagger (`https://swagger.io`) is a free tool provided by OpenAPI Spec for developing APIs. Adding Swagger is very simple to use, and it will show all the exposed methods that a calling application can call.

Using the Package Manager Console:

**Tools ➤ NuGet Package Manager ➤ Package Manager Console**

Set the default project to "microservices-map-info" (see Figure 4-13).

Default project:  microservice-map-info

***Figure 4-13.*** *Select default project for NuGet*

Now run this command:

```
Install-Package Swashbuckle.AspNetCore
```

Open the file Startup.cs and modify the methods ConfigureServices and Configure to look like this:

```
public void ConfigureServices(IServiceCollection services)
{
  services.AddTransient<GoogleDistanceApi>();
  services.AddControllers();

  services.AddSwaggerGen(c =>
  {
   c.SwaggerDoc("v1", new OpenApiInfo { Title = "My map API",
   Version = "v1" });
  });
}

// This method gets called by the runtime. Use this method to configure the
HTTP request pipeline.

public void Configure(IApplicationBuilder app, IWebHostEnvironment env)
{
  if (env.IsDevelopment())
  {
    app.UseDeveloperExceptionPage();
  }

  app.UseSwagger();

  app.UseSwaggerUI(c =>
  {
    c.SwaggerEndpoint("/swagger/v1/swagger.json",
        "My microservice for map information.");
  });

  app.UseHttpsRedirection();

  app.UseRouting();
```

```
  app.UseAuthorization();

  app.UseEndpoints(endpoints =>
  {
    endpoints.MapControllers();
  });
}
```

Now, when you run the application, you can go to this URL in your browser:

`https://localhost:5001/swagger/index.html`.

You will see a page showing the multiple available action methods. In this application, there are two ways of calling our single action method "GetDistance." One way is without specifying the action method name. The other is for when specifying that action method. Now, select one of the methods and then select the "Try it out" button. The page shows the two parameters "originCity" and "destinationCity." Put in "Dallas,TX" for the origin and "Los Angeles,CA" for the destination. Select the button "Execute." The page will call your application and then show the result.

Using Swagger is a great way to test your microservice while you are developing it. It also helps you see the structure of the HTTP call for when you modify the monolith to call the microservice.

# Leveraging gRPC

The previous way of communicating with the microservice was with REST and JSON. Now, you can leverage a binary transport mechanism for faster communication. With gRPC, communication may be faster depending on the type of data sent. It takes some time to convert an instance of a class to a message. For small, simple message payloads, you may be better off with JSON. However, as soon as the message payload size is more than tiny, the time to convert to binary is quickly justified. And with the high-performance nature of binary communication, gRPC is used for large message payloads and even streaming. gRPC is also platform agnostic, so it can be running on anything that can use HTTP/2.

gRPC uses HTTP/2 for transport and Protocol Buffers for the interface definition language (IDL). With JSON, converting an instance of a class to a stream of text relies on many rules and uses reflection. Since gRPC is a binary representation of data, the conversion effort is not as straightforward. Developers must use customizations even on simplistic data types. In this section, you will modify the microservice to leverage gRPC to learn how to trim latency with the network calls.

gRPC uses an IDL definition file, or "contract," to define the message data and must be shared on both the sender and receiver. A quick example of a "proto" file is

```
syntax = "proto3";

service SubscribeToEvent {
  rpc Subscribe (EventSubscription) returns (Subscribed)
}

message EventSubscription {
  int32 eventId = 123;
  string name = foo;
}

message Subscribed {
  string message = bar;
}
```

In this example, a service "SubscribeToEvent" is defined with the method "Subscribe." The "Subscribe" method takes in a parameter type "EventSubscription," which returns the type "Subscribed."

## Incorporating gRPC

With Visual Studio open to our microservice, you will add new folders and files and modify the project file.

1. Right-click the "microservice-map-info" project and select Add ➤ New Folder. Name the folder "Protos."

2. Create another folder from the project called Services.

3. Right-click the Protos folder and select Add ➤ New Item. In the menu, select "Protocol Buffer File." Name it "distance.proto."

4.    In the file "distance.proto," put in the following content:

```
syntax = "proto3";

option csharp_namespace = "microservice_map_info.Protos";

package distance;

service DistanceInfo {
  rpc GetDistance (Cities) returns (DistanceData);
}

message Cities {
  string originCity = 1;
  string destinationCity = 2;
}

message DistanceData {
  string miles = 1;
}
```

Now create the service file. In the Services folder, right-click and select Add ➤ Class. Name it DistanceInfoService.cs and replace the template code with this:

```
public class DistanceInfoService : DistanceInfo.DistanceInfoBase
{
  private readonly ILogger<DistanceInfoService> _logger;
  private readonly GoogleDistanceApi _googleDistanceApi;

  public DistanceInfoService(ILogger<DistanceInfoService> logger,
  GoogleDistanceApi googleDistanceApi)
  {
    _logger = logger;
    _googleDistanceApi = googleDistanceApi;
  }

  public override async Task<DistanceData> GetDistance(Cities cities,
  ServerCallContext context)
```

```
{
  var totalMiles = "0";

  var distanceData = await _googleDistanceApi.GetMapDistance(cities.
  OriginCity, cities.DestinationCity);

  foreach (var distanceDataRow in distanceData.rows)
  {
    foreach (var element in distanceDataRow.elements)
    {
      totalMiles = element.distance.text;
    }
  }

  return new DistanceData { Miles = totalMiles};
  }
}
```

Do not be surprised if you see errors and it will not compile yet. After a couple more steps, the solution will compile. And the gRPC package will build code behind the scenes for the proto file you created. For now, just save the file.

## NuGet Packages

You need to install the gRPC NuGet package to work with the proto files and code it generates. Open Package Manager Console by going to Tools ➤ NuGet Package Manager ➤ Package Manager Console. At the prompt, type in

```
Install-Package Grpc.AspNetCore
```

## Project File

Modify the project file by left-clicking the project. It will open the file in the editor. Modify the project file to include this:

```
<ItemGroup>
  <Protobuf Include="Protos\distance.proto" GrpcServices="Server" />
</ItemGroup>
```

```
<ItemGroup>
  <Folder Include="Protos\" />
</ItemGroup>
```

## Startup Modifications

To call the gRPC service, you need to add a few lines in the ConfigureService and Configure methods. Your startup file should look like this:

```
public class Startup
{
  public Startup(IConfiguration configuration)
  {
    Configuration = configuration;
  }

  public IConfiguration Configuration { get; }

// This method gets called by the runtime. Use this method to add services
to the container.
  public void ConfigureServices(IServiceCollection services)
  {
    services.AddTransient<GoogleDistanceApi>();
    services.AddControllers();
    services.AddGrpc();
    services.AddSwaggerGen(c =>
    {
      c.SwaggerDoc("v1",
          new OpenApiInfo { Title = "My map API", Version = "v1" });
    });
  }

// This method gets called by the runtime. Use this method to configure the
HTTP request pipeline.
  public void Configure(IApplicationBuilder app, IWebHostEnvironment env)
  {
```

```
if (env.IsDevelopment())
{
  app.UseDeveloperExceptionPage();
}

app.UseSwagger();
app.UseSwaggerUI(c =>
{
  c.SwaggerEndpoint("/swagger/v1/swagger.json",
  "My microservice for map information.");
});

app.UseHttpsRedirection();
app.UseRouting();
app.UseAuthorization();

app.UseEndpoints(endpoints =>
{
  endpoints.MapGrpcService<DistanceInfoService>(); //new
  endpoints.MapControllers();
});
  }
}
```

Now that gRPC has been brought into this project, a restriction arises. gRPC will not run with IIS. So, you must debug and run in production using Kestrel[2] instead of IIS. To change to Kestrel in Visual Studio, find the selection box for running a project, as shown in Figure 4-14. Then, select "microservice_map_info" by name.

---

[2] Kestrel is a cross-platform web server for ASP.NET Core applications. For more information, go to https://docs.microsoft.com/en-us/aspnet/core/fundamentals/servers/kestrel?view=aspnetcore-6.0.

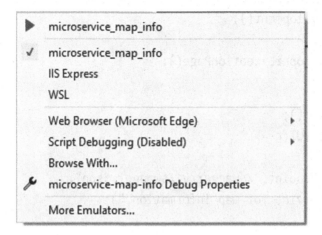

***Figure 4-14.***  *Select the launch environment*

# Testing gRPC Endpoint

Until now, you can test the connection to the REST API, but how can you test the gRPC service endpoint? You can test with a simple console application. Using a new instance of Visual Studio, create a new Console Application. Figure 4-15 shows the project type to select.

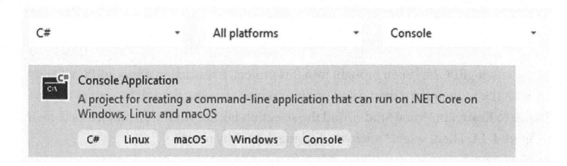

***Figure 4-15.***  *Selecting Console application type*

Select the "Next" button. Now provide a project name and location. See Figure 4-16.

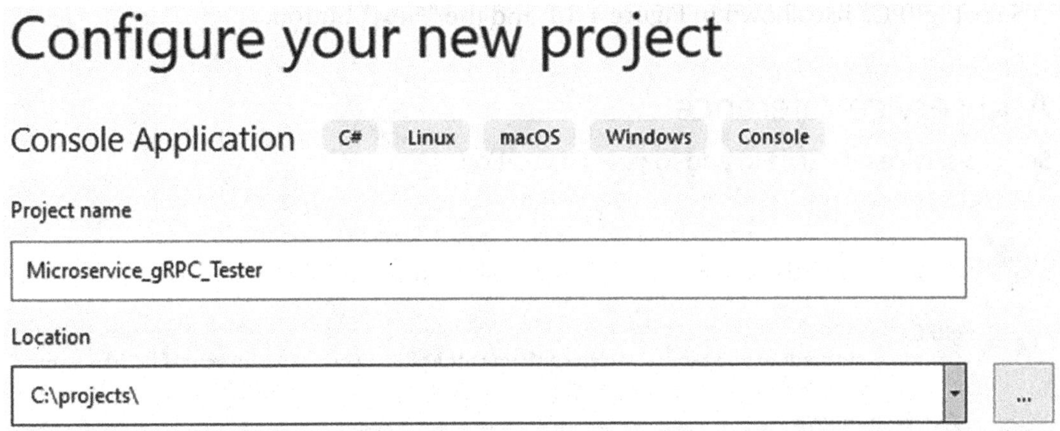

# Configure your new project

## Console Application  C#  Linux  macOS  Windows  Console

Project name

Microservice_gRPC_Tester

Location

C:\projects\

*Figure 4-16. Providing project name and folder location*

Select the "Next" button. Now the screen to add additional information appears (see Figure 4-17). Select .NET 6 if not already selected.

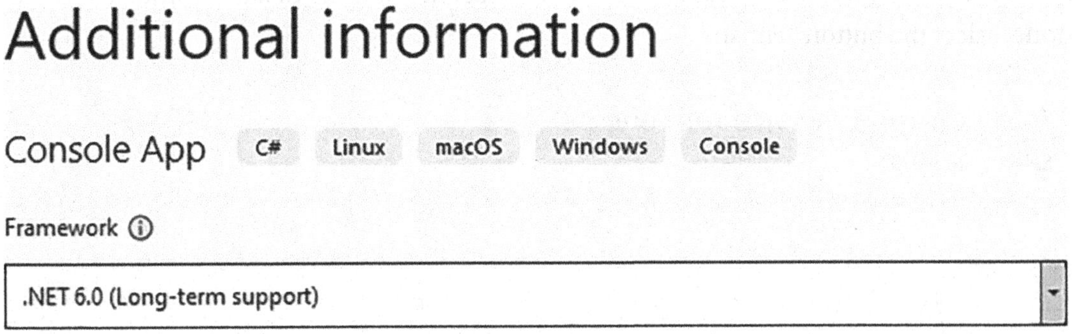

# Additional information

## Console App  C#  Linux  macOS  Windows  Console

Framework ⓘ

.NET 6.0 (Long-term support)

*Figure 4-17. Additional project information*

After creating the project, you need to make a Service Reference. Much like adding a project reference, this will add a reference based on the proto file created earlier. Right-click the project and select "Add ➤ Connected Service." When the next window appears, find the "Service References (OpenAPI, gRPC, WCF Web Service)" section and select the plus symbol.

Select "gRPC," like shown in Figure 4-18, and the "Next" button.

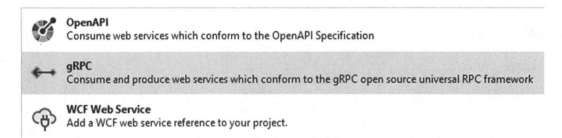

## Add service reference

Select a service reference to add to your application

**OpenAPI**
Consume web services which conform to the OpenAPI Specification

**gRPC**
Consume and produce web services which conform to the gRPC open source universal RPC framework

**WCF Web Service**
Add a WCF web service reference to your project.

*Figure 4-18.*  *Selecting service reference type for gRPC*

The service reference is based on the proto file. On this screen, shown in Figure 4-19, traverse to the folder where you created the microservice and the distance.proto file. Once done, select the button "Finish."

## Add new gRPC service reference

Select a file or URL

⦿ File

C:\Projects\microservice-map-info\microservice-map-info\Protos\distance.proto    Browse...

◯ URL

Select the type of class to be generated

Client

*Figure 4-19.*  *Adding new gRPC service reference*

Now to write some client code to contact the gRPC endpoint. Open the Program.cs file and replace the method Main with this:

```
static async Task Main(string[] args)
{
  var channel = GrpcChannel.ForAddress(new Uri("https://localhost:5001"));
  var client = new DistanceInfo.DistanceInfoClient(channel);
```

```
var response = await
    client.GetDistanceAsync(new Cities
    { OriginCity = "Topeka,KS", DestinationCity = "Los Angeles,CA" });

Console.WriteLine(response.Miles);

Console.ReadKey();
}
```

You will have to update the using statements as well. However, this is an interesting part. How does the client code know the data types and namespace for this code? When you created the Service Reference and selected the distance.proto file, code was generated based on the contents.

At this point, you can build our new gRPC endpoint tester. But before you can run it, you will need to note one more detail. Notice the URL is set to https://localhost:5001. This path needs to match that of the microservice. Looking in the microservice project, in the launchSettings.json file, you see that when running with Kestrel, for HTTPS, the URL is https://localhost:5001. Since those two URLs match, we are good for testing. Now, start the microservice. After it is running, start the console application. Using the test data of Topeka,KS, and Los Angeles,CA, you should see a returned value of "1,555 mi."

Our microservice can now accept REST-based requests using JSON as well as gRPC-based requests using binary. You will have to judge when to REST vs. gRPC as it largely depends on the size of the message payload needed in your architecture design. You will have runtime decisions based on the payload size. Instead, your architectural design, governed by your business requirements, helps shape the use of one transport method vs. another.

# Modify the Monolith

Now that the microservice is working and ready to be called, let's modify the monolith to use it. This section will alter the monolith to call the microservice to retrieve the distance between two cities.

In the Services folder, right-click and select Add ➤ Class. Provide the name DistanceInfoSvc and select the Add button. Now replace the template code with this code:

```
public interface IDistanceInfoSvc
{
  Task<(int, string)> GetDistanceAsync(string originCity,
    string destinationCity);
}

public class DistanceInfoSvc : IDistanceInfoSvc
{
  private readonly IHttpClientFactory _httpClientFactory;

  public DistanceInfoSvc(IHttpClientFactory httpClientFactory)
  {
    _httpClientFactory = httpClientFactory;
  }

  /// <summary>
  /// Call the microservice to retrieve distance between two cities.
  /// </summary>
  /// <param name="originCity"></param>
  /// <param name="destinationCity"></param>
  /// <returns>Tuple for distance and the distance type.</returns>
  public async Task<(int, string)> GetDistanceAsync(string originCity,
  string destinationCity)
  {
    var httpClient = _httpClientFactory.CreateClient("DistanceMicroservice");

    var microserviceUrl = $"?originCity={originCity}&destinationCity={desti
    nationCity}";

    var responseStream = await httpClient.GetStreamAsync(microserviceUrl);

    var distanceData = await JsonSerializer.DeserializeAsync<MapDistance
    Info>(responseStream);

    var distance = 0;
```

```csharp
    var distanceType = "";
    foreach (var row in distanceData.rows)
    {
      foreach (var rowElement in row.elements)
      {
        if (int.TryParse(CleanDistanceInfo(rowElement.distance.text), out
        var distanceConverted))
        {
          distance += distanceConverted;
          if (rowElement.distance.text.EndsWith("mi"))
          {
            distanceType = "miles";
          }

          if (rowElement.distance.text.EndsWith("km"))
          {
            distanceType = "kilometers";
          }
        }
      }
    }

    return (distance, distanceType);
}

private string CleanDistanceInfo(string value)
{
  return value
        .Replace("mi", "")
        .Replace("km", "")
        .Replace(",", "");
}

    //These classes are based on the data structure
    //returned by Google's Distance API
```

```
public class MapDistanceInfo
{
    public string[] destination_addresses { get; set; }
    public string[] origin_addresses { get; set; }
    public Row[] rows { get; set; }
    public string status { get; set; }
}

public class Row
{
    public Element[] elements { get; set; }
}

public class Element
{
    public Distance distance { get; set; }
    public Duration duration { get; set; }
    public string status { get; set; }
}

public class Distance
{
    public string text { get; set; }
    public int value { get; set; }
}

public class Duration
{
    public string text { get; set; }
    public int value { get; set; }
}
}
```

The DistanceInfoSvc class is responsible for calling the microservice and
deserializing the results. JSON is the data format for the returned distance data. The data
deserializes into MapDistanceInfo class. You can generate the classes to match JSON
data in Visual Studio by capturing the JSON payload in the clipboard. Now, go to an open
area and select Edit ➤ Paste Special ➤ JSON as Classes.

Now we need to alter the quote service to call the DistanceInfoSvc to retrieve the distance for the quote. In the QuoteSvc class, add the following code alterations.

First, alter the constructor to have the DistanceInfoSvc injected in.

```
private readonly IDistanceInfoSvc _distanceInfoSvc;

public QuoteSvc(IDistanceInfoSvc distanceInfoSvc)
{
    _distanceInfoSvc = distanceInfoSvc;
}
```

Now alter the method that creates the quote to leverage DistanceInfoSvc class.

```
public async Task<Quote> CreateQuote(string originCity, string
destinationCity)
{
    var distanceInfo = await _distanceInfoSvc
        .GetDistanceAsync(originCity, destinationCity);

    // other code here for creating a quote

    var quote = new Quote {Id = 123,
        ExpectedDistance = distanceInfo.Item1,
        ExpectedDistanceType = distanceInfo.Item2};

    return quote;
}
```

Update the appSettings.json file to hold the location of the microservice.

```
"DistanceMicroservice": {
    "Location": "https://localhost:6001/mapinfo"
}
```

We need to update the Startup.cs file to register the DistanceInfoSvc and provide the HttpClient. In the ConfigureServices method, add the following code:

```
services.AddScoped(typeof(IDistanceInfoSvc), typeof(DistanceInfoSvc));

var distanceMicroserviceUrl =
    Configuration.GetSection("DistanceMicroservice:Location").Value;
```

```
services.AddHttpClient("DistanceMicroservice", client =>
{
  client.BaseAddress= new Uri(distanceMicroserviceUrl);
});
```

The line that registers IDistanceInfoSvc will inject instances of DistanceInfoSvc where used in constructors. In this case, when instantiating the QuoteSvc class, an instance of DistanceInfoSvc is injected. The next section gets the URL to the microservice and provides it to the HttpClient base address. Using the AddHttpClient method allows for retrieving an instance of HttpClient. The key benefit of doing it this way is that another instance of the HttpClient is not generated with each call to the microservice.

# Service Discovery

So far, the caller (monolith in our case) requires knowing the IP address of where the microservice instance is hosted. Even if there was only one microservice instance, the caller should not have the IP because another instance could replace the microservice with a new IP address. However, there should never be just one microservice instance in production. You might have one microservice but with multiple instances for high availability. Each microservice instance has an IP address. Should the caller (monolith in our case) know the IP address of each microservice instance? If one instance dies or another is created, how will you update the monolith?

Callers of a microservice should not have the responsibility to know about every instance of microservice. That creates a tightly coupled architecture. Instead, the caller should only know about one IP address, which is a load balancer. Using a load balancer, you have a separation of concerns between the caller and the microservice instances.

The ability for a load balancer to know about the multiple microservice instances is service discovery. For this purpose, many products are available, such as Apache's ZooKeeper, HashiCorp's Consul, Eureka by Netflix, and even Nginx.

# Summary

We went over interprocess communication methods for calling a microservice. Specifically, in this chapter, we covered the RPC communication style. We also covered the need to design the API first to better understand how the microservice is called and the payload structure. We then went over transport mechanisms and the details of REST and gRPC. Then we built the first microservice that leveraged Google's Distance API. We then incorporated the ability to call Google's Distance API with the Web API front-end controller. Then we modified the microservice to leverage gRPC for binary payload. Next, we modified the monolith to call the microservice. Finally, we noted how service discovery is an additional part of the architecture to prevent hard-coding IP addresses and handle multiple microservice instances.

# CHAPTER 5

# Microservice Messaging

So far, you have learned how to create microservices using RPC communication. You also learned how it is synchronous communication requiring a request and a response. In this chapter, you will create two microservices using messaging's asynchronous communication method to fulfill some business needs regarding invoice management.

## Issues with Synchronous Communication

Before we dive into messaging communication, let us first understand why messaging is a viable option. Imagine this scenario; you are a coach of a sports team for kids. An issue comes up that causes the rescheduling of a game. You start down a list of people and call them one by one. You call the other coaches, plus the umpires/judges and *all* of the parents.

Now imagine that call one of the parents that oversee the concession stands. That parent then calls the owner of the concession stands and discovers they cannot attend on the proposed date. You called the parent, and the parent called the owner. Each step in the communication chain has transitive latency. This transitive latency is problematic for you, who never intended to spend so much time trying to communicate with others.

Other issues exist for you and the other coaches. The list of people to contact varies. They also vary by purpose. Just because a coach is contacted does not mean all the parents must be contacted as well. And it is never known who has the correct list of contact information.

This direct communication is extremely inefficient. It allows for all sorts of communication issues. What would happen if anyone were not notified of the schedule change? What if the chain of communication involved other downstream pieces? And what if there is a failure to notify them? This allows for cascading failures.

© Sean Whitesell, Rob Richardson, Matthew D. Groves 2022
S. Whitesell et al., *Pro Microservices in .NET 6*, https://doi.org/10.1007/978-1-4842-7833-8_5

This way of contacting others is a huge drain on you and the other coaches. You agreed to be the coach to help the kids, not worry about communication issues. Each call has the potential of not being answered and information failing to be sent and understood. Also, each call takes the coaches' time because they are synchronous. Each caller must wait for someone to answer, receive the message, and acknowledge what needs to happen next.

# Limits of RPC

The preceding real-life scenario is an example of RPC communication. Each call you and the coaches made required waiting for a response. This shows the biggest drawback of RPC with microservices; processes must wait for a response, that is, synchronous communication.

Another issue with this type of communication is handling the number of simultaneous calls. For example, if more calls are coming in than the microservice can handle, the caller will see either severe latency or no contact at all. This forces the caller to use retry policies or the circuit breaker pattern.

Scaling microservices horizontally requires a load balancer. The load balancers must also be performant not to add any latency. And just because another instance of a microservice exists does not mean it is instantly registered in the load balancer. So, there is an effort to register the microservice instance in the load balancer.

Then there is the other issue of adding other microservices to a business process. If the caller is only aware of one microservice, then it must be altered to know about the other microservices. This means more code changes to each caller that must be aware of the others. And how is versioning to be handled? There are even more code changes to handle adapting to a different version.

# Messaging

With the scenario of you as the coach, what if there was a way to broadcast the information once? Perhaps group text or an email would suffice. Then everyone receives that information independently, and each recipient reacts accordingly. That is the purpose of messaging.

Using messaging in the microservices architecture allows independent pieces to communicate without knowing the location of each other. In the preceding scenario, each coach would have to have a list of the other coaches and how to reach them. Also, they each need to know how to reach the parents and anyone else involved in a game.

Messaging solves many of the problems identified in the preceding example story. If the coach had a messaging system in place, contacting some people or everyone would be easier. Also, adding, removing, and updating contact information would be simpler. So, where does messaging fit in an architecture?

# Architecture

With messaging, there is a shift in the way of thinking about microservices. You can use simple messaging architecture to reach a microservice in a disconnected way. But moreover, using messaging with microservices allows for a dynamic and reactive architecture. With an event-driven architecture, the microservices react to messages sent as a response to an event. Perhaps a user has committed to the creation of an order. Or maybe there is a change to the inventory of an item.

# Reasons to Use Messaging

There are multiple reasons to use the messaging communication style over the RPC style. The list of reasons includes

- Loosely coupled

- Buffering

- Scaling

- Independent processing

## Loosely Coupled

By using messaging, the sender and the microservices (message consumers) are loosely coupled. The sender of a message does not need to know anything about the microservices receiving the message. This means that microservices do not need to know the endpoints of others. It allows for the swapping and scaling of microservices without any code changes.

This provides autonomy for the microservices. With autonomy, the microservices can evolve independently. This allows for microservices to only be tied together where they fit to fulfill business processes and not at the network layer.

## Buffering

With the microservice architecture, there are opportunities for downtime or intermittent network connection issues. Message brokers utilize queues that provide a buffer of the messages. During times of issues, the undeliverable messages are stored. Once the consumers are available again, the messages are delivered. This buffering also retains sequencing. The messages are delivered in the order they were sent. Maintaining the message order is known as First In, First Out (FIFO).

## Scaling

The ability to scale a microservice architecture is paramount. For any production applications or distributed processing, you will have multiple instances of your microservices. This is not just for high availability but allows messages to be processed with higher throughput.

## Independent Processing

Messaging allows a microservice architecture solution to change over time. You can have a solution to generate orders and manage the shipping of the products. Later, you can add other microservices to perform additional business processes by having them become message consumers. The ability to add microservices to business processes as consumers allows them to be independent information processors.

# Message Types

There are multiple types of messages, depending on the need for communication. These message types play a role in fulfilling various responsibilities in business processes.

## Query

Consider the scenario of contacting your favorite store to see if they have the latest game in stock. (Pretend they do not yet have a site to sell online.) You want to purchase three copies quickly, but the store is not open. You send them an email or perhaps filling out an inquiry form on their website for that information. This is using a query message type in an asynchronous communication style. Although the query could be done synchronously, like a phone call, it does not have to be done that way.

When the store opens, they reply that they do have the game in stock. The reply also includes how many are currently in stock and suggestions on other similar games. A reply to a query is the Document message type. The document contains the information requested and any supporting information.

## Command

You reply confirming you want to secure those three copies, and you are on your way to the store. The message to the store letting them know that they are to hold the items aside for you is a command. The command message type instructs what the consumer is to do without explicitly requiring a reply.

## Event

You arrive at the store and purchase the games. Later, you receive an email about the purchase. The store thanks you for the purchase and includes a digital receipt. That email was sent due to an event in their system. An order was created for you, and as a result, you received the email.

When you purchased the games, the system notified other areas of the system about the order. The event kicked off processes in other parts of the store's system. Each independent process received that event and reacted. For example, the system processed the payment, took the item out of inventory, and notified the shipment department of where the games were to be sent.

The architecture of having multiple consumers listening to the same event is called Publish/Subscribe (Pub/Sub). The publisher of the event sends out the message for others to process. The consumers subscribe to the event and process the message differently. For example, the payment processor consumer will act on the message differently than an inventory management consumer.

# Message Routing

For messages to go from a publisher to the consumers, there must be a system to handle the messages and the routing. This system provides message routing to the consumers that have subscribed to the different messages. There are two types of these systems: brokered and broker-less.

## Broker-less

A broker-less system, like ZeroMQ, sends messages directly from the publisher to the consumer. This requires each microservice to have the broker-less engine installed. It also requires each endpoint to know how to reach others. As you scale your microservices, it quickly becomes harder to manage the endpoint list.

Because there is no central message system, it can have lower latency than a brokered system. This also causes a temporal coupling of the publisher to the consumer. This means that the consumer must be live and ready to handle the traffic. One way to handle the chance of a consumer not being available is to use a distributor. A distributor is a load balancer to share the load when you have multiple instances of a microservice. The distributor also handles when a consumer is unavailable, sending a message to another instance of your microservice.

## Brokered

A brokered system like ActiveMQ, Kafka, and RabbitMQ provides a centralized set of queues that hold messages until they are consumed. Because the messages are stored and then sent to consumers, it provides a loosely coupled architecture. The storing of messages until they are consumed is not a high latency task. It simply means the publisher does not have to store the messages but can rely on the broker.

Designing the use of a broker is about first understanding the business needs of each application and microservice. This topology will consist of various producers and consumers, each with their own messaging needs. Some producers only need to send messages and are not subscribing to other messages. Other producers will send messages for one business while also subscribing to other messages. As you will see in the code examples, our test client sends commands regarding invoices. It also subscribes to the message that the invoice was created. This means that although you can use a broker, the applications are not totally unaware of other applications, so there is still a topological coupling.

An advantage of using a broker is that if a message fails in the processing by a consumer, the message stays in queue until it can pick it up again or another process is ready to process it.

In this chapter, we will use the MassTransit library. It provides some abstractions that allow us to get running quickly. MassTransit can use RabbitMQ, among others, to provide the message transport we need.

# Consumption Models

There are multiple models for receiving messages you will see with multiple consumers. You will use one or both models. Two models are described in the following.

## Competing Consumers

Various business processes need to have a message processed by only one consumer. For example, a *create invoice* message should only be processed once. If multiple instances of a consumer processed it, duplicate information could be stored and sent out to other microservices. Figure 5-1 depicts competing consumers.

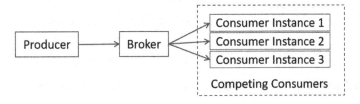

***Figure 5-1.*** *Competing consumers*

An example of a competing consumer, Figure 5-2, is the Invoice Microservice. When you create multiple instances of the Invoice Microservice, they each become a competing consumer.

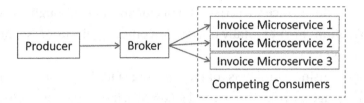

**Figure 5-2.** *Invoice microservice instances as competing consumers*

You should have multiple instances of a microservice for scaling, availability, and distribution of load. A microservice is designed to subscribe to a specific queue and message type. But when there are multiple instances of that microservice, you have a competing consumer scenario. When a message is sent, only one of the microservice instances receives the message. If that instance of the microservice that has the message fails to process it, the broker will attempt to send it to another instance for processing.

## Independent Consumers

There are times when other microservices must also consume the message. This means that these microservices do not compete with other consumers. They receive a copy of the message no matter which competing consumer processes the message.

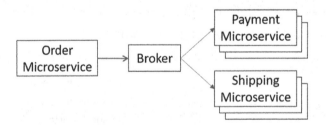

**Figure 5-3.** *Independent consumers*

These independent consumers process the messages for their specific business processing needs. In the preceding example, Figure 5-3, a message is sent from the Order Microservice. The message needs to be received by one instance of the Payment Microservice and one instance of the Shipping Microservice. Here the Payment and Shipping microservices are not competing with each other. Instead, they are independent consumers. Also, note that each instance of a Payment Microservice is a competing consumer to itself. The same is true for the Shipping Microservice instances.

Having independent consumers allows for a Wire Tap pattern (see Figure 5-4). An example of this has a front-end component that sends a command to the Order Microservice to revise an order. In RabbitMQ, you can have an exchange that is bound to another exchange. This allows copies of messages to be sent to another consumer, even though the exchange is set up with direct topology.

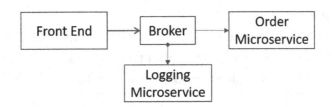

*Figure 5-4.*  *Wire Tap pattern*

# Delivery Guarantees

As we evaluate our business needs and design a messaging topology solution, we must also consider that there will be times when messages either cannot be delivered or are delivered again. Message delivery disruption can allow for the possibility of causing duplication of data or other side effects. There are many reasons why messages fail delivery. Network failures/interruptions happen often enough that we must take them into account. Also, there can be issues with hardware, bugs in our code, or even timeouts. As great as brokers are, they cannot solve all of the problems. So, we must design for those issues when we build our applications.

When issues occur, there is a chance of duplicate messages being sent, so our consumers must handle the messages in an idempotent manner. That is, treat every message with the possibility that it has already been processed before. Exactly how to do that is per message type and business needs. Some messages may include a timestamp, and as they are processed, only messages with later timestamps are processed. And the latest timestamp is stored by the consumers to compare the timestamp in the next message. This also means that competing consumers must have a way for all instances to know the latest timestamp.

There are a few patterns regarding the delivery of messages that apply per message type we design. As each consumer may consume multiple message types, consider how these patterns apply to their needs.

# At Most Once

This delivery guarantee is for when your system can tolerate the cases when messages fail to be processed. An example is when receiving temperature readings every second. If the broker delivers the message, but the consumer fails to process it, the message is not resent. The broker considers it delivered regardless of the consumer's ability to complete any processing of the message.

Another term for this delivery guarantee is "Fire-and-Forget." The principle is the same. The publisher sends a message without any assumption it is delivered or processed. This also offers the highest performance since there is no state management required.

# At Least Once

The "at least once" delivery guarantee is where you will spend the most effort designing the consumers to handle messages in an idempotent manner. If a message fails to be given to a consumer, it is retried. If a consumer receives a message but fails during the process, the broker will resend that message to another consumer instance.

An example scenario: you have a consumer that creates a database entry for a new order, then that instance dies. It did not send an acknowledgment to the broker that it was done with the message. So, the broker sends that message to another consumer instance. There the message is processed and inadvertently creates a duplicate database entry.

Although most broker systems have a flag that is set when it sends a message again, you are safer to assume the message is a duplicate anyway and process accordingly. For example, if the message is to create an order, search the database of another order by that customer on that date for those same items. Then if an order exists, you have confidence that the previous attempt got that far in the business operation.

Because microservices architecture is an implementation of distributed computing, there is a lot to consider. Here we are referring to how messages are handled. There is also much to understand with distributed transactions which is outside the scope of this book. I highly recommend a book, *The Art of Immutable Architecture* by Michael Perry, published by Apress. In Perry's book, there is a specific section on Idempotence and Commutativity applicable to handling messages.

# Once and Only Once

Another name for this delivery guarantee is "Exactly Once," which is the hardest to accomplish. Many argue it does not exist. When you need a message to be processed only once, how do you know it was only processed once? How do you know the message is not a duplicate? Essentially, how do you know the intended state has not already succeeded?

The point here is that guaranteeing a message was only delivered and processed once requires state management involving the consumers and the broker system. This addition of state management may be far more trouble than designing for the other delivery guarantees.

# Message Ordering

If the entire message system were single threaded, then there would be a guarantee of the order of messages. However, that would be an extremely inefficient system and quickly discarded. Instead, we use messaging systems that process messages as efficiently as possible. But this puts the onus on developers to build an architecture that can tolerate the reception of out-of-order messages.

An example scenario is that of a message sent to an Order Microservice to create a new order. Another message to a different instance of the same microservice is sent with an update to the order. During the processing of the first message, an error occurs, and the message is not acknowledged. The broker then sends that message to the next microservice instance that is available. Meanwhile, the message with the update to the order is being processed. The microservice code must decide how to update an order that does not exist yet.

One suggestion is for each instance of the microservice to share the same data store. Then messages received out of order could be stored temporarily and then reassembled when the order's creation message is processed. Of course, there is a lot to manage to do this successfully. Thankfully there is an easier way.

In the book *The Art of Immutable Architecture*, Perry notes that operations should be commutative as it applies here. This means that if the messages do not arrive in the correct order, the result should be the same as if they arrived in the correct order. So, how is our code supposed to handle the information commutative?

We cannot force the order of the messages, but we can design for handling messages out of order. In our scenario, the message with the order update can include all the information that was in the message to create the order. Since the order has not yet been created, there is no order number. So, the update message was sent knowing that it was an update to an order not yet created. Including the original information in the update message allows a consumer to create the order and apply the update in cases where the order does not exist. When the message to create the order is received, it is ignored as it now already exists.

# Building the Examples

Since the microservice we will create in this chapter is meant to process invoices for the company, we need to understand the various states of an invoice. Those listed here are simple examples. You should get with your subject matter experts or domain experts to understand the applicable "real world" invoice states during processing.

- New
- Late
- Modified
- Paid
- Closed

The invoice microservice we will build in this chapter will first have the responsibility of creating an invoice. It may seem like the monolith would be responsible for creating the invoice. But since a microservice is responsible for persisting data, then it should own that data. So, this microservice will receive a request to create an invoice. And part of that process will persist it to a database.

Of course, the microservice we will build here is only an example of a fully featured microservice for processing invoices. This microservice will provide a starting point for you to build more business functionality as you deem necessary.

# Building the Messaging Microservices

To demonstrate microservice messaging, we will create three projects: One for the Invoice Microservice. Another for a Payment Microservice. Then a test client will take the place of a monolith. The test client will act as a front-end service with information for the Invoice Microservice to create an invoice. Then the Invoice Microservice will publish a message about the newly created invoice. The Payment Microservice and the test client will both receive the message that the invoice was created. For the test client, it is confirmation the invoice was created. In a real-world scenario, it could display the invoice number to the user. The Payment Microservice serves as a quick example of a downstream microservice that reacts to the creation of the invoice.

---

**Disclaimer**    The code examples are not meant to be production worthy. They are just enough to help demonstrate concepts.

---

# Running RabbitMQ

You have some options when running RabbitMQ. It can run on a server, on your computer, or in a Docker container. If you would like to install RabbitMQ, go to `https://rabbitmq.com/download.html`. In our examples, we will run RabbitMQ from a Docker container. Docker Desktop is required to be installed. To install Docker Desktop, go to `https://docker.com/products/docker-desktop`.

I did note that we will be using MassTransit for messaging. We will be running MassTransit on top of RabbitMQ. MassTransit provides a layer of abstraction and makes coding easier. It can run on top of RabbitMQ, Azure Service Bus, ActiveMQ, and others.

With Docker Desktop installed, go to a command prompt and enter

```
docker run -p 5672:5672 -p 15672:15672 rabbitmq:3-management
```

If you prefer to run the RabbitMQ instance detached from the console:

```
docker run -d -p 5672:5672 -p 15672:15672 rabbitmq:3-management
```

You can look at the RabbitMQ Management site by going to `http://localhost:15672`. The default username and password for RabbitMQ are *guest* and *guest*.

With RabbitMQ running, now we will create the microservices. We will start with the microservice for invoices.

# First Project

For the first project, we will create a class library on which the other projects will depend. This project will contain the interfaces and classes that become our messages.

In Visual Studio 2022, select the option to Create a New Project. Then select the Class Library option (see Figure 5-5).

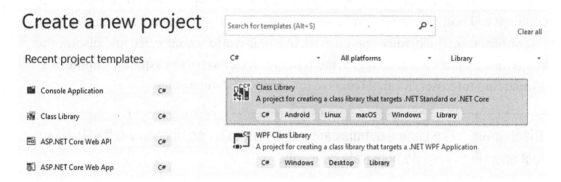

***Figure 5-5.***  *New class library*

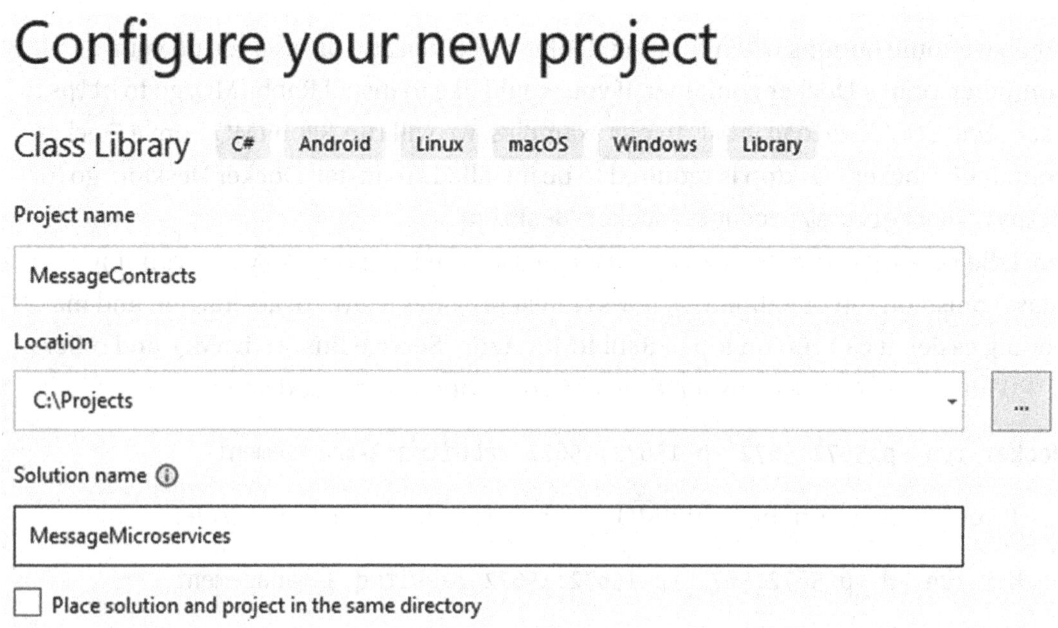

# Configure your new project

## Class Library   C#   Android   Linux   macOS   Windows   Library

Project name

MessageContracts

Location

C:\Projects

Solution name ⓘ

MessageMicroservices

☐  Place solution and project in the same directory

***Figure 5-6.***  *Naming and selecting file location*

Figure 5-6 shows the screen for the project name MessageContracts. Provide a location for your projects, and then for the solution name, use MessagingMicroservices. Make sure the checkbox is not selected to place the solution in the same directory as the project. When done, select the "Next" button.

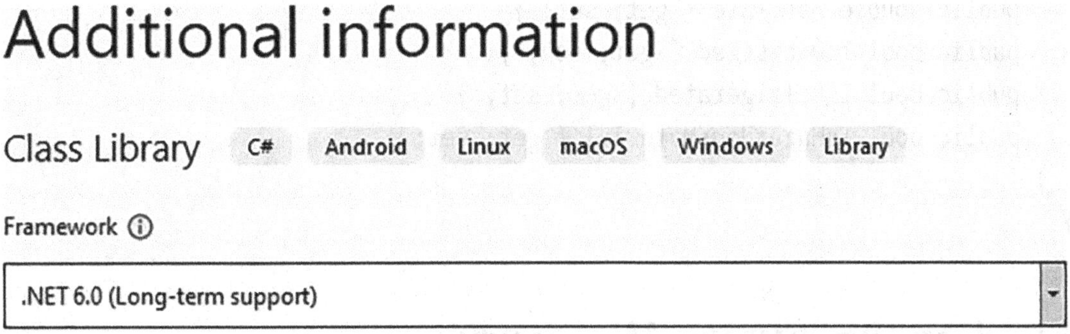

# Additional information

Class Library    C#    Android    Linux    macOS    Windows    Library

Framework ⓘ

.NET 6.0 (Long-term support) ▾

***Figure 5-7.*** *Additional project options*

If not already selected, choose the framework for .NET 6 (see Figure 5-7). Then, select the "Create" button. After creating the project, rename the Class1.cs file to MessageContracts.cs. Then replace all the code in that file with the following code:

```
using System.Collections.Generic;

namespace MessageContracts
{
  public interface IInvoiceCreated
  {
    int InvoiceNumber { get; }
    IInvoiceToCreate InvoiceData { get; }
  }

  public interface IInvoiceToCreate
  {
    int CustomerNumber { get; set; }
    List<InvoiceItems> InvoiceItems { get; set; }
  }
```

```
public class InvoiceItems
{
  public string Description { get; set; }
  public double Price { get; set; }
  public double ActualMileage { get; set; }
  public double BaseRate { get; set; }
  public bool IsOversized { get; set; }
  public bool IsRefrigerated { get; set; }
  public bool IsHazardousMaterial { get; set; }
}
}
```

# Building the Invoice Microservice

Now we will create the first microservice. This microservice is for processing invoices. As an example of a microservice using messaging, it will receive a command to create an invoice. It will then publish an event about the new invoice once created.

Right-click the solution and select Add ➤ New Project.

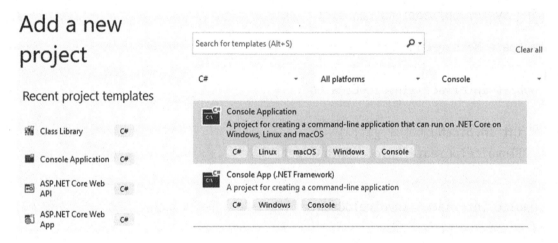

***Figure 5-8.*** *New console application*

Select the option for Console Application and then select the "Next" button (see Figure 5-8).

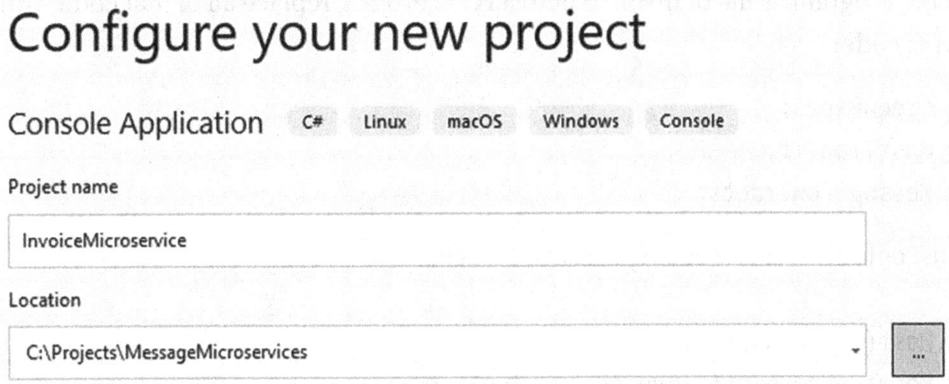

# Configure your new project

Console Application   C#   Linux   macOS   Windows   Console

Project name

InvoiceMicroservice

Location

C:\Projects\MessageMicroservices

**Figure 5-9.** *Project name and location*

Now give the project the name of InvoiceMicroservice and then select the "Next"
button (see Figure 5-9). Choose the .NET 6 framework and then select the "Create"
button. This project also needs to have the MassTransit library with RabbitMQ
installed. In the Package Manager Console, make sure the Default Project has the
InvoiceMicroservice selected. Then at the prompt, enter

```
Install-Package MassTransit.RabbitMQ
```

We now need to connect this project to the MessageContract project. We will
be writing code that is dependent on interfaces and classes in the MessageContract
namespace. Right-click the InvoiceMicroservice project and select Add ➤ Project
Reference. Figure 5-10 shows an example of selecting the project MessageContracts.

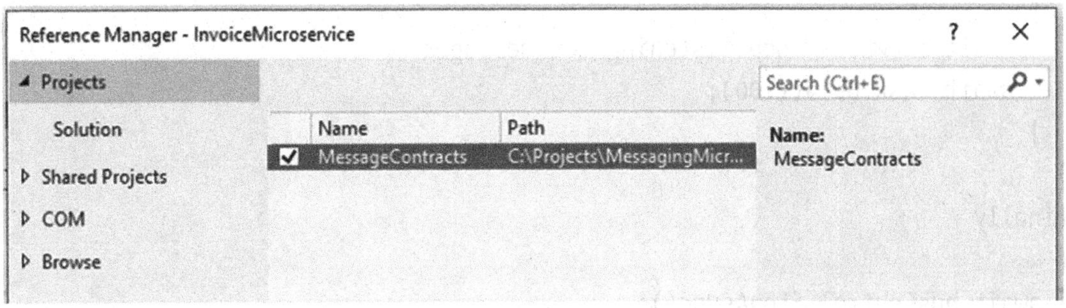

| | Name | Path | |
|---|---|---|---|
| ✓ | MessageContracts | C:\Projects\MessagingMicr... | Name:<br>MessageContracts |

Reference Manager - InvoiceMicroservice

▲ Projects — Solution, ▷ Shared Projects, ▷ COM, ▷ Browse — Search (Ctrl+E)

**Figure 5-10.** *Project dependency*

Select the checkbox left of MessageContracts and then select OK.

In the Program.cs file of InvoiceMicroservice project, replace all of that code with the following code:

```
using GreenPipes;
using MassTransit;
using MessageContracts;

var busControl = Bus.Factory.CreateUsingRabbitMq(cfg =>
{
  cfg.Host("localhost");
  cfg.ReceiveEndpoint("invoice-service", e =>
  {
    e.UseInMemoryOutbox();
    e.Consumer<EventConsumer>(c =>
      c.UseMessageRetry(m => m.Interval(5, new TimeSpan(0, 0, 10))));
  });
});

var source = new CancellationTokenSource(TimeSpan.FromSeconds(10));
await busControl.StartAsync(source.Token);

Console.WriteLine("Invoice Microservice Now Listening");

try
{
  while (true)
  {
    //sit in while loop listening for messages
    await Task.Delay(100);
  }
}
finally
{
  await busControl.StopAsync();
}
```

```csharp
public class EventConsumer : IConsumer<IInvoiceToCreate>
{
  public async Task Consume(ConsumeContext<IInvoiceToCreate> context)
  {
    var newInvoiceNumber = new Random().Next(10000, 99999);

    Console.WriteLine($"Creating invoice {newInvoiceNumber} for customer:
    {context.Message.CustomerNumber}");

    context.Message.InvoiceItems.ForEach(i =>
    {
      Console.WriteLine($"With items: Price: {i.Price}, Desc:
      {i.Description}");
      Console.WriteLine($"Actual distance in miles: {i.ActualMileage}, Base
      Rate: {i.BaseRate}");
      Console.WriteLine($"Oversized: {i.IsOversized}, Refrigerated:
      {i.IsRefrigerated}, Haz Mat: {i.IsHazardousMaterial}");
    });

    await context.Publish<IInvoiceCreated>(new
    {
      InvoiceNumber = newInvoiceNumber,
      InvoiceData = new
      {
        context.Message.CustomerNumber,
        context.Message.InvoiceItems
      }
    });
  }
}
```

# Building the Payment Microservice

Now we will create the PaymentMicroservice project. This project will serve as an example of a downstream microservice that reacts to creating an invoice. Right-click the solution and select Add ➤ New Project.

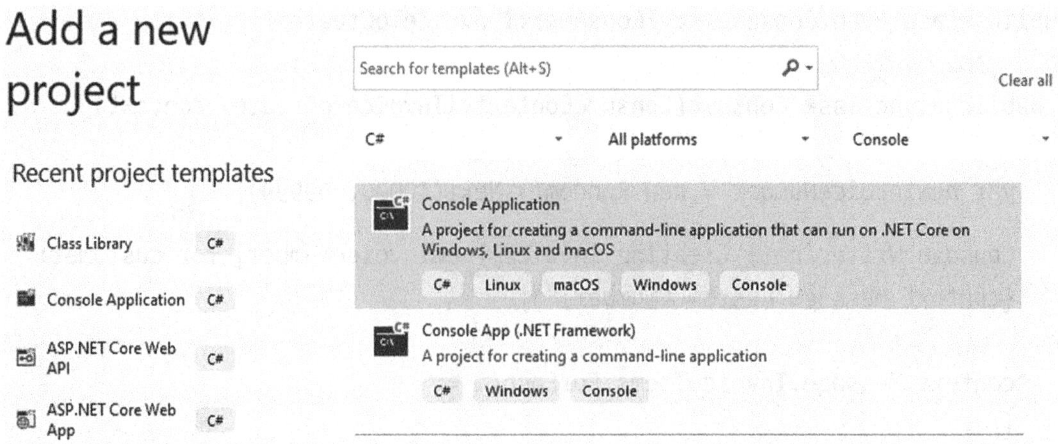

## Add a new project

C# ▾          All platforms ▾          Console ▾

### Recent project templates

**Console Application**
A project for creating a command-line application that can run on .NET Core on Windows, Linux and macOS

C#    Linux    macOS    Windows    Console

Class Library          C#

Console Application    C#

**Console App (.NET Framework)**
A project for creating a command-line application

C#    Windows    Console

ASP.NET Core Web API    C#

ASP.NET Core Web App    C#

***Figure 5-11.*** *New console application*

Select the option for Console Application and then select the "Next" button (see Figure 5-11).

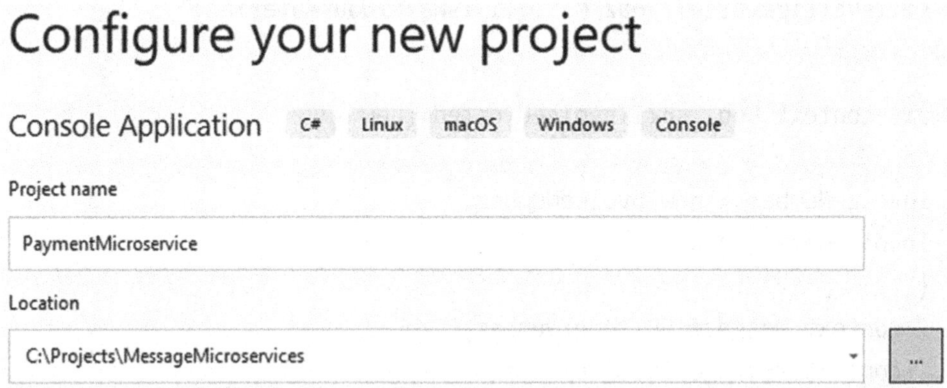

## Configure your new project

Console Application    C#    Linux    macOS    Windows    Console

Project name

PaymentMicroservice

Location

C:\Projects\MessageMicroservices                              ▾    ...

***Figure 5-12.*** *Project name and location*

For the project name, use PaymentMicroservice and then select the "Next" button (see Figure 5-12). Now select .NET 6 for the framework and select the "Create" button. This project also needs to have the MassTransit library with RabbitMQ installed. In the Package Manager Console, make sure the Default Project has the PaymentMicroservice selected. Then at the prompt, enter

```
Install-Package MassTransit.RabbitMQ
```

We now need to connect this project to the MessageContract project. We will be writing code that is dependent on interfaces and classes in the MessageContract namespace. Right-click the InvoiceMicroservice project and select Add ➤ Project Reference.

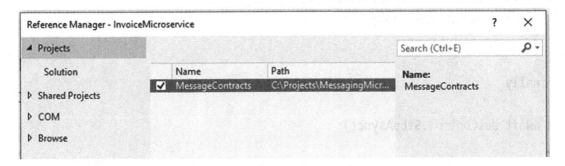

***Figure 5-13.*** *Project dependency*

Select the checkbox left of MessageContracts and then select OK (see Figure 5-13). In the Program.cs file of PaymentMicroservice project, replace all of that code with the following code:

```
using GreenPipes;
using MassTransit;
using MessageContracts;

var busControl = Bus.Factory.CreateUsingRabbitMq(cfg =>
{
  cfg.Host("localhost");
  cfg.ReceiveEndpoint("payment-service", e =>
  {
    e.Consumer<InvoiceCreatedConsumer>(c =>
      c.UseMessageRetry(m => m.Interval(5, new TimeSpan(0, 0, 10))));
  });
});

var source = new CancellationTokenSource(TimeSpan.FromSeconds(10));
await busControl.StartAsync(source.Token);
Console.WriteLine("Payment Microservice Now Listening");
```

```
try
{
  while (true)
  {
    //sit in while loop listening for messages
    await Task.Delay(100);
  }
}
finally
{
  await busControl.StopAsync();
}

class InvoiceCreatedConsumer : IConsumer<IInvoiceCreated>
{
  public async Task Consume(ConsumeContext<IInvoiceCreated> context)
  {
    await Task.Run(() =>
      Console.WriteLine($"Received message for invoice number: {context.
      Message.InvoiceNumber}"));
  }
}
```

At this point, you do want to make sure the code will compile. But there is nothing to run just yet.

## Building a Test Client

We need to create a project that will play the role of what could be in a monolithic application. For simplicity, we will just have the code send a request for a new invoice when the application starts. Once again, right-click the solution and select Add ➤ New Project.

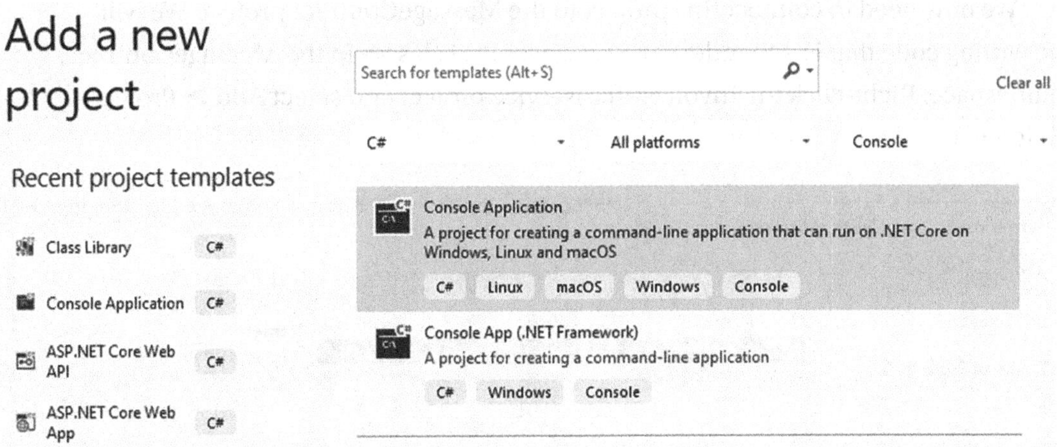

# Add a new project

Search for templates (Alt+ S)

Clear all

C#    ▾      All platforms    ▾      Console    ▾

## Recent project templates

- Class Library    C#
- Console Application    C#
- ASP.NET Core Web API    C#
- ASP.NET Core Web App    C#

**Console Application**
A project for creating a command-line application that can run on .NET Core on Windows, Linux and macOS

C#    Linux    macOS    Windows    Console

**Console App (.NET Framework)**
A project for creating a command-line application

C#    Windows    Console

**Figure 5-14.** *New console application*

Select the option for Console Application and then the "Next" button (see Figure 5-14).

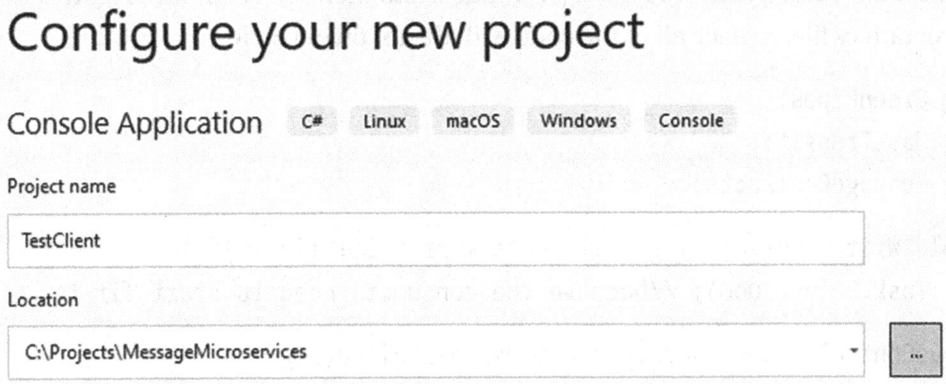

# Configure your new project

## Console Application    C#    Linux    macOS    Windows    Console

Project name

TestClient

Location

C:\Projects\MessageMicroservices

**Figure 5-15.** *Project name and location*

For the project name, use TestClient and then select the "Next" button (see Figure 5-15). Select .NET 6 for the framework and then select the "Create" button. This project also needs to have the MassTransit library with RabbitMQ installed. In the Package Manager Console, make sure the Default Project has the PaymentMicroservice selected. Then at the prompt, enter

```
Install-Package MassTransit.RabbitMQ
```

We now need to connect this project to the MessageContract project. We will be writing code that is dependent on interfaces and classes in the MessageContract namespace. Right-click the InvoiceMicroservice project and select Add ➤ Project Reference.

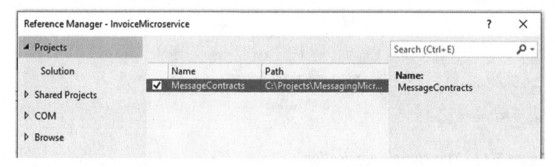

***Figure 5-16.*** *Project dependency*

Select the checkbox left of MessageContracts and then select OK (see Figure 5-16). In the Program.cs file, replace all of the code with the following code:

```
using GreenPipes;
using MassTransit;
using MessageContracts;

Console.WriteLine("Waiting while consumers initialize.");
await Task.Delay(3000); //because the consumers need to start first

var busControl = Bus.Factory.CreateUsingRabbitMq(cfg =>
{
  cfg.Host("localhost");
  cfg.ReceiveEndpoint("invoice-service-created", e =>
  {
    e.UseInMemoryOutbox();
    e.Consumer<InvoiceCreatedConsumer>(c =>
      c.UseMessageRetry(m => m.Interval(5, new TimeSpan(0, 0, 10))));
  });
});
```

```csharp
var source = new CancellationTokenSource(TimeSpan.FromSeconds(10));

await busControl.StartAsync(source.Token);
var keyCount = 0;
try
{
  Console.WriteLine("Enter any key to send an invoice request or Q to
  quit.");

  while (Console.ReadKey(true).Key != ConsoleKey.Q)
  {
    keyCount++;
    await SendRequestForInvoiceCreation(busControl);
    Console.WriteLine($"Enter any key to send an invoice request or Q to
    quit. {keyCount}");
  }
}
finally
{
  await busControl.StopAsync();
}

static async Task SendRequestForInvoiceCreation(IPublishEndpoint
publishEndpoint)
{
  var rnd = new Random();
  await publishEndpoint.Publish<IInvoiceToCreate>(new
  {
    CustomerNumber = rnd.Next(1000, 9999),
    InvoiceItems = new List<InvoiceItems>()
          {
              new InvoiceItems{Description="Tables", Price=Math.Round(rnd.
              NextDouble()*100,2), ActualMileage = 40, BaseRate = 12.50,
              IsHazardousMaterial = false, IsOversized = true, IsRefrigerated
              = false},
```

```
        new InvoiceItems{Description="Chairs", Price=Math.Round(rnd.
        NextDouble()*100,2), ActualMileage = 40, BaseRate =
        12.50, IsHazardousMaterial = false, IsOversized = false,
        IsRefrigerated = false}
    }
  });
}

public class InvoiceCreatedConsumer : IConsumer<IInvoiceCreated>
{
  public async Task Consume(ConsumeContext<IInvoiceCreated> context)
  {
    await Task.Run(() => Console.WriteLine($"Invoice with number: {context.
    Message.InvoiceNumber} was created."));
  }
}
```

We need multiple applications to start at the same time. Right-click the solution and select Set Startup Projects. In the dialog window, select the option for Multiple startup projects. Then change the action of each console application from None to Start. Be sure to leave the MessageContracts project action set to None. Then select OK (see Figure 5-17).

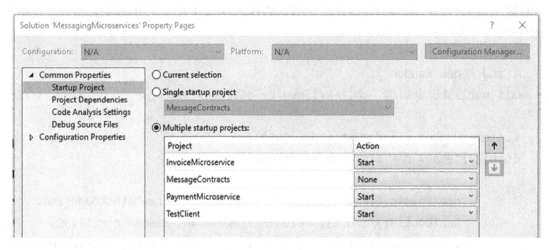

*Figure 5-17.* *Setting start action on multiple projects*

# Testing What We Have

We need to test and prove that messages are being sent from the Test Client to the invoice Microservice. Then we need to make sure that the message that is sent from the Invoice Microservice is received by the Payment Microservice and the Test Client. Select either the F5 button or the menu option to start the applications (see Figure 5-18).

***Figure 5-18.*** *Start debug run option*

With RabbitMQ running, start the applications in Visual Studio. This will launch the Test Client, Invoice Microservice, and Payment Microservice. Three windows will show on the screen. On the Test Client screen, press any key, and it will trigger a command message for the Invoice Microservice to create an invoice with the information in the message (see Figure 5-19).

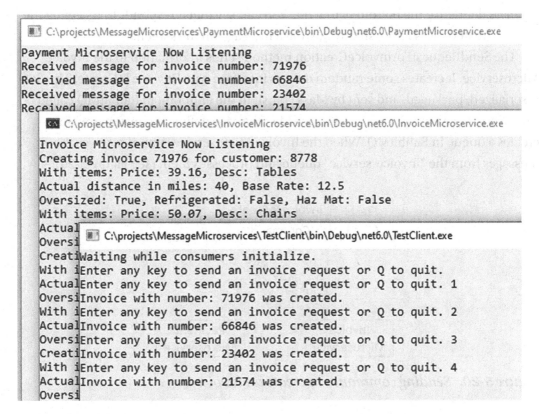

***Figure 5-19.*** *Example of running the microservices and test client*

# Play-by-Play Explanation

Now that you have a working application, we will go over some details to better understand how the different pieces work. We will start with the TestClient application. This project intends to be a quick and not full-featured example to fulfill the purpose of a monolith. The monolith in our storyline is an existing application that needs to be modified to send information to the newly created invoice microservice. In this case, it will use messaging instead of a direct call with RPC.

Looking at the example code, you see that it creates an instance of a messaging bus with MassTransit using RabbitMQ. It sets the host to the address, "localhost," where the RabbitMQ instance in Docker is running. Of course, hard-coding a value like this is generally bad. It is only hard-coded here for the sake of the example.

We then set up a Receive Endpoint. This is because our test client application will also listen for messages in the queue named "invoice-service-created." Also defined is the InvoiceCreatedConsumer, which tells MassTransit that our code wants to listen to messages sent with the message type of InvoiceCreated. The InvoiceCreatedConsumer is a class defined at the bottom of that file. You can see that it responds to receiving the InvoiceCreated message by simply posting a message on the screen.

The SendRequestForInvoiceCreation method sends information to the Invoice Microservice. It creates some random data as interface type IInvoiceToCreate. The data is serialized, packaged, and sent by MassTransit to the endpoint in RabbitMQ called "invoice-service." In our case, the Invoice Microservice defines a consumer which creates a queue in RabbitMQ. When the Invoice Microservice runs, it receives the messages from the "invoice-service" queue and processes them (see Figure 5-20).

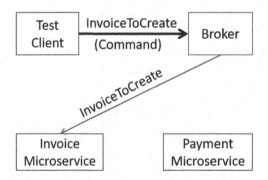

***Figure 5-20.*** *Sending commands to create an invoice*

Looking in the Invoice Microservice code, you see the RabbitMQ host being defined and the "invoice-service" Receive Endpoint setting. The EventConsumer class is of type IConsumer that is of type IInvoiceToCreate. This is reacting to the messages with information for this service to create an invoice. Here you could save information to a database, logging, etc. Notice that when the microservice creates an invoice, it then publishes an event called IInvoiceCreated (see Figure 5-21).

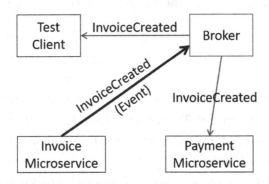

***Figure 5-21.*** *Sending events as a result of invoice creation*

When the new invoice is published as an event, one or more subscribers could receive the same message. In this case, the test client that sent the original information and is a subscriber receives the event message. Also, the other example Payment Microservice is a subscriber. The idea here is that another microservice wants to know and react to the invoice creation event. Then it can do whatever processing is deemed necessary for payment processing based on the new invoice.

# Drawbacks of Messaging

Although there are numerous reasons for implementing messaging, it is not without drawbacks. Messaging solutions require effort and time to understand the many pieces that must be decided. Expect to create several proofs of concept to try out the many designs. You will need to judge each design based on complexity, ease of implementation, and manageability variations.

After a messaging solution has been chosen, you then have the infrastructure to create and manage. The messaging product, RabbitMQ, for example, must run on a server someplace. Then for high availability, you must create a cluster on multiple servers. With the additional servers, you have more infrastructure to maintain.

Troubleshooting is also much harder. Since microservices can reside on numerous servers, there may be many log files to comb through when there is an error. You will have to understand if only one microservice failed to receive and process a message and which microservice instance failed.

Since messages can end up in a Dead Letter Queue, you may have to replay that message or decide to delete it. Then, decide if the timeout setting for the DLQ is sufficient. You will also need to verify the messaging system of choice is fully functioning.

# Summary

We covered a lot in this chapter. There is so much more to learn with messaging, even if not used with microservices. This chapter provided a high-level overview of messaging with a couple of example microservices. Here you learned that RPC-style communication has many drawbacks.

You also learned about the reasons to use messaging. Messaging is a communication style that helps keep microservices loosely coupled. It also provides buffering, scaling, and independent processing of messages. Each microservice can stay as an independent application, written in the best language for the business need.

In this chapter, you also learned about message types. Commands are for when a microservice is being directed to execute a specific business operation. Queries are for retrieving data, and Events are for alerting subscribers about the fact something has occurred. In our code examples, a command was used to have the Invoice Microservice create an invoice. When that invoice was created, it published an Event. Subscribers like Payment Microservice and the Test Client received the published message and reacted independently with that information.

You also learned that message routing could be done by brokered or broker-less systems. They each have pros and cons that must be evaluated depending on the various business needs you will have. And note, depending on what business needs you are trying to solve, you may have a mix of solutions. Just because a broker-less system solves one aspect of your needs does not mean it will solve them all.

With messaging, you learned about different types of consumers. When you have a consumer subscribed to a queue and scale-out that consumer, multiple consumers compete for the message. Competing consumers help to ensure that only one microservice is processing a specific message. Using independent consumers means that differing microservices can receive the same message. You saw this with the Test Client and Payment Microservice. They each receive the message when an invoice is created. Using independent consumers is useful when another subscriber should receive a copy of the message. Another example could be logging or a data warehouse solution where they need a copy of the message regardless of what other business processes are doing.

You also learned about delivery guarantees and that you must consider that message delivery is not easy. Many circumstances can cause a message to fail to be delivered or processed. As much as we want a message to be delivered once and processed every time, the real world has factors that require developers to build more robust consumers. We must have our consumers be idempotent in case a duplicate message is sent. And our consumers must handle commutative messages as they can be delivered out of expected order.

We then made some code examples using the MassTransit library that uses RabbitMQ as the message transport. You saw how the Test Client, which represents the monolith in our story, can send a command for an invoice to be created. Then the Invoice Microservice, serves as the single source of truth for invoices, generated the invoice and published an Event with the details of the new invoice. The Payment Microservice and the Test Client are independent consumers receiving the Event sent from the Invoice Microservice.

# CHAPTER 6

# Decentralizing Data

Microservices architecture is an implementation of a distributed system. This means that we may need to separate computational load across multiple systems for reasons like governance. Now that microservices exist to handle business functionality across systems, we need to discuss how to handle the data. In this chapter, we will go over decentralizing data and suggestions for implementing different ways to handle data across multiple microservices.

The developer, Kathy at Code Whiz, has now made multiple microservices. She made microservices for retrieving distance information to increase quote accuracy. Kathy also made microservices for handling invoices and other related functionality. But now is the time for Kathy to consider if the database system that the client, Hyp-Log, uses is sufficient or if other databases should be created.

## Current State

Most monolithic applications' code has grown over time, and this usually includes the centralized database. Considering one of the most common database types is relational, multiple tables in one database make it is easy to serve several business processes. Queries can join tables, making it relatively easy to gather data. This type of database works very well until business process changes require a different way of handling data. There are relational database systems like Microsoft's SQL Server and Oracle. There are also non-relational database systems, some of which are called No-SQL. Azure Cosmos DB and AWS DynamoDB are two examples. The database of choice is largely dependent on the data model you choose.

Businesses must change and adapt over time to stay relevant. Some adapt to new requirements in regulations and compliance mandates. Many businesses change because the industry changes, and they cannot be left behind. Perhaps a new product line can help supply income that supports them for the next set of changes. To stay competitive, businesses and their processes must change.

137

© Sean Whitesell, Rob Richardson, Matthew D. Groves 2022
S. Whitesell et al., *Pro Microservices in .NET 6*, https://doi.org/10.1007/978-1-4842-7833-8_6

You have been learning how microservices may help with the endeavors for a business to handle change. Just as applications evolve as the business changes, so must the data models and schemas. You may be knowledgeable about how data is modeled in your monolith. Developing microservices allows for data modeling changes as you understand the needs of the changing business processes applied to microservices and the monolith. There are several database types to choose from, and their pros/cons help the success of microservices.

Most monolithic applications have data models that store changes by searching for the record and applying the update. The current state is the only thing stored. There might be a history table, and they generally include changes across multiple tables and have little if any query performance. While this way of storing records is still valid for many scenarios, with microservices, there are other data models to consider.

# The Rule

There is a general "rule" stating that if a microservice persists data, it should own that database. This could be a database or a data store. The difference being a database is a system with the sole purpose of housing and managing data. A data store could be a database but could also be a file, a messaging system like Kafka, or anything else that can house data. These two terms may be interchangeable in this chapter depending on the use case.

So, must we adhere to this rule that a microservice is to own its own database? Many organizations have dedicated database administrators (DBAs), and they are not usually excited about another database to manage. It is not easy for a database to simply exist when dealing with availability, patching, logging, backups, capacity planning, security, and many other details. Adding more databases also adds to additional possibilities of failures and support calls.

Depending on the size of your architecture, you may be able to have microservices without decentralizing your database. But if this is true, why does the rule even exist? The reason is that at some point in the growth of microservices, you may be in a position where the schema needs of one microservice impact the needs of another microservice. Just as a monolith has grown over time with additional functionality and bug fixes, so do the data schemas. Code to handle the processing of an order must rely on the database and schema to properly manage that data. Over time, with changes to functionality, you may create new columns or additional tables. Consider also the changes to any stored procedures or functions. If these changes impact the evolution of other microservices, then it becomes a clear indicator of the need to separate data to their respective microservices.

Each microservice exists to be the processor of their business functionality, their domain. Each microservice also needs to be the sole manager of the single source of truth, the data.

Without the ability to manage the single source of truth, you risk losing data integrity. This means that if more than one application uses a database, you risk having incomplete data in various tables because the requirements and validations may not be the same in each application.

# Database Choices

There is a huge advantage of having a separate database for a microservice. If, for example, your monolithic application uses SQL Server, and you build a new microservice for handling incoming telemetry data from field sensors. Having a separate database than what the monolithic application uses allows you to pick a different database type depending on the data modeling needs. You may consider using a data store like Azure Table Storage for telemetry data processing because it stores non-relational structured data.

For order data, it is possible to use a database system like Azure Cosmos DB. Azure Synapse or AWS Redshift might be preferred for a high volume of data with microservices that perform data analysis. The point is that you can choose different database types that best fit the processing needs of the data.

# Availability

Every microservice has a chance of failure. This could be from a server host rebooting, a container rebooting, a bug in the code, or when the database becomes unreachable. No microservice can have 100% availability. We measure the availability of our system using "nines." If a system has four nines, it is 99.99% available as it uses four nines in the percentage description. Considering how many minutes are in a year, 525,600, a system that has four nines of availability means it may have up to 52.56 minutes of downtime.

With microservices relying on other microservices, we get an understanding of the availability (see Figure 6-1). To get an overall calculation of the availability, multiply the percentage of each microservice. Here we would get 99.98% × 99.95% × 99.99% which equals 99.92% of availability.

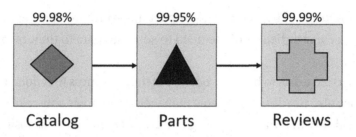

*Figure 6-1.*  *Example of availability*

With microservices that are called in parallel, the method of calculation does not change (see Figure 6-2). Looking at the following microservices, we take the percent of availability of each microservice to 99.98% × 99.95% × 99.99% × 99.94%. This gives us a total availability of 99.86%.

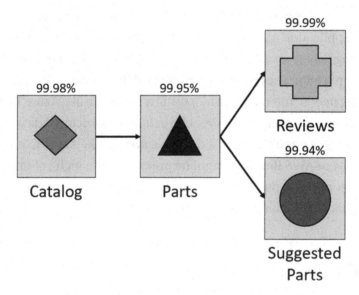

*Figure 6-2.*  *Example of availability with parallel execution*

The opportunity of downtime must consider how and where you are hosting your microservices. Downtime occurring data centers may take down more than one microservice and other dependent systems like databases and storage accounts. Systems like Kubernetes can help with some downtime issues. When a pod fails, Kubernetes attempts to create a new instance of that pod for resiliency.

# Sharing Data

As we explore decentralizing the data to different databases, we quickly see a new issue.

There are other processes fulfilled by other microservices that still need data, but now from other microservices. Perhaps you have a shipping microservice that needs information about the order. How does it get that data?

One option is to simply have the shipping microservice call the order microservice to retrieve the necessary data (see Figure 6-3). This is a reasonable solution but not without its challenges. As microservices are calling each other to retrieve data, it is possible to have a rather chatty network. As the network calls increase, so could the latency. As the requests for data increase, so does the load on the related databases.

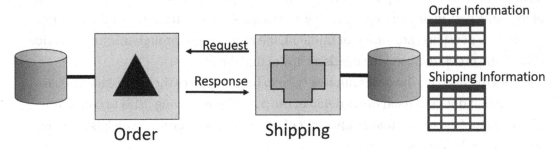

***Figure 6-3.*** *Sharing data*

Consider one microservice calls another microservice that must also call another. Each microservice call only adds to the latency, and the business processes have an increased opportunity of failing. Looking at Figure 6-4, if the call to the Reviews microservice takes 1.5 seconds, the Part microservice takes 2.1 seconds, and the Catalog microservice takes 2.4 seconds to execute, you have a total latency of 6 seconds. This should challenge your architectural decisions. Do the calls really need to be synchronous? Can the calls be done asynchronously?

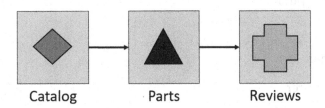

***Figure 6-4.*** *Inline microservice calls*

Latency is not the biggest issue we have. It is something to consider, but what about handling the fact that now data is in two or more databases? How is that data kept in sync? Or perhaps we ask this differently. With business processes needing data to be in multiple databases, how do we keep the data consistent? When downtime occurs in one microservice but not another, what happens to the data consistency? We will cover this topic in the section for transactional consistency.

# Duplicate Data

The other option is to duplicate data. That sounds absurd. Why separate databases just to duplicate data later? This is not as bad as it seems at first. Consider an example of having a microservice for parts you sell online. The parts microservice is the manager of the parts data in its own database. It is the single source of truth for all things related to parts. As new parts are added or updated, the requests go through this microservice. What if the order microservice needs a copy of that data?

With the need for the order microservice to have a copy of the parts data, you also notice that it does not need every detail of the part. The following list is to convey the idea of a lot of detail that makes up a part of the parts microservice, which is the single source of truth database:

- Id
- Part number
- Name
- Description
- Category
- Classification
- Size description
- Color
- Container
- Manufacturer
- Manufacturer's part number

- Manufactured date

- Replaces part number

- Discontinued date

The order microservice needs a copy of the part information **but** only enough information to fulfill the requirements of an order. It does not need a copy of when a part was discontinued or when it was replaced. The order microservice only needs details about a part, such as a name and some description details. Now, in the order microservice database, there is a table for the part information. This list is an example of what details could be in this parts table to fulfill the needs of processing orders:

- Part Id

- Part number

- Name

- Description

- Size description

- Color

Now that there are some duplicate data across microservices, the next challenge is keeping the data in sync. For example, what if the application administrator fixes a typo in the description of a part? How does the duplicate information in the order microservice get updated? This is where using messaging helps (see Figure 6-5).

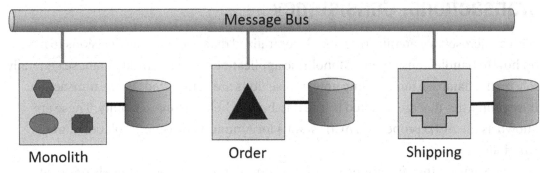

***Figure 6-5.*** *Example of an order system with messaging*

A message of *OrderShippingAddressUpdated* is sent and processed by the shipping microservice as well as the order microservice (see Figure 6-6). The shipping microservice processes the update by finding the shipping address for the specified order in the database and applying the change. The order microservice can also process the message by searching its database for the specified order and correct the address.

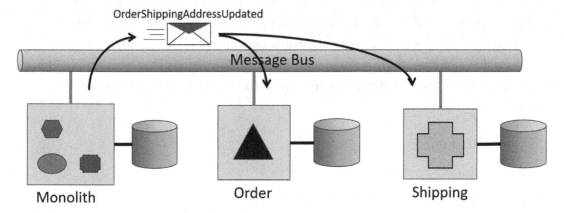

*Figure 6-6.*  *Messaging example*

This is a simple way of keeping multiple microservices with some duplicate data in sync without requiring the microservices to be aware of each other. By keeping microservices unaware of each other, your architecture is loosely coupled and allows the microservices to continue to evolve independently.

# Transactional Consistency

With a microservice architecture and decentralized data, we have big decisions to make on how to handle transactions. Monolithic applications with a central database generally rely on the database for handling how transactions are committed. These transactions have properties that are handled by the database to help ensure reliability. These are known as the ACID properties. ACID stands for Atomic, Consistent, Isolation, and Durability.

Transactions that are atomic will either commit the change completely or not at all. This helps ensure that the intended change is not partially committed. Consistency guarantees the intended change is not altered during the transaction. Isolation is made so that the transaction is not altered by other transactions. The durability guarantee is so that the committed change remains in the system until another transaction occurs to change that data. This is for handling times when there is a system failure right after a transaction commits. For example, the committed change is saved and can survive a reboot.

With distributed systems like microservices, there is an increased chance of failures. Attempting to do distributed transactions across multiple microservices is difficult and adds transactional latency and many failure scenarios. With each possible type of failure, you have to build in compensating transactions. This complicates the architecture.

## CAP Theorem

With data decentralized, we need to understand how to handle times when the database is unavailable for the related microservice. Eric Brewer created the CAP theorem that states it is impossible to provide more than two guarantees during a time of failure. The CAP theorem has three guarantees: **C**onsistency, **A**vailability, and **P**artition tolerance. Because microservices communicate over a network, we design them to handle the times when there is an issue on the network, known as partition tolerance. This means that if a microservice communication fails, it must handle that condition, such as using retry policies. Because network interruptions are easily possible, we must decide the behavior of microservices during those times.

This leaves us with the choice of Availability or Consistency. When we decide that a microservice should favor Availability, we are saying that it will continue being available for callers when the microservice cannot reach its database. When receiving a request for data, it will return the last known data even if it is out of date from what is in the database. Changes to data are cached, and when the connection is re-established to the database, it will sync up any changes.

The option of Consistency is for when the microservice must either return up-to-date information or an error. Consistency here is not the same as the consistency in the ACID guarantees. Consistency in ACID is about trusting the data is not altered during a transaction. The Consistency in CAP is about the data returned in a query during a network partition.

Consider a game application on a mobile device. If the application favors consistency, then when there is a network communication issue, the application does not continue working. However, if it favors availability, then it continues to operate with the last known information it has and synchronizes the data when the connection is restored.

# Transactions Across Microservices

With the data decentralized, we need to analyze our business processes to understand their data needs and how best to keep the data in the various microservices consistent. We start by understanding the roles the microservice fulfills in these business processes. Some processes have activities that are sequential because of their dependency on a flow of committed transactions (see Figure 6-7).

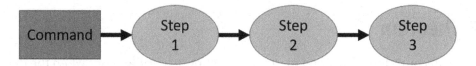

*Figure 6-7.* *Sequential business processes*

Other processes can be done in parallel, or a fan-out design, as their activities are not dependent on other transactions (see Figure 6-8).

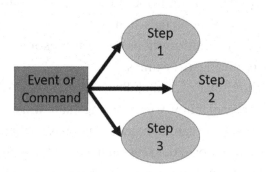

*Figure 6-8.* *Parallel activity*

The individual processes covered by the microservices still need to complete before the business process as a whole is considered complete. Regardless of choice to use sequential or fan-out design, the collection of transactions needs to be managed, so we understand when the business process is complete and, just as important, when they fail to complete. This maintainable collection of transactions is called a saga.

# Sagas

A saga is a mechanism for managing potentially long-lived transactions in a distributed system. Depending on the processing needs of the transactions, you may choose one of three saga patterns to manage the transactions. The three patterns are Routing Slip, Choreography, and Orchestration.

Note that sagas do not provide atomicity across the transactions. Each microservice included in a saga has atomicity to their database but not across other databases (see Figure 6-9).

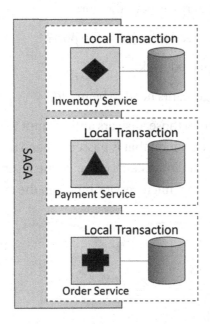

***Figure 6-9.*** *Example of saga with local transactions*

A saga is not a distributed transaction. A distributed transaction holds a lock on resources across microservices and has a lot of issues when dealing with failure cases. Also, distributed transactions cannot tolerate a large time span like sagas. A saga is for coordinating a set of local transactions that may take fractions of a second to complete or potentially days depending on the business process needs and availability of microservices.

# Routing Slip

When using the routing slip pattern, information passes from one microservice to another. As a microservice receives the routing slip, it acts accordingly based on the information provided, including storing information in its database. For an example of information in a routing slip, consider what it would take to make flight and cruise reservations. This approach is with the premise that you will make a cruise line reservation only after a flight reservation has successfully been completed. Consider the following questions that need to be answered to make these reservations:

- What day does the cruise leave the port?

- What time do you need to arrive at the port?

- When are you expected back?

- What flight arrangements need to be made?

Your application will obtain those answers and attempt to make those reservations. The routing slip contains information that is passed to each microservice. Each microservice contacts independent systems to create the reservations. The routing slip has those answers and includes what microservice is next in the call chain (see Figure 6-10).

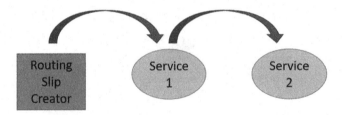

***Figure 6-10.***  *Routing slip activities*

If a microservice has an error, it updates the routing slip based on its information and sends it to the previous microservice. This way, each microservice knows if it is performing actions based on the forward progression or performing a compensating transaction (see Figure 6-11). The error condition could be from a required reservation not being made or an issue with the microservice itself. Each state of the transactions is kept with the routing slip.

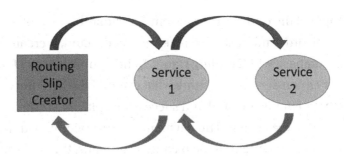

***Figure 6-11.*** *Routing slip error condition handling*

The routing slip pattern is useful for sequential operations that require preconditions to be met. Although this example assumes the order of reservations, you should challenge if this pattern is the right one to use. Do you require a cruise ship reservation to be made before the flight reservation? What if the flight reservation comes first? Or can the operations be done in parallel? The next two patterns discuss how to handle operational needs in parallel.

## Choreography

With choreography, the microservices communicate using events. As the operations complete, they send events with information about the succeeded transaction. Other microservices receive the events they subscribe to so they can perform their actions (see Figure 6-12).

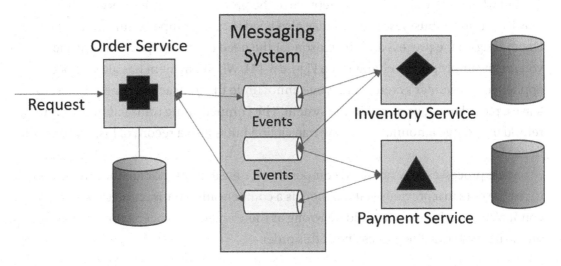

***Figure 6-12.*** *Choreography*

With the example of the online order system, consider this flow of activity (see Figure 6-13). After the order microservice receives a command, it creates an order and saves it to its local database with Pending status. It then publishes an *OrderCreated* event. The inventory microservice consumes that event. If the inventory microservice validates the number of items on hand and successfully places a reserve on those items, it publishes an *ItemsReserved* event. The payment microservice consumes that message and attempts to process a payment. If the payment succeeds, the payment microservice publishes a *PaymentProcessed* event. The order microservice consumes that event and updates the status of the order accordingly.

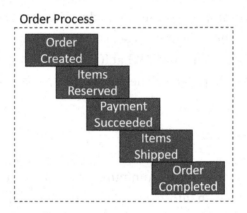

*Figure 6-13.*  *Order creation process*

But what if there is a failure someplace in the process? Each microservice that plays a part in the business process may also need to have compensating transactions. Depending on the process and the reason for the need to revert a previous transaction, you might simply undo a change (see Figure 6-14). When payment has already been applied to a customer's credit card, you cannot undo the transaction. And it is best to leave a record that it occurred in the system. The compensating transaction then is to refund the charge amount. It is a new transaction but is also a record of history for audit needs.

Some processes may not need compensating transactions, nor are they required to restore data to a previous state. If there is a compensating transaction to change the count of an item in stock, it could be wrong as there could have been another transaction on the items during the processing of this order.

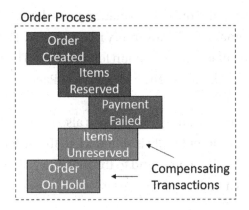

***Figure 6-14.*** *Order process with compensating transactions*

## Orchestration

With orchestration, microservices are contacted using commands directly from the central process manager. Just like with choreographed sagas, the manager maintains the state of the saga.

Using the online order system example, the order microservice acts as the central controller sometimes called the orchestrator (see Figure 6-15). As a request comes in, the order microservice issues a command directly to other microservices in turn as they process and complete their steps.

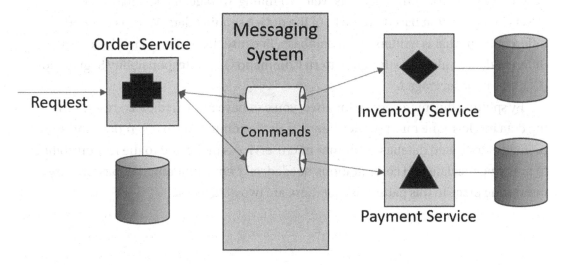

***Figure 6-15.*** *Orchestration*

After creating and saving the order information to its database, the order microservice issues a command to the inventory microservice. The inventory microservice receives the command and places a reservation for the items. The order microservice then issues another command to the payment microservice. Payment is processed, and the order goes to shipping.

The ability to create compensating transactions also needs to be applied here. If the payment fails to process, a different reply is sent back to the order microservice. The order microservice then sends another command to the inventory microservice to release the reservation on the items. Then the order status is set to PaymentCorrectionNeeded.

# CQRS

Some business processes have different data models for the writing vs. the reading. Consider the scenario of a system that receives telemetry data from devices in the field (see Figure 6-16). This data comes in from many devices several times per second. The data model used to write the data to a database is simple. It contains fields like pressure values of different sensors, battery voltage, and temperature. The data model also has properties like device Id, sensor Id, and a date/timestamp.

Retrieving the data is for a different purpose, so the read data model is vastly different than the write data model. The read data model includes computed values based on values from other fields as well as a rolling average. It also includes value offsets for calibration based on the Id of the device sending data. What is queried is different than what is written to the database. Because the write and read use vastly different data models, the design pattern Command Query Responsibility Segregation (CQRS) can be leveraged.

By splitting the microservice into two, you can have more dedicated resources for the data models. One microservice handles all the commands to insert data and stores them in a dedicated database. Another microservice is dedicated to the responsibilities of querying the data and computations needed, all from a different database. A very interesting piece to this pattern is that there are two databases.

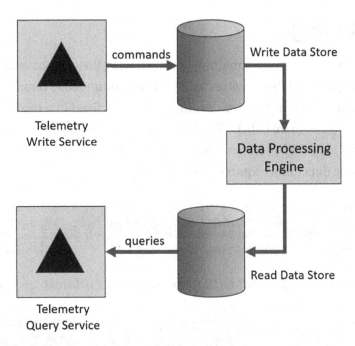

*Figure 6-16.* *Example of CQRS with telemetry data*

Having two databases, you can have the database for writes be tuned for handling volumes of incoming data. The read database can be tuned with indexes to support retrieving the necessary data. It also does not have to be the same database type as the write database. Commands may come in as JSON documents, but the read database can be relational to store a materialized view of a cumulation of data.

There are a few benefits of using CQRS. Security is applied differently for the data models. You can scale the microservices independently. And there is a separation of complexity between the microservices.

The challenge now is getting data from the write database to the read database. There are multiple ways of doing this. Depending on your needs, this can be done with log shipping, data streams, messaging, or even another microservice. Because the read database is separate from the write database, the data may be behind or stale. You must be able to handle eventual consistency. With eventual consistency, the data in a database or database cluster will become consistent at a later time. Business processes are affected by this and will need to have procedures to handle those conditions.

The CQRS pattern, much like the event sourcing pattern, should not be everywhere. It should not be used if your data model or business processing needs are simple. If CRUD-like operations will suffice, then that is more likely the better option.

# Event Sourcing

Many applications store data in a manner of only having the current value. Updates occur to replace data, and the previous value is not automatically retained (see Figure 6-17). Building on the previous example, a typo is fixed in a record for the shipping address (see Figure 6-18). The new value replaces the current value. For most applications, this model of operations is fine. But for some business processes, this model of handling data lacks required additional details.

| Order Id | Customer Id | Creation Date Stamp | Payment Terms | Shipping Address | ... |
|----------|-------------|---------------------|---------------|------------------|-----|
| 24156 | 10232 | 20170531163456 | 30 Days | 123 Any Sreet ... | |

*Figure 6-17.* *Example of record with typo in shipping address*

| Order Id | Customer Id | Creation Date Stamp | Payment Terms | Shipping Address | ... |
|----------|-------------|---------------------|---------------|------------------|-----|
| 24156 | 10232 | 20170531163456 | 30 Days | 123 Any Street ... | |

*Figure 6-18.* *Example of record after typo fixed*

Event sourcing is a design pattern for persisting data. It can be used to store the events that affect items like an order, invoice, or a customer's account. Events like *OrderCreated* and *OrderStatusUpdated* are stored so that the events can be replayed to get the current value. This allows for history to be kept with objects at all times. This is not just a history of changes to an order but is also proof of how an order got to the latest state. By using event sourcing, you have the records needed for processes that must adhere to regulation and compliance mandates. Data should never be directly updated or deleted. Instead, to delete a record, use a "soft delete" that sets a property in your data to signal that is to be considered by your application as a deleted record. This way, you still have the history of events.

The entries stored are the events that have happened to the state of the objects. The events are essentially domain events. In Domain-Driven Design (DDD), the domain events are noted as past tense. This is because they are events as opposed to commands.

The event payload is the key to each change of state. As each event occurs, you store the payload. That payload could be a simple JSON document that has just enough detail to support the event. For example, this JSON document has an event type of *OrderCreated*. It also has the details about the initial state of the order.

154

```json
{
  "Event":{
    "Type":"OrderCreated",
    "Details":{
        "OrderId":1234,
        "CustomerId":98765,
        "Items":[
        "Item1":{
                "ProductId":"ABC123",
                "Description":"WhizBang Thing",
                "UnitPrice":35.99
        }
      ]
    }
  }
}
```

Before the customer pays for their order, they add another item.

```json
{
  "Event":{
    "Type":"ItemsAdded",
    "Details":{
      "Items":[
      {
       "ProductId":"FOO837",
        "Description":"Underwater Basket Weaving Kit",
        "UnitPrice":125.99
      }
      ]
    }
  }
}
```

The event payload of the new item does not contain the other item in the order. It only has the details of an item to add to the order. The shipping and taxes can also be applied.

```
{
  "Event":{
    "Type":"ShippingAmountApplied",
    "Details":{
      "OrderId":1234,
      "Amount":15.00
    }
  }
}

{
  "Event":{
    "Type":"TaxAmountApplied",
    "Details":{
      "OrderId":1234,
      "Amount":7.58
    }
  }
}
```

Now the customer attempts to make a payment, but it fails. The event is also captured.

```
{
  "Event":{
    "Type":"PaymentFailed",
    "Details":{
      "OrderId":1234,
      "TransactionId":837539
    }
  }
}
```

Perhaps the customer makes a partial payment. They could pay from a gift card that does not have enough balance to pay the whole amount.

```json
{
  "Event":{
    "Type":"PartialPaymentApplied",
    "Details":{
      "OrderId":1234,
      "Amount":10.00,
      "TransactionId":837987
    }
  }
}
```

Then the customer applies another payment.

```json
{
  "Event":{
    "Type":"PartialPaymentApplied",
    "Details":{
      "OrderId":1234,
      "Amount":174.56,
      "TransactionId":838128
    }
  }
}
```

Figure 6-19 shows an example of a table that stores events on orders. The details and amount fields are data pulled from the event body. Separating data like this can help the read process when calculating a total. Notice that the order ID is used as a correlation ID. This allows you to query for the order ID and get all related change entries.

| Event | Order ID | Details | Amount |
|---|---|---|---|
| OrderCreated | 1234 | Order | 0.00 |
| ItemsAdded | 1234 | Items... | 35.99 |
| ItemsAdded | 1234 | Items... | 125.99 |
| ShippingAmountApplied | 1234 | Shipping | 15.00 |
| TaxAmountApplied | 1234 | Tax | 7.58 |
| PaymentFailed | 1234 | Payment | 184.56 |
| PartialPaymentApplied | 1234 | Payment | 10.00 |
| PartialPaymentApplied | 1234 | Payment | 174.56 |
| ItemsShipped | 1234 | Inventory | |
| OrderCompleted | 1234 | Order | |

*Figure 6-19.* *Records of order activity*

Event sourcing is great for processes handling financial transactions, medical records, and even information for lawsuits. Anything that needs a track record of change might be a candidate for this pattern of data handling. However, this pattern is not for everything, and you may be headed toward overengineering. If a process does not need state change tracking, then the event sourcing pattern may not serve you as well as you would like. Also, you may see an increase in data storage cost with event sourcing.

# Scenarios

Another benefit of event sourcing is how it can offset the role of the system. It is no longer in charge of the state of the data. Instead, a person is in charge. The system receives all events and also provides a report noting missing events. The following scenarios help explain some uses of event sourcing.

## Scenario 1

Using an inventory management system, a person loading a truck scans a box before putting it on a truck. The system says the box does not exist. The person has to stop what they are doing and find a way to have the box entered into the system. The state of the object must be corrected before it can be placed on the truck. But the box does exist!

With event sourcing, the event of scanning the box and placing it on a truck continues even if the box is believed not to exist. The event is still captured in the system, and an additional entry is sent to an exception report. This allows people to manage the state of an object without stopping the flow of business.

This also shows another condition. You may have an event of a box being scanned before the event that it exists. Now that an administrator has added the item to the system, an event is created. That event of creation is in the database after the event of the box being placed on a truck. Having a creation event after an activity event is tolerable. For one, it shows that there was an issue that a person had to fix. You could also have specific events to have a sequence number prior to other events. Then your timestamps are in order for evidence tracking. And queries will show the order based on a sequence number.

## Scenario 2

The items in the box from scenario 1 are for an order on an online system. The online system sold the items to the customer, but the items were not in stock. The order was able to take place without the inventory in stock. The order event triggered a process to get the items to fulfill the order. The order system did not need to act on a true count of the items in inventory.

The idea of selling an item that could be out of stock is a matter of policy and not architecture. This allows people to decide how to handle such events. For example, one policy could be to alert the customer that the items are delayed, and they can cancel the order. Another option is to expedite shipping from a different warehouse to the customer. The business gets to decide how to handle the events.

# Eventual Consistency

So many things in the world around us are eventually consistent. Actions like deposits and debits to our bank accounts, to sports scores as the changes are sent to scorekeepers and reporters are examples of events that are eventually made consistent over time. As much as we may want a deposit made immediately available once it hits the account, most systems do operate with the emphasis on availability over consistency. If we design our microservices architecture with the expectation of strong consistency, then we risk terrible latency. This is because the microservices are independent applications communicating over a network. Most of the time, everything is working fine, and there are no delays in achieving consistency. We must design our systems for when those times of delay occur.

What does it mean to have eventual consistency instead of strong consistency? A microservice using a transaction to its own database may use strong consistency. This means that every node in the database cluster must meet a quorum and agree on the change. Again, most of the time, this is fine. However, because some database systems use nodes, there is a chance of issues. Then, a quorum may not be met, and the transaction is rejected. What if you are using a database in the cloud and it is multiregional? Using strong consistency may require a quorum to be met on multiple nodes in different regions. This only adds latency.

Must the changed data be immediately readable? This is the challenge. Writing data to multiregional systems is allowed to take the time it needs when the changed data is not expected to be read immediately. When the need to read the changed data is a bit relaxed, you are better off with eventual consistency. Going back to the example of the bank account, it uses eventual consistency. You may be able to query the database and see the deposit. But other systems related to the transaction may not see the change immediately.

If you queried the order database directly with an online order system, you would see the new order. But the report microservice may not have that data yet. So, some reports and dashboards are seconds or minutes behind. Depending on some processes, it may be the following day before a report is created reflecting the previous day's events.

For microservices to attempt strong consistency, they have to make synchronous API calls to each other. This requires each microservice to complete its steps before the next microservice can proceed. This not only increases latency but also has a higher failure rate. Anything that stops a microservice instance from completing a task will cause a failure the caller must handle. This also includes error conditions such as invalid data, bugs in code, or an unknown condition.

Leveraging the asynchronous messaging patterns mentioned earlier, you can provide eventual consistency across microservices. This allows microservices to process as soon as they can without the dependency of another service. By allowing eventual consistency, microservices can stay loosely coupled without demanding unnecessary restraints.

# Data Warehouse

Some companies use a data warehouse, sometimes referred to as Data Lake, to store massive amounts of data, or "Big Data." This data comes from many different sources and allows for differing data models to be stored for varied purposes. A data warehouse is a collection of data stores for storing massive amounts of data that do not have to be the same type (see Figure 6-20).

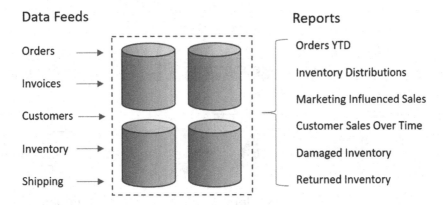

***Figure 6-20.***  *Example of multiple data feeds*

Data warehouses allow companies to collect data both for historical compliances and for reporting. SQL Server is an Online Transactional Processing (OLTP) type database system. The main purpose is for handling normalized data in transactions using ACID properties. The Online Analytical Processing (OLAP) type database system stores denormalized data for analytics, data mining, and business intelligence applications.

With the locking nature of most OLTP database systems, it is best never to use them as a source for reports. The massive reads on those databases have locks that can interfere with write activities. Instead, the data should be copied and any conversions applied in an OLAP database system. This allows for data processing to be done on other servers without impeding transactions. It also allows for data to be retrieved and utilized with different data models than what was used when the data was written.

You can use Extract, Transform, Load (ETL) tools such as Azure Data Factory, Microsoft SQL Server Integration Services (SSIS), and Informatica PowerCenter for moving and transforming data to an OLAP database.

ETL tools can be used for pulling data into a data warehouse, but it is also possible for data to be sent instead. As a microservice is writing data to a database, it can also send that data on a message bus that is received by an endpoint in the data warehouse.

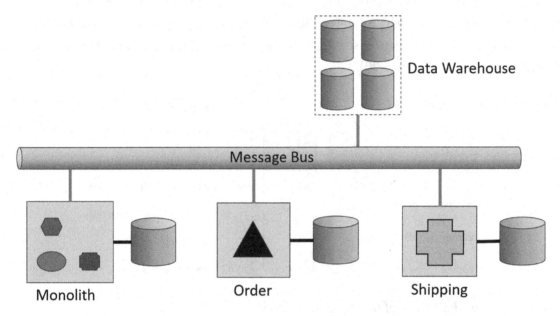

***Figure 6-21.*** *Microservices architecture using a data warehouse*

Patterns like CQRS can be used to feed data warehouse solutions. Having a data warehouse provides a separation of databases used by microservices (see Figure 6-21). The data in the data warehouse can now be leveraged in many various ways. One of which is a way of combining data from multiple sources into a materialized view.

# Materialized View

A materialized view is a way of viewing data that differs from the way it is stored. But it is more than a way of viewing data. Using materialized views allows for showing raw data as well as any computed data based on those values. Materialized views are meant to be rebuilt from a data source and never modified by the applications.

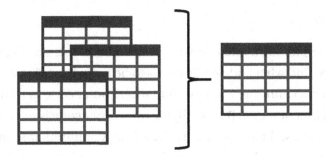

**Figure 6-22.** *Materialized view*

Materialized views allow applications to retrieve predefined views of data (see Figure 6-22). This helps with performance and adaptability. These materialized views can be used for reporting and dashboards. The data could be sales vs. forecasted sales for the month or year. It can help see sales trend lines. Even the ability to how well customers are able to use your application can benefit future changes.

# Splitting the Monolith

There are many challenging details when it comes to splitting functionality out of a monolith to a new microservice. Every challenge may make you question if using microservices is the right approach. So, where should we begin?

Let us start with the approach that the code has not yet separated from a monolith. With so much infrastructure to put in place for even the smallest code base to be a microservice, start small. You should consider putting in place a Continuous Integration/Continuous Deployment (CI/CD) pipeline for code releases. A team of developers dedicated to managing the requirements, coding standards, tests, and bugs should also be in place first. Even testing strategies (discussed in Chapter 7) need to be thought out and implemented. No matter the size of the code you intend to pull from a monolith without infrastructure in place, you will have a much harder time developing and managing the microservice. If you find that even with the smallest code things are not working for you, reconsider if microservices is the correct approach.

# Moving Code

One approach to developing a microservice from a monolith is starting with code. You do some analysis to find what code really needs to be pulled out. If you are pulling out the functionality for accounting, you must find where other code in the monolith is using that domain functionality. By identifying what other code is using accounting functionality, you can list the areas where refactoring is required. Instead of calling the accounting code in memory, it must now call the microservice by either an HTTP API or with messaging. For the examples here we will assume the use of HTTP API.

The monolith now calls the accounting microservice by the API. This is in the right direction but the microservice is still tied to the same database used by the monolith (see Figure 6-23). As discussed earlier in this chapter, staying in this position will allow for contention of the schema changes and challenge data integrity. And there are likely other parts of the monolith that are using tables that the accounting microservice will need once extracted. The accounting microservice needs to be the single source of truth of the accounting data.

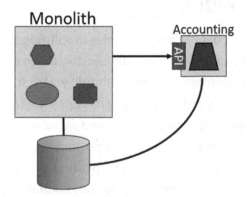

***Figure 6-23.*** *Monolith sharing database with single microservice*

Another problem is also presented here. The accounting functionality may require contacting other domain functionality that is still in the monolith (see Figure 6-24). In this case, we add an API to the monolith for the accounting microservice to call. We now have a circular reference that should otherwise be avoided. However, this is one of those migration steps that can buy you time. Having this circular reference helps to get the accounting microservice developed as well as highlighting areas for change that might otherwise never be identified. This position is tolerable **if** this is not the final state. Do not go to production with this position unless you have a solid plan to continue the migration in the next sprint.

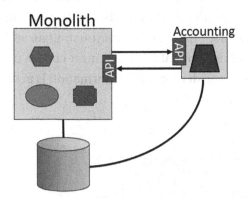

***Figure 6-24.*** *Accounting microservice calls back to monolith*

Having a new API to the monolith only adds complexity to the architecture and is more to manage. And circular dependencies should always be avoided. It is only mentioned here as it is a reasonable migration step to get you to a solid architecture. Going through this development highlights tightly coupled code and allows you to attempt to refactor to be more loosely coupled. Ultimately, you want to be in a position where the accounting microservice is not reliant on code in the monolith (see Figure 6-25). You may have to further segregate domain functionality and leave some in the monolith. For example, if functionality for accounts payable cannot be refactored well, then split the microservice even further. Perhaps you have a microservice just for handling accounts receivable business processes.

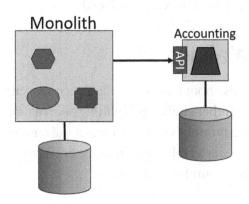

***Figure 6-25.*** *Accounting microservice with its own database*

# Strangler Pattern

The strangler pattern is useful for refactoring code to a microservice. You start by adding an interception layer between the caller and the accounting code (see Figure 6-26). The interception layer you create can direct the calls to either the functionality still in the monolith or redirect to call the microservice. As you migrate additional functionality to the accounting microservice, the interception layer code is updated to redirect calls accordingly. A resource to consider for more information is at `https://www.amazon.com/gp/product/B081TKSSNN`.

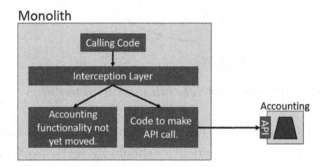

***Figure 6-26.*** *Strangler pattern using interception layer*

# Feature Flags

An option to consider that controls the flow of processes is feature flags (also known as feature toggle). With feature flags the execution of code in the monolith is governed by the settings of the individual flags you set up. The settings for the flags are usually in configuration files. They can also be set using values you place in a database. One product of feature flags to check out is LaunchDarkly.[1]

# Splitting the Database

We went over several details about how to handle data transactions and different data storage models. Now for another challenge, splitting apart a database. For this section, we are going to assume the monolith is using a relational database like SQL Server. Looking at Figure 6-27, there is a table for shipments and another table for accounting that has a final amount for a round-trip shipment.

---

[1] `https://launchdarkly.com`

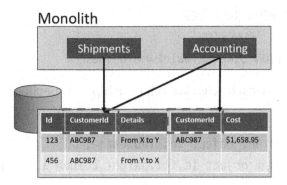

**Figure 6-27.**  *Analyzing data*

From the image we can see the accounting code is using information from two tables. These two tables have a foreign key relationship on the CustomerId column. The accounting department may use this information for reporting current sales per customer or month-to-date and year-to-date reports. What is not shown is how the data is managed. Are there stored procedures or functions being used? What about an Object Relational Mapper (ORM) like Entity Framework? Since the attempt is going to be to move accounting functionality to a microservice, that code needs to have the accounting data under its control. This helps with data integrity management.

We know the accounting table will move to the database for the accounting microservice. We need to identify the foreign key constraints, stored procedures, and functions using the connected tables. To find the stored procedures that use a table by name, use the following command:

```
SELECT Name
FROM sys.procedures
WHERE OBJECT_DEFINITION(OBJECT_ID) LIKE '%TableNameToFind%'
```

To find functions that include the table name:

```
SELECT
    ROUTINE_NAME,
    ROUTINE_DEFINITION ,
    ROUTINE_SCHEMA,
    DATA_TYPE,
    CREATED
```

```
FROM INFORMATION_SCHEMA.ROUTINES
WHERE ROUTINE_TYPE = 'FUNCTION'
AND ROUTINE_DEFINITION LIKE '%TableNameToFind%'
```

To find tables that have a foreign key relationship to a specified table:

```
SELECT
    OBJECT_NAME(f1.parent_object_id) TableName,
    COL_NAME(fc1.parent_object_id,fc1.parent_column_id) ColName
FROM
    sys.foreign_keys AS f1
INNER JOIN
    sys.foreign_key_columns AS fc1
        ON f1.OBJECT_ID = fc1.constraint_object_id
INNER JOIN
    sys.tables t
        ON t.OBJECT_ID = fc1.referenced_object_id
WHERE
    OBJECT_NAME (f1.referenced_object_id) = 'TableNameHere'
```

Kathy, the Code Whiz developer, has been hard at work understanding the existing database structure and data models. She used the queries shown earlier to help identify the connected resources to determine if there are supporting tables that need to move with the accounting table. Kathy created a map of the tables specific to the accounting functionality. She then added to the map the resources that had a relationship to the accounting tables.

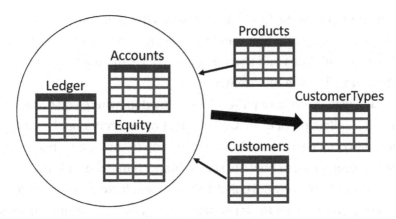

***Figure 6-28.*** *Direction of data dependencies*

Kathy noted the direction of the dependencies (see Figure 6-28). Some tables need information from accounting objects. Some tables were used by the accounting objects. As Kathy identifies the dependencies, she is able to analyze further if there is data that should be copied to the database for the accounting microservice. This is possible using the knowledge you learned in the previous section on sharing and duplicating data.

Much more information can be found on splitting monoliths to microservices at https://www.amazon.com/gp/product/B081TKSSNN.

# Summary

Decentralizing data is far from easy and plays a critical role in the evolution of architecture. As you learned in this chapter, there may be a point where applications using the same tables and schema need to have their own databases. This does not mean separate database servers though. By having separate databases, the applications are in more control of the data integrity. Also, it allows you to choose a different database type based on your needs.

You also learned that it is permissible to have duplicate data in various databases. This allows for microservices to work autonomously with just enough information to fulfill the needs of business processes.

We also went over handling data transactions distributed across microservices. As business processes span microservices, local transactions are used to manage changes in data. Managing a collection of transactions may involve the patterns like routing slip and sagas.

You learned about using the CQRS pattern when the write model differs greatly from the read model. This model difference and processing needs may impact performance, so splitting the responsibilities into a write microservice and another for reads provides a clean way of handling the data requirements.

Event sourcing was shown as a pattern of storing data where you do not store the current value but a collection of events. The collection of events can be queried, and the values computed to obtain the latest known values up to that time. This is useful when processes need to keep proof of how the state of data changed over time.

We also went over how eventual consistency is used instead of strong consistency. By allowing different systems to get the latest state change at a later time provides systems with more availability.

Then we touched on how some companies use data warehouses and materialized views based on data that came from other sources. This allows the growing changes to how data is read and reported on from impacting the performance of the microservices.

You also learned some ideas to split code from a monolith with the strangler pattern and feature flags. The best way for you is only known after you try them to which pattern best fits your scenarios. Splitting up a database to allow data to move to another database to be owned by a microservice is just as tedious as splitting code. So, you learned ways of looking for stored procedures and functions that use a table by name. Also, you learned how to identify foreign key constraints.

# CHAPTER 7

# Testing Microservices

Kathy, the developer at Code Whiz, has made a few microservices and is concerned with proving they work as expected. She knows that the microservices are crucial for their client Hyp-Log, our hypothetical company in this book. Kathy looks at the various ways of testing microservices.

This chapter will go over why testing is important, what to test and what not to test, and various approaches to testing. We will also build an example of contract testing for REST-based communication. Then we build tests for messaging-based microservices.

Remember that each microservice is an independent application deserving of all the attention as any other application. A microservice has a focus on domain functionality. And they are pieces of a larger architectural solution. As such, these microservices have testing requirements just like any other application. However, they have more testing requirements because they are interconnected to form a bigger picture of that architectural solution.

The development of microservices adds complexity to the architecture. It allows bugs not to be found until much later in the development process or after deploying to the production environment. And these bugs are costly.

## Cost of Errors

Testing plays a crucial and often underrated role in software development. Too often, we are required to rush code development only to have errors in understanding what the business/users need and how we implement those needs. For Kathy and the other developers at Code Whiz, this is no exception.

---

**Note** You should build tests throughout the development of any application. Test-Driven Development (TDD) is a highly recommended methodology to consider.

---

171

Numerous studies prove that the cost of fixing a bug grows exponentially from time of gathering requirements to when found in production. It is cheaper to identify and fix bugs as early as possible in the software development life cycle.

The cost of fixing bugs is not only monetary but also in the loss of confidence. If you hire a contractor to add an electrical outlet and it randomly functions, you would be rather upset. If you buy a new car and it breaks down after a month, you would be upset as well. We require quality effort from others. That requirement applies to software development as well. Does that mean perfection every time? No, but it does mean we are to give our best attempt.

The role of microservices in a distributed architecture increases the likelihood of bugs inadvertently getting into the code. Given the additional complexity of a microservices architecture, the cost of these bugs is much more than an N-tier style application. The cost only adds the need for not only more testing but also more types of testing. Before we talk about testing details, let us first go over some items that do not need testing.

# What Not to Test

There is so much to test with any system to verify accuracy, performance, and overall quality. However, there are some things that testing would be a waste of time. Instead of creating a test to verify an external system/dependency exists, write tests that prove your code is handling the times when a connection to a system is expected but fails.

Other things you should not test are items like the .NET Framework. The .NET Framework is already well tested before release. Though that does not make it bug-free, it removes the need for you to test it. Testing the framework is like testing the frame of a new car before buying. Generally, we test the car operates well without proving it will hold on to all the tires. The caveat to this is that when you are learning something about a framework or library, testing is a fantastic way to learn.

# What to Test

As important as it is for us to test our code, we must test in appropriate ways and at the right time. A microservice does not exist alone. It is part of an architecture for specific business purposes, meaning testing is required at multiple layers of code and from multiple perspectives. Testing microservices includes not only testing the code but also performance as well as handling failures.

# Code

In the book *Succeeding with Agile,* Mike Cohn presents a test pyramid (see Figure 7-1). The pyramid depicts various layers of testing with an emphasis on the number of tests. The bottom of the pyramid is the widest part, suggesting more unit tests than other test types. Above that is the service test and at the top is User Interface (UI) test. These are sometimes called end-to-end (E-to-E) tests and usually require human execution.

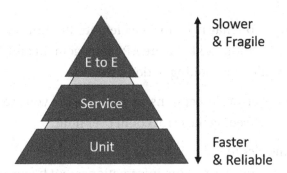

***Figure 7-1.*** *Testing pyramid*

Others have added to the pyramid, noting that not only are there more unit tests than service tests and E-to-E tests, but they also expect the cheapest execution cost. That is, they are to be easy to automate and can be run repeatedly throughout the day. The tests at the top of the pyramid are the most expensive. They are hard to automate and generally take a lot of time and resources of people.

# Performance

Each microservice is purpose built to solve various problems with business processes. So, knowing how they fulfill their responsibilities for those business processes is as important as knowing they are stable and performant.

After the microservices are working and accurate, then consider making them performant. It does not matter how fast any code runs to a wrong answer. Make it work, make it accurate, and then make it fast.

There are several metrics to consider when evaluating the performance of a microservices architecture. The following list provides a few metrics to consider when gauging the health of the microservices. More details are in Chapter 9 addressing cross-cutting concerns.

- CPU/RAM – Is the microservice showing signs there is a need to scale the number of instances? Perhaps you need to provide more CPU or RAM for the microservice instance.

- Network connections – Is the microservice handling new requests and responsive?

- Messaging – How many messages can be processed in a given time period?

- Rate limiting – You may need to consider rate-limiting access to the microservices. Products like Azure API Management and AWS API Gateway provide rate-limiting options.

- The number of errors/exceptions/retries – Ensure you are logging information and seeing the error count over time.

- Capturing metrics to bill a customer – You may need to add another microservice to receive custom information about business processes that you can use to bill your customers.

## System Failure Handling

During the transition from a monolithic architecture to a full microservices architecture, Netflix created some Open Source Software (OSS) packages. One of which is Chaos Monkey (`https://github.com/Netflix/chaosmonkey`). Chaos Monkey can be used to randomly turn off virtual machines or containers, which provides the challenge of making sure you add in resilience handling protective measures. You can run Chaos Monkey in your test environment, but you can also run it in your production environment. Because there is always a chance of a virtual machine or container going away, the architecture must handle those scenarios. Running Chaos Monkey in your production environment guarantees those system-level failures will occur. Have you prepared for those situations? How well are you expecting the unexpected?

## Security

Imagine that you have developed a microservice to process payroll functionality. And further, imagine that this microservice will process your paycheck. Attention to detail increases, and you strive for the best code development. But what about security?

Assuredly the microservices will exist on a private network. You are sure that no Internet traffic can get to the microservice. However, incoming traffic is not the problem here. It is common to use 3rd party public NuGet packages, but do we ever review the code in that package? We must protect microservices from the traffic coming into the network and traffic going out that is not warranted. Unwanted code can sniff the network and attempt to send information to an external site. And that code could be in another microservice. Consider reviewing the recommendations by the OWASP organization (`https://owasp.org/www-project-top-ten`).

Using a service mesh like Istio (`https://istio.io`) provides a way to secure traffic between microservices. A service mesh may help keep the communication encrypted/secure and should be used even on a private network. Now that you have made a microservice that processes your paycheck, you need also to control who can call it. Just having a microservice available on the network allows it to be callable by anyone. But by using Istio, you can also control the authorization on microservices. Now, only the permitted caller can reach sensitive information provided by a microservice.

# Testing Levels

A modified test pyramid shows more explicit layers where microservices interact (see Figure 7-2). The following image is the pyramid revised for use with testing microservices. It has six levels as opposed to the original three levels. The pyramid test levels are Unit, Integration, Component, Contract, Service, and End-to-End (E to E).

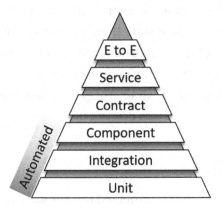

***Figure 7-2.***  *Extended testing pyramid*

# Unit Testing

The unit tests should be automated and run against code that is the smallest piece of independent business logic (see Figure 7-3). These tests are for verifying the accuracy of an algorithm, for example, a method that takes in various information and returns a tax rate. Is the tax rate correct? Is the calculation correct every time with the same information? If not, then you probably have a factor, like time, that is changing.

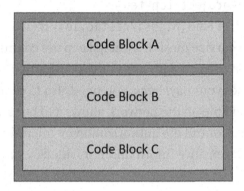

***Figure 7-3.*** *Code blocks*

Unit tests have fast execution time compared to the other testing types on the pyramid. And unit tests should not connect to any other code module or 3rd party systems like a database, file, or messaging system.

You can prove that the code at the most basic level is performing accurately by having unit tests. It also helps to prove your understanding of the business requirements. If you have misunderstood a requirement, then the tests will help show that given certain conditions, the answer is wrong, and something needs to change.

Unit tests should not test logic that resides outside of the boundary of the algorithm. For example, testing an algorithm for tax rates does not test for connections to a database or other outside systems. Testing processes that rely on code external to itself are integration tests.

# Integration Testing

Integration tests are for code blocks connected to a resource either in another module or an external system like a database, file, or messaging system (see Figure 7-4). Tests here are for algorithms that work with other algorithms. These other methods may be in another class. In those cases, you see class dependencies.

Integration tests also help to prove dependency injection is working with the registered classes. Because of the dependencies of other classes and sometimes 3rd party systems, you usually find there to be fewer integration tests than unit tests. However, these tests are usually more involved and have more setup and teardown code.

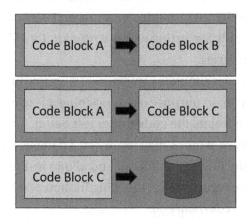

***Figure 7-4.*** *Code blocks calling outside of boundary*

## Component Testing

With a microservice architecture, you can think of microservices as components (see Figure 7-5). And code in a monolith that calls a microservice is also a component. These components are the pieces that are communicating to each other to distribute the computational needs. This level of testing is about testing these components in isolation. We are not ready to have them talking to each other just yet.

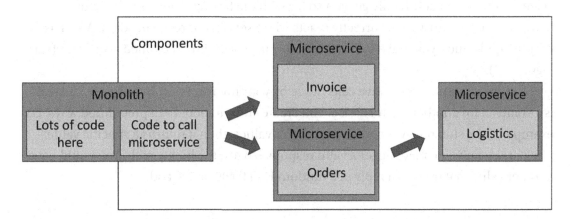

***Figure 7-5.*** *Microservices as components*

# Mocking

There are a couple of options we have here for testing the components. Consider a scenario where code is calling a microservice owned by a different development team. The purpose here is to test the code that makes the call without the other microservice being available. That provider microservice may not yet be available or may require resources of its own not ready for testing without preparation. Mocking is the type of testing that is useful in the cases.

A mock object is code that simulates an external resource like a database or simply another dependency. The main purpose of a mock object is to allow tests to provide a replica of a dependency to isolate the code under test better.

For testing microservices, a mock may represent a database or another microservice. It replaces the object on the other end of a call and allows testing a microservice without specific dependencies (see Figure 7-6). A mocking framework that works well is called "moq" at `https://github.com/moq/moq`.

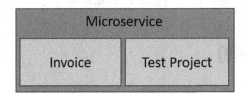

***Figure 7-6.*** *Test project as a mock*

# Stub

Having a mock object will only get you so far with the testing. There is still the need to make sure a microservice correctly reacts when sending or receiving data. A stub is custom application you make to serve various purposes with predefined responses (see Figure 7-7).

The use of a stub is to receive calls made by your microservice. In this case, the stub is a stand-in for another microservice. You create stubs to behave in predefined ways. For example, if the stub receives certain parameter values, then it returns a specific value. The parameter value may trigger a valid response to test the happy path. You could have another value that triggers a reply of a random HTTP 400 or 500 code.

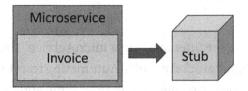

***Figure 7-7.*** *Stub testing object*

Using expectations of requests and responses prove how the code handles conditions, and that code changes have not broken anything. Another idea is to have the stub wait an extremely long time before replying to test the microservice's ability to handle timeout issues.

# Contract Testing

Microservices receive a payload of data by either an API call or messaging. Either way, the data needs to be in the expected format. This format is the contract. Contract testing is about verifying that calls from components to microservice are communicating with the agreed-upon data format.

Each microservice plays a part in the architecture. Therefore, it must be known as early as possible the format of the data. Of course, requirements change, and so must the code, data format, tests, and any mocks/stubs. During development, it can be malleable as needed to fulfill the business requirements. If there are changes to the contract of a microservice already in production, you will handle the change by versioning the API or the contract itself.

## Consumer-Driven Contract Testing

When creating code that calls or "consumes" a microservice, you test the code that works with the contract. This type of testing is called consumer-driven contract testing. The test verifies your code that handles the data in the contract.

By leveraging consumer-driven contract testing, the developers of the consumer can both define the contract and code to that definition. For the developers working on the provider microservice, they too can code and test using the same tests defined by the developers of the consumer.

Later in this chapter, we will have a step-by-step coding example of creating a consumer-driven contract testing set of projects. See the section called "Consumer-Driven Contract Testing Deep Dive."

# Service Testing

At this level, you are testing the interaction to a microservice. The components are now talking to each other without mocks or stubs. Automating tests here is possible but hard to accomplish. If you are the developer of both the calling and the receiving sides, then automating is easier. However, with microservices developed by other teams, testing is usually manual. These tests are also more expensive in time and money because they involve people doing more test preparations. With service testing, you are verifying conditions like

- Use of network

- API interaction

- Sending or receiving messages

- Failure from network or CPU/memory exhaustion

# End-to-End Testing

End-to-end testing is the most expensive level. It requires people to test the system as a whole. Here administrators might create users for the system and perhaps making new customer accounts, load requests, invoices, etc. End-to-end testing is about exercising the business logic from a user's perspective. The users do not care about what the system does to process an invoice. They just need to have the confidence that it does and that the system handles not only when correct data is used but also with invalid data. Does your new microservice handle network issues like partitioning and latency and incorrect data by a user?

# Consumer-Driven Contract Testing Deep Dive

In this section, we will create examples of consumer-driven contract testing. We will create two services, one being the consumer and the other as the provider. You will see how to use the PactNet library to generate an output file. The provider microservice uses this file to confirm it has not broken the contract. For more information on the Pact framework, check out `https://pact.io`.

# Consumer Project

In Visual Studio 2022, we are going to create the first microservice. The first step is to create a new project. Select "ASP.NET Core Web API" from the list of options (see Figure 7-8).

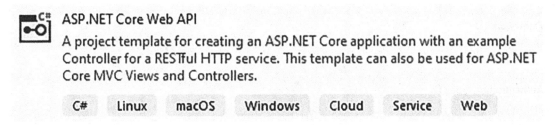

**ASP.NET Core Web API**
A project template for creating an ASP.NET Core application with an example Controller for a RESTful HTTP service. This template can also be used for ASP.NET Core MVC Views and Controllers.

| C# | Linux | macOS | Windows | Cloud | Service | Web |

***Figure 7-8.***  *Project type ASP.NET Core Web API*

Select Next and configure the project name and location (see Figure 7-9). This first project is named OrderSvc-Consumer. It is not required to have "consumer" or "provider" in the name. Those terms are used with the project name to help keep the purpose of the projects obvious.

# Configure your new project

ASP.NET Core Web API | C# | Linux | macOS | Windows | Cloud | Service | Web |

Project name

    OrderSvc-Consumer

Location

    C:\Projects

Solution name ⓘ

    OrderSvc-Consumer

☐ Place solution and project in the same directory

***Figure 7-9.***  *Project name and location*

Select the Framework option for .NET 6 and then the "Create" button (see Figure 7-10).

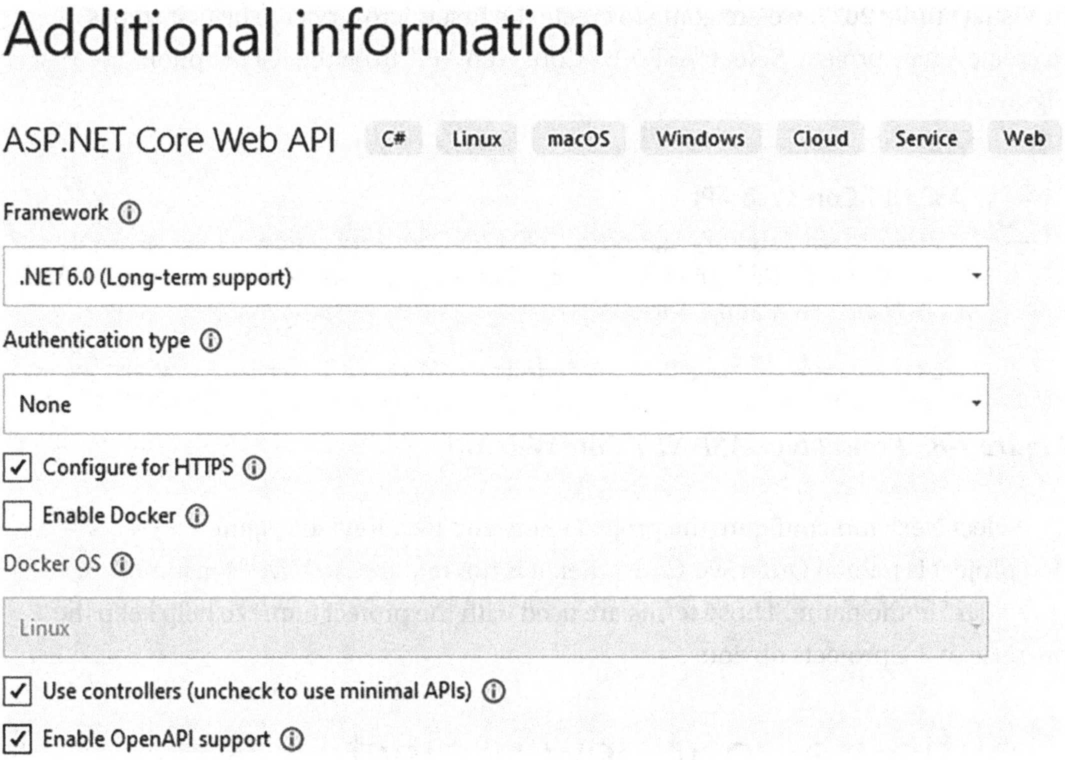

# Additional information

ASP.NET Core Web API   C#   Linux   macOS   Windows   Cloud   Service   Web

Framework ⓘ

.NET 6.0 (Long-term support)    ▾

Authentication type ⓘ

None    ▾

☑ Configure for HTTPS ⓘ

☐ Enable Docker ⓘ

Docker OS ⓘ

Linux    ▾

☑ Use controllers (uncheck to use minimal APIs) ⓘ

☑ Enable OpenAPI support ⓘ

*Figure 7-10.  Additional project options*

This service does not need any real code except for one model. The test code here and the mock in the next section will use the DiscountModel class. Create a new class called DiscountModel.

```
public class DiscountModel
{
  public double CustomerRating { get; set; }
  public double AmountToDiscount { get; set; }
}
```

# Consumer Test Project

Now we will add a test project. In this example, we are using the xUnit test framework. The PactNet library is not dependent on a specific testing framework. So, you are welcome to pick the testing framework with which you are the most comfortable. Begin by right-clicking the solution and selecting Add ➤ New Project. Now select the project type xUnit Test Project and then the "Next" button (see Figure 7-11).

***Figure 7-11.*** *Selecting the xUnit Test Project type*

Now provide a Project Name and a Location of where to create the new project. You will then choose an appropriate Target Framework. Select the version that matches the main project, which for this book should be .NET 6.0. Now select the "Create" button.

After you create the test project, make a project reference to the project you are testing. In this example, the project reference uses the OrderSvc-Consumer.

You will need to add a NuGet package for the contract testing. First, you need to know which package you choose is based on the OS you are running the tests on (see Figure 7-12). If you are running on Windows, then select the PactNet.Windows library. If running on Linux, select the PactNet.Linux library based on if running on 32 bit (x86) or 64 bit (x64). There is also a library option for OSX.

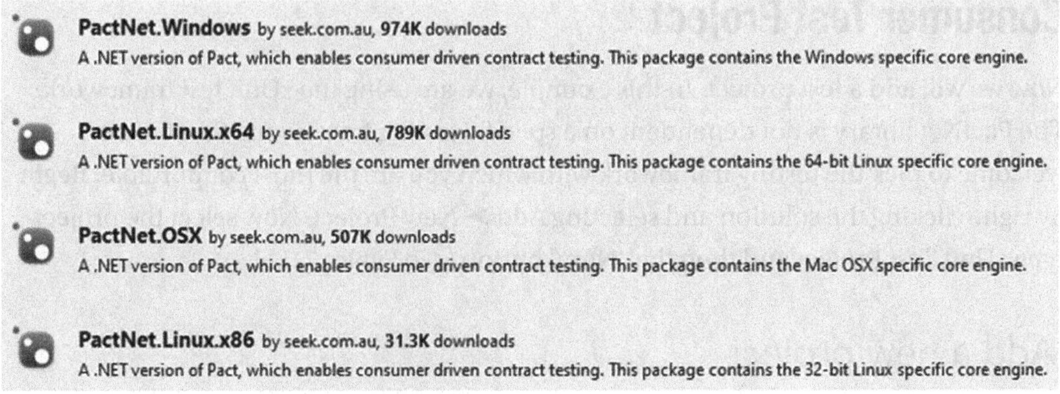

**Figure 7-12.** *PactNet library options*

The integration test calls a mock service instead of calling the real discount microservice. In your test project, create a new class called DiscountSvcMock. Then apply the following code:

```
public class DiscountSvcMock : IDisposable
{
  private readonly IPactBuilder _pactBuilder;
  private readonly int _servicePort = 9222;
  private bool _disposed = false;
  public IMockProviderService MockProviderService { get; }
  public string ServiceUri => $"http://localhost:{_servicePort}";

  public DiscountSvcMock()
  {
    var pactConfig = new PactConfig
    {
      SpecificationVersion = "2.0.0",
      PactDir = @"c:\temp\pact\OrderSvcConsumer",
      LogDir = @"c:\temp\pact\OrderSvcConsumer\logs"
    };

    _pactBuilder = new PactBuilder(pactConfig)
        .ServiceConsumer("Orders")
        .HasPactWith("Discounts");
```

```
    MockProviderService = _pactBuilder.MockService(_servicePort,
      new JsonSerializerSettings
        {
          ContractResolver = new CamelCasePropertyNamesContractResolver(),
          NullValueHandling = NullValueHandling.Ignore
        });
    }

  protected virtual void Dispose(bool disposing)
  {
    if (!_disposed)
    {
      if (disposing)
        {
        _pactBuilder.Build();
      }
      _disposed = true;
    }
  }

  public void Dispose()
  {
    Dispose(true);
  }
}
```

In your test class, modify it to the following code. It creates a test that is reliant on the mock service you just created. Because of the mock service, you do not need to run the service itself. Running the test will leverage PactNet and the mock service.

```
public class DiscountSvcTests : IClassFixture<DiscountSvcMock>
{
  private readonly IMockProviderService _mockProviderService;
  private readonly string _serviceUri;

  public DiscountSvcTests(DiscountSvcMock discountSvcMock)
  {
```

```csharp
    _mockProviderService = discountSvcMock.MockProviderService;
    _serviceUri = discountSvcMock.ServiceUri;
    _mockProviderService.ClearInteractions();
  }

  [Fact]
  public async Task GetDiscountAdjustmentAmount()
  {
    var discountModel = new DiscountModel { CustomerRating = 4.1 };

    _mockProviderService
      .Given("Rate")
      .UponReceiving("Given a customer rating" +
        ", an adjustment discount amount will be returned.")
      .With(new ProviderServiceRequest
        {
          Method = HttpVerb.Post,
          Path = "/discount",
          Body = discountModel,
          Headers = new Dictionary<string, object>
          {
            {"Content-Type","application/json; charset=utf-8"}
          }
        })
      .WillRespondWith(new ProviderServiceResponse
        {
          Status = 200,
          Headers = new Dictionary<string, object>
          {
            {"Content-Type","application/json; charset=utf-8"}
          },
          Body = new DiscountModel
          {
            CustomerRating = 4.1,
            AmountToDiscount = .41
          }
        });
```

```
    var httpClient = new HttpClient();
    var response = await httpClient
            .PostAsJsonAsync($"{_serviceUri}/discount"
            ,discountModel);
    var discountModelReturned =
      await response.Content.ReadFromJsonAsync<DiscountModel>();

    Assert.Equal(
      discountModel.CustomerRating
      ,discountModelReturned.CustomerRating
    );
  }
}
```

The output of the executed test has two main items. There is an assert statement in the test. But there is also a file created in the folder C:\temp\pact\OrderSvcConsumer. You can change the location for the files; however, you will need to provide the same path when creating the provider microservice later.

Looking at the output file that PactNet has created, we can see the details that PactNet required us to set up and the information used by the provider when that service uses this same file.

```
{
  "consumer": {
    "name": "Orders"
  },
  "provider": {
    "name": "Discounts"
  },
  "interactions": [
    {
      "description": "Given a customer rating, an adjustment discount
      amount will be returned.",
      "providerState": "Rate",
      "request": {
        "method": "post",
        "path": "/discount",
```

```
      "headers": {
        "Content-Type": "application/json; charset=utf-8"
      },
      "body": {
        "customerRating": 4.1,
        "amountToDiscount": 0.0
      }
    },
    "response": {
      "status": 200,
      "headers": {
        "Content-Type": "application/json; charset=utf-8"
      },
      "body": {
        "customerRating": 4.1,
        "amountToDiscount": 0.41
      }
    }
  }
],
"metadata": {
  "pactSpecification": {
    "version": "2.0.0"
  }
}
}
```

You can see the request is making a POST to the path "/discount." It uses "application/json" as the content type as well as the "charset=utf-8." Also noted is the body of the request containing the details of the DiscountModel type. The property "amountToDiscount" shows 0.0, default value of a double since a value was not given.

Also, in the file is the expected response. It includes an HTTP status code of 200, matching headers, and a body. The body includes the supplied customer rating as well as the expected result of calling the real service. Remember, it called the mock service, so all of these details are the setup of expectations. When the provider microservice uses this file, the test library compares the value to the value in the defined response object in this file.

# Provider Project

Now that we have made a consumer-driven contract integration test with PactNet, we will create a provider microservice to use the output file. Begin by creating a new ASP. NET Core Web API project (see Figure 7-13).

This example will be a fully working microservice. However, the business logic will be just enough to prove the point and help with testing.

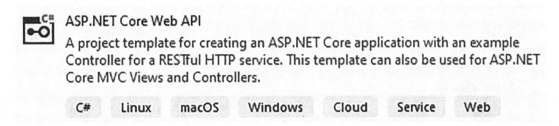

**Figure 7-13.**  *Project type ASP.NET Core Web API*

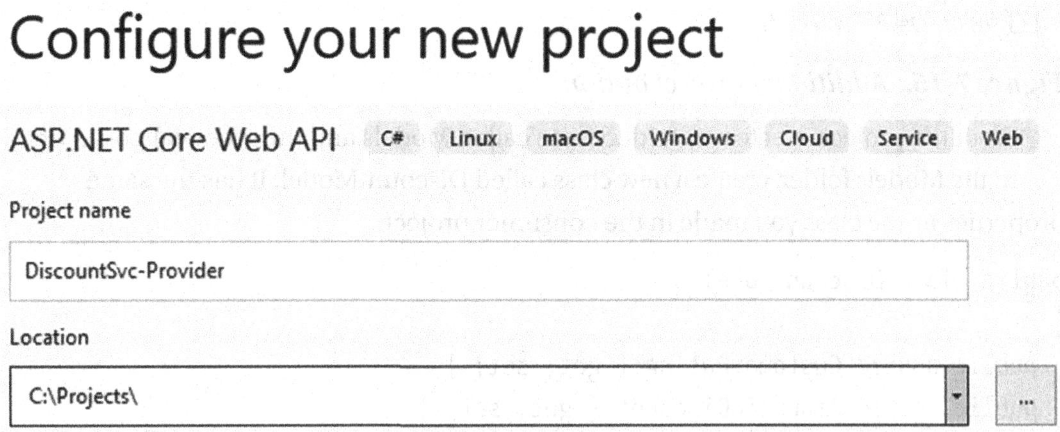

# Configure your new project

ASP.NET Core Web API    C#    Linux    macOS    Windows    Cloud    Service    Web

Project name

DiscountSvc-Provider

Location

C:\Projects\

**Figure 7-14.**  *Project name and location*

Provide a project name and location and then select the "Next" button (see Figure 7-14). Now, select the framework .NET 6 and then the "Create" button (see Figure 7-15).

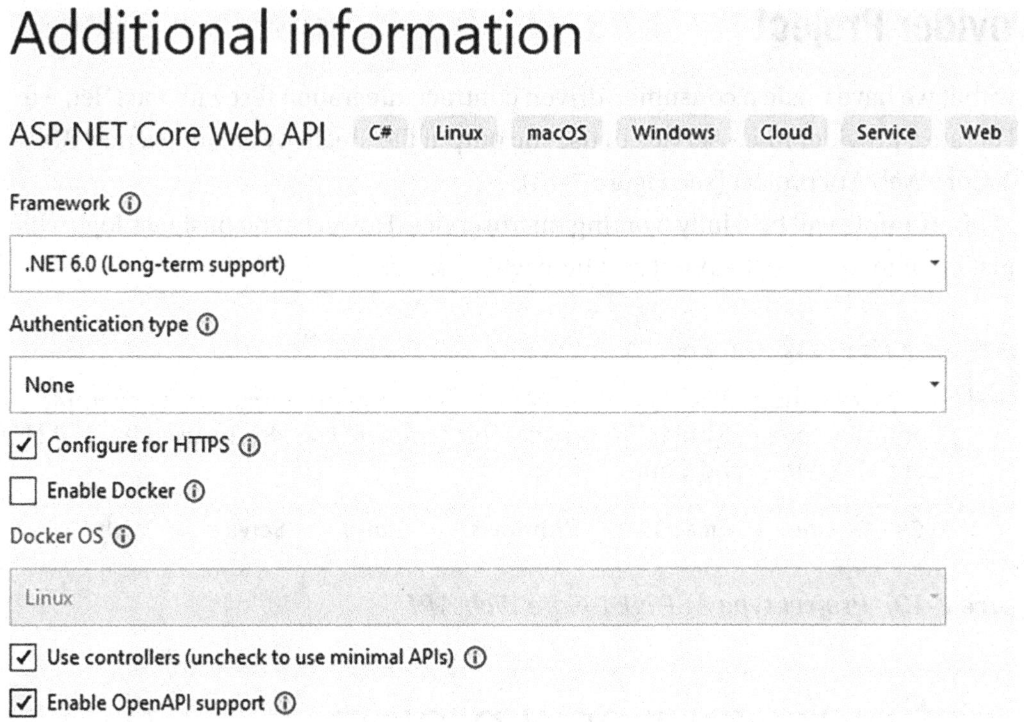

# Additional information

ASP.NET Core Web API   C#   Linux   macOS   Windows   Cloud   Service   Web

Framework ⓘ

> .NET 6.0 (Long-term support)                                              ▾

Authentication type ⓘ

> None                                                                       ▾

☑ Configure for HTTPS ⓘ
☐ Enable Docker ⓘ
Docker OS ⓘ

> Linux                                                                       ▾

☑ Use controllers (uncheck to use minimal APIs) ⓘ
☑ Enable OpenAPI support ⓘ

***Figure 7-15.*** *Additional project options*

From the project, create two folders, one called Models and the other called Services.

In the Models folder, create a new class called DiscountModel. It has the same properties as the class you made in the consumer project.

```
public class DiscountModel
{
  public double CustomerRating { get; set; }
  public double AmountToDiscount { get; set; }
}
```

In the Services folder, create a new class called DiscountService.

```
public class DiscountService
{
  public double GetDiscountAmount(double customerRating)
  {
    return customerRating / 10;
  }
}
```

190

The code is just enough to provide a working example. In Program.cs file, replace existing code with this:

```
using DiscountSvc_Provider.Models;
using DiscountSvc_Provider.Services;

var builder = WebApplication.CreateBuilder(args);

// Add services to the container.

builder.Services.AddControllers();
builder.Services.AddTransient<DiscountService>();

var app = builder.Build();

// Configure the HTTP request pipeline.

app.UseHttpsRedirection();

app.UseAuthorization();

app.MapControllers();
app.UseRouting();

app.UseEndpoints(endpoints =>
{
  var svc = endpoints
      .ServiceProvider
    .GetRequiredService<DiscountService>();

  endpoints.MapPost("/discount", async context =>
  {
    var model = await context.Request
  .ReadFromJsonAsync<DiscountModel>();

    var amount = svc.GetDiscountAmount(model.CustomerRating);

    await context.Response
      .WriteAsJsonAsync(
        new DiscountModel
        {
```

```
            CustomerRating = model.CustomerRating,
            AmountToDiscount = amount
        });
    });
});

app.Run();
```

In the Properties folder, edit the file launchSettings.json. Here we will modify the profile called DiscountSvc_Provider. Because this is a microservice and no real need for anything to be shown to a browser, the setting "launchBrowser" value is false. We are also changing the port used in the "applicationUrl" setting to be something other than the default 5000. This is only required if you run multiple Web API projects for web apps that attempt to open and use the same port.

```
"DiscountSvc_Provider": {
  "commandName": "Project",
  "dotnetRunMessages": "true",
  "launchBrowser": false,
  "applicationUrl": "http://localhost:8080",
  "environmentVariables": {
    "ASPNETCORE_ENVIRONMENT": "Development"
  }
}
```

## Provider Test Project

Now create the test project. The instructions here are the same as what you did for the consumer project. Right-click the solution and select Add ➤ New Project.

***Figure 7-16.*** *Adding the xUnit test project*

Select the project type for xUnit Test Project and then select the "Next" button (see Figure 7-16).

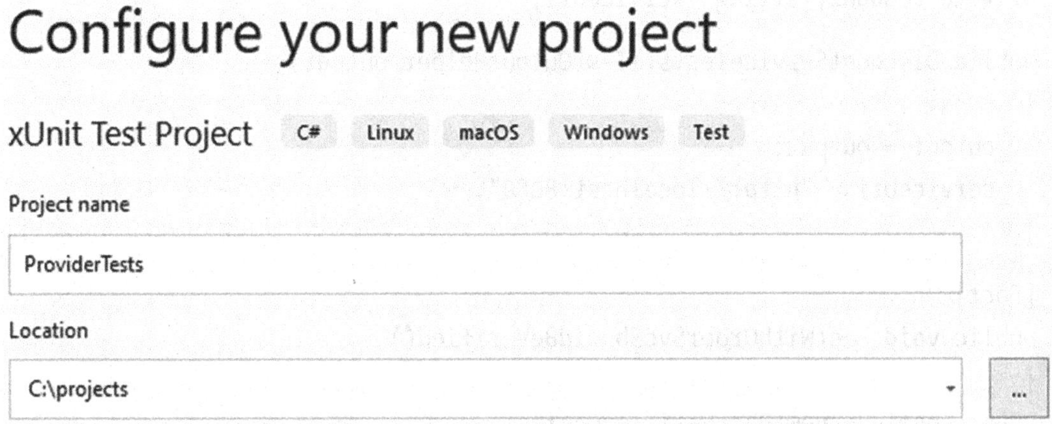

# Configure your new project

xUnit Test Project   C#   Linux   macOS   Windows   Test

Project name

ProviderTests

Location

C:\projects

***Figure 7-17.*** *Project name and location*

Provide the project name ProviderTests and location (see Figure 7-17). Now, select the framework .NET 6 and then the "Create" button (see Figure 7-18).

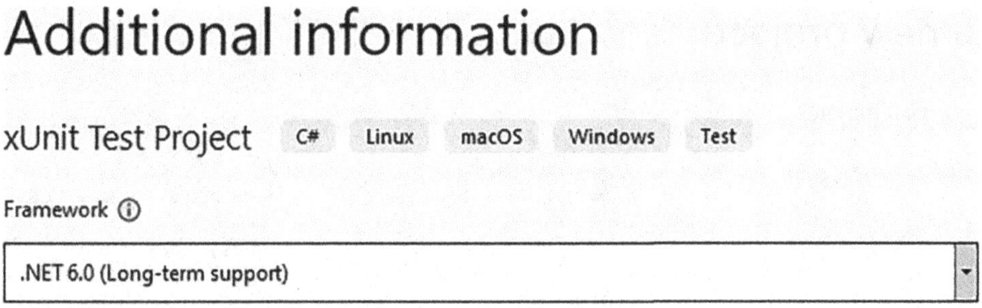

# Additional information

xUnit Test Project   C#   Linux   macOS   Windows   Test

Framework ⓘ

.NET 6.0 (Long-term support)                                                    ▾

***Figure 7-18.*** *Additional project options*

Add library reference to PactNet for Windows or Linux based on what OS you are running the tests on. Create a class called DiscountServiceTests and then apply the following code:

```
public class DiscountServiceTests : IDisposable
{
  private readonly ITestOutputHelper _output;
  private bool _disposed = false;
  private readonly string _serviceUri;

  public DiscountServiceTests(ITestOutputHelper output)
  {
    _output = output;
    _serviceUri = "http://localhost:8080";
  }

  [Fact]
  public void PactWithOrderSvcShouldBeVerified()
  {
    var config = new PactVerifierConfig
    {
      Verbose = true,
      ProviderVersion = "2.0.0",
      CustomHeaders = new Dictionary<string, string>
      {
        {"Content-Type", "application/json; charset=utf-8"}
      },
```

```
    Outputters = new List<IOutput>
    {
      new XUnitOutput(_output)
    }
  };

  new PactVerifier(config)
    .ServiceProvider("Discounts", _serviceUri)
    .HonoursPactWith("Orders")
    .PactUri(@"c:\temp\pact\OrderSvcConsumer\orders-discounts.json")
    .Verify();
}
protected virtual void Dispose(bool disposing)
{
  if (!_disposed)
  {
    if (disposing)
    {
      //
    }
      _disposed = true;
  }
}

public void Dispose()
{
  Dispose(true);
}
}
```

Now create a new class called XUnitOutput and apply the following code:

```
using Microsoft.VisualStudio.TestPlatform.Utilities;
using Xunit.Abstractions;
using IOutput = PactNet.Infrastructure.Outputters.IOutput;
```

```
public class XUnitOutput : IOutput
{
  private readonly ITestOutputHelper _output;

  public XUnitOutput(ITestOutputHelper output)
  {
    _output = output;
  }

  public void Write(string message, OutputLevel level)
  {
    _output.WriteLine(message);
  }

  public void WriteLine(string line)
  {
    _output.WriteLine(line);
  }

  public void WriteLine(string message, OutputLevel level)
  {
    _output.WriteLine(message);
  }
}
```

There are a few specific items in that code worth mentioning. First, the service URI is the location of the provider project. The test will not succeed unless that project is running. We will need to start that application before running the tests. Second, you must supply the values for "ServiceProvider" and "HonoursPactWith." The values applied here match those in the output Pact contract file generated from the consumer test. Lastly, notice the file path to the file just mentioned. The file path can be an absolute path or a relative path.

With everything compiling, start the Discount Service provider application. You can do this by opening a console window or terminal and traversing to the folder location of the project file and using the .NET CLI.

```
dotnet run
```

With the provider running, now execute the test that will run against the Pact contract file. Right-click the test and select Run (see Figure 7-19).

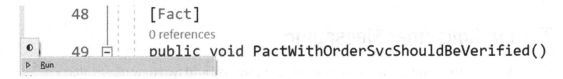

*Figure 7-19.* *xUnit test to execute*

After a small amount of time, you should see a successful test run (see Figure 7-20). The test uses the information in the Pact file to call the Discount microservice at that port location.

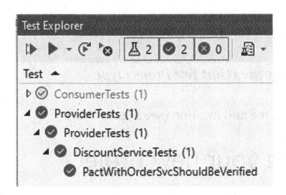

*Figure 7-20.* *Successful test run*

The conclusion is that you can test for breaking changes when the contract changes. Because many things are affected when a contract changes, there must be communication between the developers of each microservice. The caveat to this is when working with 3rd party or external services. The Google API service, for example, does not have to adhere to requests or contracts of consumers.

# Testing Messaging-Based Microservices

In the last section, you learned how to test microservices that use REST-based communications. The challenge now is testing microservices that communicate using messaging. In Chapter 5, you built two microservices that used MassTransit to send messages to each other.

In the code you wrote in Chapter 5, the Payment Microservice receives and reacts to the "InvoiceCreated" message sent by the Invoice Microservice. We will now write different tests – one for the consumer and another for the producer.

## Testing Consumer Messaging

Since the code in Chapter 5 is all-in-one solution, we will add two new test projects. In reality, the microservices are not likely to be in one solution. Begin by adding a new xUnit test project (see Figure 7-21).

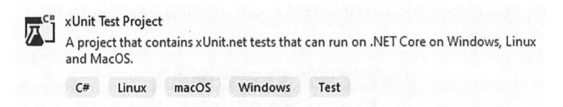

**Figure 7-21.** *Selecting the xUnit Test Project type*

Provide a project name and location (see Figure 7-22).

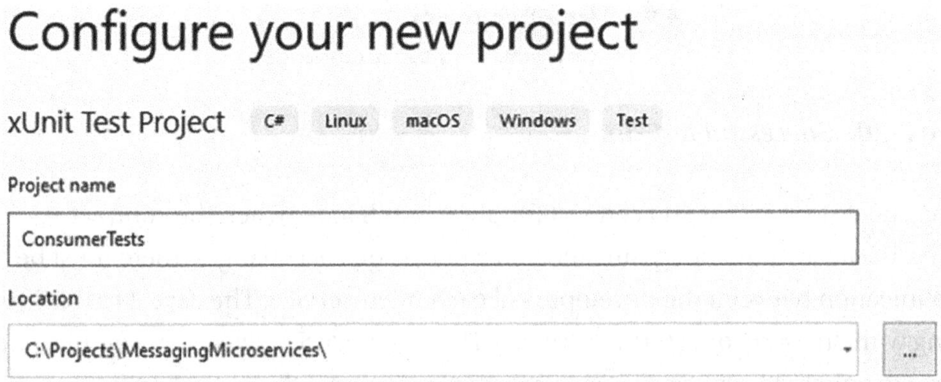

## Configure your new project

xUnit Test Project    C#    Linux    macOS    Windows    Test

Project name

ConsumerTests

Location

C:\Projects\MessagingMicroservices\

**Figure 7-22.** *Project name and location*

Now, select the framework .NET 6 and then the "Create" button (see Figure 7-23). The choice of .NET is not critical but best to use the same version as the other projects in the solution.

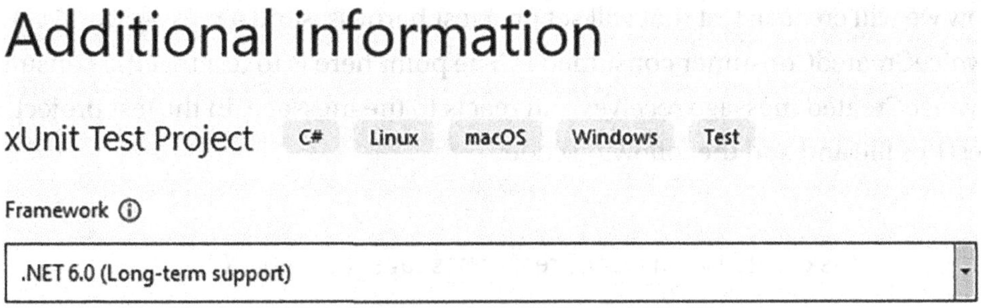

# Additional information

xUnit Test Project   C#   Linux   macOS   Windows   Test

Framework ⓘ

.NET 6.0 (Long-term support) ▾

***Figure 7-23.*** *Additional project options*

Now make a project reference to the Payment Microservice project (see Figure 7-24).

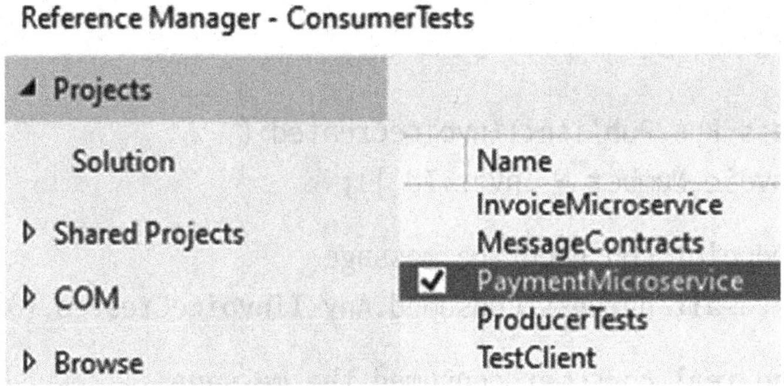

Reference Manager - ConsumerTests

| ◢ Projects | | |
| --- | --- | --- |
| Solution | | Name |
| | | InvoiceMicroservice |
| ▷ Shared Projects | | MessageContracts |
| ▷ COM | ☑ | PaymentMicroservice |
| | | ProducerTests |
| ▷ Browse | | TestClient |

***Figure 7-24.*** *Setting project reference*

You also need NuGet dependencies MassTransit.TestFramework and FluentAssertions. Get the latest available version of each (see Figure 7-25).

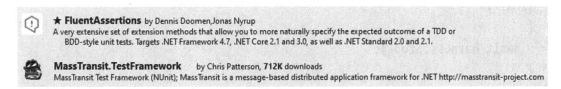

★ **FluentAssertions** by Dennis Doomen,Jonas Nyrup
A very extensive set of extension methods that allow you to more naturally specify the expected outcome of a TDD or BDD-style unit tests. Targets .NET Framework 4.7, .NET Core 2.1 and 3.0, as well as .NET Standard 2.0 and 2.1.

**MassTransit.TestFramework**   by Chris Patterson, **712K** downloads
MassTransit Test Framework (NUnit); MassTransit is a message-based distributed application framework for .NET http://masstransit-project.com

***Figure 7-25.*** *Selecting MassTransit.TestFramework*

Now we will create a test that will set up a test harness, send a message, and verify the InvoiceCreatedConsumer consumed it. The point here is to test that the consumer of the IInvoiceCreated message receives and reacts to the message. In the test project, open UnitTest1.cs file and add the following code:

```
[Fact]
public async Task Verify_InvoiceCreatedMessage_Consumed()
{
  var harness = new InMemoryTestHarness();

  var consumerHarness = harness.Consumer<InvoiceCreatedConsumer>();
  await harness.Start();

  try
  {
    await harness.Bus.Publish<IInvoiceCreated>(
        new {InvoiceNumber = InVar.Id });

    //verify endpoint consumed the message
    Assert.True(await harness.Consumed.Any<IInvoiceCreated>());

    //verify the real consumer consumed the message
    Assert.True(await consumerHarness.Consumed.Any<IInvoiceCreated>());

    //verify there was only one message published
    harness.Published.Select<IInvoiceCreated>().Count().Should().Be(1);
  }
  finally
  {
    await harness.Stop();
  }
}
```

In this code, you can see the use of the In-Memory Test Harness by MassTransit. The test harness allows us to use a fake bus for sending messages. The message IInvoiceCreated is created and published. There is also a test to verify that the test harness consumed the message and the specific InvoiceCreatedConsumer class consumes the message.

Open the Test Explorer window by selecting Test from the top menu and then selecting Test Explorer (see Figure 7-26). After the test shows in the list, right-click the test and select Run (see Figure 7-27).

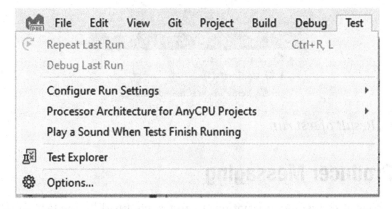

***Figure 7-26.*** *Open Test Explorer window*

***Figure 7-27.*** *Run tests*

You should see the results in the Test Explorer (see Figure 7-28).

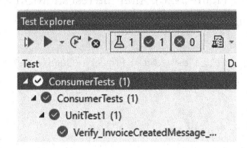

***Figure 7-28.*** *Result of test run*

# Testing Producer Messaging

Now we need to write a test for a provider of a message. Just like the last section, right-click the solution and add a new project. Select the project type xUnit Test Project (see Figure 7-29).

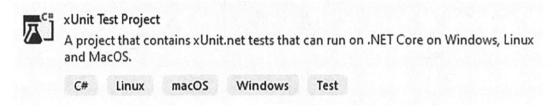

***Figure 7-29.*** *Selecting the xUnit Test Project type*

Now give the project the name ProducerTests and provide a location for the project files (see Figure 7-30).

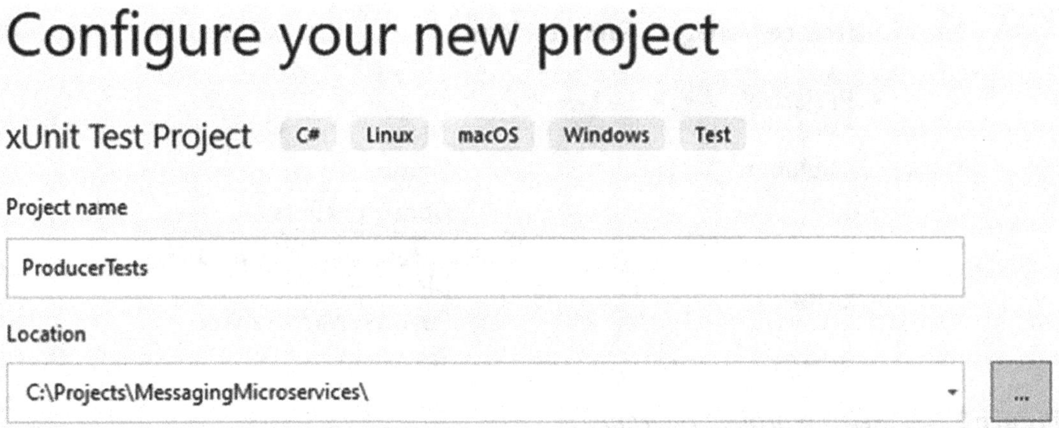

# Configure your new project

xUnit Test Project   C#   Linux   macOS   Windows   Test

Project name

ProducerTests

Location

C:\Projects\MessagingMicroservices\

***Figure 7-30.*** *Project name and location*

Now select .NET 6 for the Target Framework (see Figure 7-31).

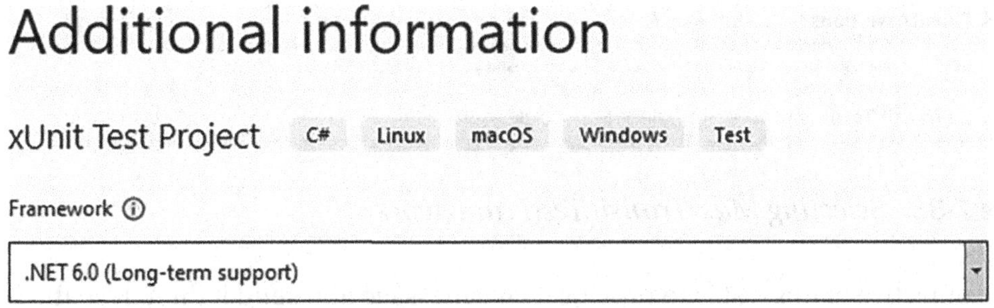

# Additional information

xUnit Test Project   C#   Linux   macOS   Windows   Test

Framework ⓘ

.NET 6.0 (Long-term support)

***Figure 7-31.*** *Additional project options*

The test project needs a project reference connection to the Invoice Microservice project (see Figure 7-32).

Reference Manager - ProducerTests

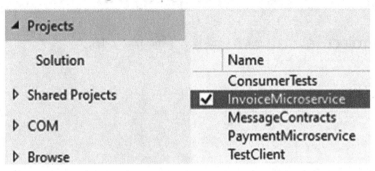

*Figure 7-32.* *Setting project reference*

Now add NuGet dependencies MassTransit.TestFramework and FluentAssertions.
The latest versions are fine (see Figure 7-33).

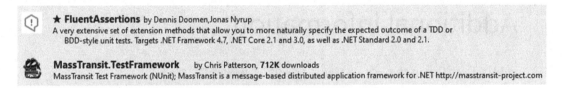

*Figure 7-33.* *Selecting MassTransit.TestFramework*

The objective of this test is to provide a fake message and send it directly to the
consumer. The test harness supplies a bus for the fake message and allows us to test the
reception of the message. The EventConsumer class in the Invoice Microservice receives
and reacts to the IInvoiceToCreate message.

In the UnitTest1.cs file, add the following code:

```
[Fact]
public async Task Verify_InvoiceToCreateCommand_Consumed()
{
  //Verify that we are receiving and reacting
  //to a command to create an invoice
  var harness = new InMemoryTestHarness();
  var consumerHarness = harness.Consumer<EventConsumer>();

  await harness.Start();
```

```
try
{
  await harness.InputQueueSendEndpoint.Send<IInvoiceToCreate>(
    new {
      CustomerNumber = 19282,
      InvoiceItems = new List<InvoiceItems>()
      {
        new InvoiceItems
        {
          Description="Tables",
          Price=Math.Round(1020.99),
          ActualMileage = 40,
          BaseRate = 12.50,
          IsHazardousMaterial = false,
          IsOversized = true,
          IsRefrigerated = false
        }
      }
    });

  //verify endpoint consumed the message
  Assert.True(await harness.Consumed.Any<IInvoiceToCreate>());

  //verify the real consumer consumed the message
  Assert.True(await consumerHarness.Consumed.Any<IInvoiceToCreate>());

  //verify that a new message was published
  //because of the new invoice being created
  harness.Published.Select<IInvoiceCreated>().Count().Should().Be(1);
}
finally
{
  await harness.Stop();
}
}
```

After sending the fake message to the InputQueueSendEndpoint, verify the test harness consumed the message. Then the EventConsumer is checked to verify it has also consumed the message. The reaction of receiving the IInvoiceToCreate message is to send another message. We then verify the publication of the IInvoiceCreated message. You know that message as it is the same as the consumer messaging tests you wrote in the last section.

Using the Test Explorer window, right-click the new test in the list and select Run (see Figure 7-34).

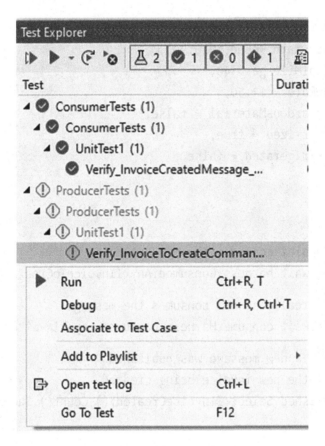

**Figure 7-34.** *Run test*

You should see the results in the Test Explorer (see Figure 7-35).

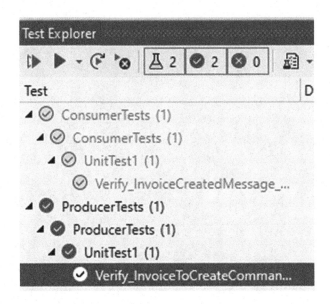

***Figure 7-35.*** *Result of test run*

# Summary

In this chapter, we went over how testing plays a critical role in developing any software application. You learned that the cost of errors rises as the project continues development and certainly after deployment to production. So, testing must be considered in the early stages of development and reviewed constantly. Methodologies like Test-Driven Development should be considered as it helps reduce opportunities in a lot of cases. Also, tests should evolve just as the code and architecture change.

You also learned that knowing what to test is as important as knowing how to test them. And knowing what not to test saves time and keeps you focused on error or system failure scenario handling.

We went over the testing pyramid by Mike Cohn and the modified one as it applies to microservices architecture. The modified pyramid shows different types of tests based on what you are testing and why.

Then you learned how to do contract testing for microservices that work together via REST communication. You also created code that uses the Pact library to test the contract between microservices. To finish this chapter, you learned how to implement testing on microservices that work together using messaging communication.

# CHAPTER 8

# Containerization

Containers and containerization are not, strictly speaking, necessary when building microservices. However, there are many benefits in using containers. In this chapter, we'll take an introductory look at two popular tools for building and orchestrating containers: Docker and Kubernetes (respectively). We'll build a Docker image, share it on Docker Hub, and then learn how to deploy it to AKS (Azure Kubernetes Service) with Kubernetes.

## Why Containers?

A container is a package of software that runs in isolation. You can think of it like a lightweight virtual machine (like VirtualBox or VMWare). Lightweight because while a virtual machine must include a guest operating system (Windows, Linux, etc.), a container's abstraction is one step higher and virtualizes the host operating system. While it's not the only one, Docker is a very popular containerization tool and the only one covered in this chapter.

While this chapter will not cover containerization in depth, it's important to understand the benefits of containers and why you would want to use them. Even if you aren't yet working on a microservice architecture, you can still benefit from using a containerization tool like Docker.

## It Works on My Machine!

Oftentimes when faced with a bug reported by the QA team, developers like myself will try to reproduce it. When I was unable to reproduce the bug, I would comment, "It works on my machine." At some point, a frazzled project manager might respond by saying, "Fine, let's ship your machine to the customer."

© Sean Whitesell, Rob Richardson, Matthew D. Groves 2022
S. Whitesell et al., *Pro Microservices in .NET 6*, https://doi.org/10.1007/978-1-4842-7833-8_8

Later, John Ioannidis quipped on Twitter, "And that's how Docker started." While John is making a joke, it's not far from the truth. Containers allow developers to run a software package locally with everything needed built into the container. This reduces the need to make sure the correct versions of all the dependencies are synchronized. It also reduces the need to try and figure out what local environmental conditions are different from person to person, machine to machine.

With a Docker image, you can almost literally "ship your machine to the customer." In fact, the metaphor of the ship container is used throughout the Docker website and logo. By having a standard container that boats, trucks, and trains can optimize for, the boat, truck, and train operators don't need to have specific knowledge of what's in the container to effectively transport it.

# Onboarding

Containers and container composition can also aid getting new developers and new team members up to speed, and reduce the "yak shaving" and installation of components, tools, and dependencies.

In my current role, as an example, I work with a lot of back-end server software. I run multiple databases like Couchbase Server, SQL Server, and PostgreSQL, along with communication software like RabbitMQ, Kafka, and Apache NiFi. Not to mention my own ASP.NET Core containers (like the one you will build later in this chapter). Installing this software in containers with Docker allows me to spend more time helping people solve problems.

Not only does it make it easier and faster for me to install (and uninstall software) but also to switch between versions. For instance, let's say I'm running Couchbase Server 7.0 directly on my Windows operating system. Now, let's say there's a question on Stack Overflow about Couchbase Server 6.6.1. Here are the steps I'd potentially have to take:

1. Back up data from Couchbase Server 7.0.

2. Uninstall Couchbase Server 7.0 from Windows.

3. Download and install Couchbase Server 6.6.1 to Windows.

4. Work through and answer the Stack Overflow question.

5. Uninstall Couchbase Server 6.6.1 from Windows.

6.  Install Couchbase Server 7.0.

7.  Restore the backed-up data into Couchbase Server 7.0.

On the other hand, with Docker, I can "stop" a 7.0 instance, "start" a 6.6.1 instance, work on the question, and then resume using 7.0 – without discarding or having to back up/restore 7.0's state in the process. Further, when you see Docker in action later in this chapter, you'll see how efficient this process is, especially compared with virtual machines or even bare-metal installations.

And by using a composition file (for Docker Compose this is a file in YAML format), the systems, servers, and software that a new developer needs to get started on a project can be declared in a small YAML file that can be checked into source control. In this docker-compose.yml example, three services are all defined declaratively.

[docker-compose.1.yml] (https://github.com/Apress/pro-microservices-in-.net-6/blob/main/Chapter8/examples/docker-compose.1.yml)

Don't worry about the specifics of this file too much. Let's look at a reduced version:

[docker-compose.2.yml] (https://github.com/Apress/pro-microservices-in-.net-6/blob/main/Chapter8/examples/docker-compose.2.yml)

This composition file (typically called docker-compose.yml) is telling us that the project consists of three components: a web application, a Microsoft SQL Server instance, and a Couchbase Server instance. Not only does this YAML file describe them, but also Docker-Compose will take this YAML file and make it happen. Without this file, we'd need to install Microsoft SQL Server, install Couchbase Server, and install (or more likely compile and run) our ASP.NET web application manually.

As long as Docker is installed, a new developer on your team can pull down the latest from your source code repository and get started much faster than a developer who has to download, install, and manage each database, queueing system, web server, etc., themselves instead. Not to mention potential issues that could arise with environment factors, operating system versions, software versions, and more.

# Microservices

As you've learned so far, a microservice architecture consists of many more services than a typical monolithic architecture. This multiplies the "works on my machine" issue and thus multiplies how useful a containerization tool like Docker is.

In addition, using Docker to standardize the development and delivery of microservices simplifies the overall delivery of your microservice architecture. Docker provides a single standard deliverable (an image) from which to build containers. While doing so, it still provides developers flexibility to choose whatever technologies, patterns, and tooling they need to use. So long as it can be packaged into a container, it can be shipped.

Let's get hands on to see Docker in action.

# What Is Docker?

Before installing and using Docker, let's cover some basic Docker terms. The Docker Engine is the process that will be a go-between your operating system and individual Docker containers. Each container is created with a Docker image that acts like a blueprint. In object-oriented programming terms, an image is like a class and a container is like an object.

You can create Docker images yourself, by using a base image and layering on one or more images. Image creation is defined by a Dockerfile. You can also tap into Docker Hub, which has a huge community of images created by software companies, open source projects, and individuals. Public images available on Docker Hub will be used in this chapter, and Docker Hub is the default location to "pull" images from. Docker Hub can also host private images. And there are other image repositories available like Azure Container Registry (ACR) which can store images for private use.

The general process for interacting with images and containers works like this:

1. Use Docker to create an image.

2. Push the image to Docker Hub.

3. Others can pull your image from Docker Hub.

4. Once you have an image, run a container based on that image.

Later on, when we're building an image for a microservice, we do not have to publish it to Docker Hub in order to use it. But eventually you will want to publish your image to an image repository so that it can be found by an orchestration tool (like Kubernetes).

# Installing Docker

Let's get Docker running and explore some of the basic concepts. You might already have Docker running on your system. To verify, open a command line and execute

```
docker -v
```

If the Docker version number is displayed, then you already have Docker installed and can skip down to "Docker Basics."

Otherwise, head over to `https://docker.com` and click "Get Started." Look for Docker Desktop (assuming you're running Windows or Mac) as seen in Figure 8-1. I'm using Docker Desktop for Windows, but the process for Mac should look very similar.

*Figure 8-1.* *Docker Desktop*

For Windows, an installer called "Docker Desktop Installer.exe" (Figure 8-2) will start to download. When it's finished, execute the installer.

*Figure 8-2.*  *Installer*

The latest version is Docker 3.0.x at the time of writing this chapter. You will be taken through a short installation wizard (Figure 8-3).

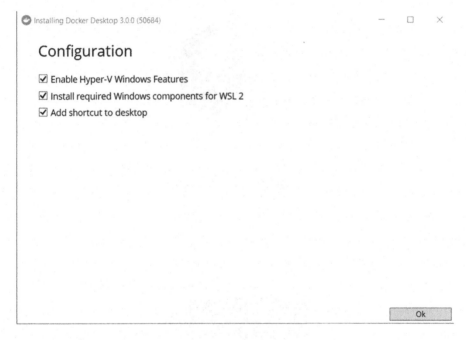

*Figure 8-3.*  *Configuration*

The first step of the wizard will present you with some checkbox options. For Windows you will need Hyper-V capabilities installed and enabled. If you are using software like VirtualBox or VMWare, you may have Hyper-V turned off or may not have it installed.

WSL (Windows Subsystem for Linux) 2 is not required to use Docker, but I recommend installing it if you can.

Docker will begin to unpack and install (Figure 8-4).

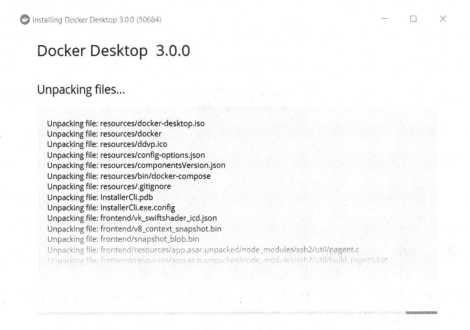

***Figure 8-4.*** *Installing Docker Desktop 3.0.0*

The last step of the wizard will tell you that installation has succeeded (Figure 8-5). Docker is now installed. You should now see an icon with the Docker logo in the Windows task bar or the Mac menu bar.

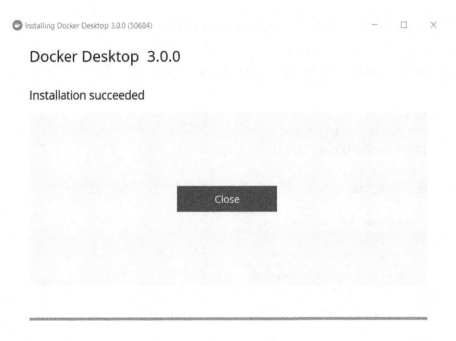

**Figure 8-5.**  *Installation complete*

Note that from time to time, Docker may prompt you about updates that can automatically be installed.

You may also be prompted by Docker to try a tutorial. You are welcome to run through this on your own if you'd like. Before proceeding with the next section of this chapter, make sure to verify that Docker is available from the command line:

```
docker -v
```

Keep this command line open, because now we're ready to explore some Docker basics.

# Docker Basics

Docker is a powerful, complex tool with many capabilities. But for this chapter we're only going to focus on a few: creating, starting, and stopping containers, listing containers and images, removing containers and images, and inspecting a container. Later when we build an image, we'll let Visual Studio do some of the work for us.

# Docker run

To create a container from an image, enter this at the command line:

```
docker run -d --name myWebSite -p 8080:80 nginxdemos/hello
```

Let's break down what each part of this command means.

## run

The run command will first create a container and then start it.

## -d

The -d specifies that this image will be run in detached mode. Detached mode simply means that you will get the command prompt back, instead of turning over control of the input/output to Docker.

## --name myWebSite

The --name option allows you to give a useful name to the container you want to run. If you don't specify a name, Docker will assign it a randomly generated name that will consist of an adjective and a scientist's name (e.g., grumpy_turing). In this example, I'm giving the container a name of "myWebSite."

## -p

The -p option specifies a port mapping. This is a crucial concept in Docker. With Docker for Desktop, all containers run inside of the same Docker host. Much like a firewall or your home router, the ports for each container must be "exposed" or "mapped" for external use. With -p 8080:80, I'm telling Docker that for the myWebSite container, I want you to expose its port 80, but map it to port 8080 externally. This means when I make requests to access the image via port 8080, all of those requests get forwarded to the image's port 80.

## nginxdemos/hello

Finally, I specify the name of an image to build the container from. Docker will first look at my local image registry to see if I've created an image by this name. If it doesn't find it, then by default it will look on Docker Hub for the image (which is what will happen in this case). The image will be downloaded/cached to my local registry. I've chosen nginxdemos/hello because it's a very slim, simple image that will be adequate for a demo.

After running this command, you should see output similar to this:

```
> docker run -d --name myWebSite -p 8080:80 nginxdemos/hello
Unable to find image 'nginxdemos/hello:latest' locally
latest: Pulling from nginxdemos/hello
550fe1bea624: Pull complete
d421ba34525b: Pull complete
fdcbcb327323: Pull complete
bfbcec2fc4d5: Pull complete
0497d4d5654f: Pull complete
f9518aaa159c: Pull complete
a70e975849d8: Pull complete
Digest: sha256:f5a0b2a5fe9af497c4a7c186ef6412bb91ff19d39d6ac24a4997eaed2b0
bb334
Status: Downloaded newer image for nginxdemos/hello:latest
8f5d46c1863312050f13699aff80cff61614657ae596c8edf227d6550d9eadc2
```

After running this, you now have a container running. And because we mapped port 80 of the container to port 8080 of the host, you should be able to enter "localhost:8080" into your browser of choice and see the NGINX hello world (Figure 8-6).

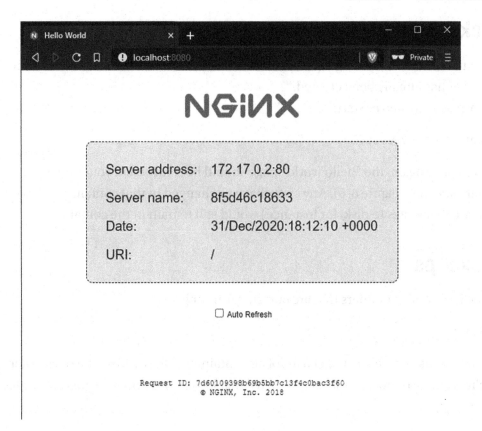

*Figure 8-6.*  *NGINX*

# Docker stop

To stop this container, use the "stop" command like

```
docker stop myWebSite
```

"myWebSite" is whatever name you've given the container (or that Docker has automatically assigned if you neglected to use --name earlier).

Once you execute this stop, you can try visiting "localhost:8080" from your browser. But this time, your browser won't return anything, because the container is no longer running.

# Docker start

To get the container running again, you don't need to use "docker run," because the container has already been created.

Instead, use docker start:

```
docker start myWebSite
```

And once again, the "hello world" page should be returned in your browser at "localhost:8080" (Figure 8-6). Any state that was changed in that container (if it were a database that writes to disk, for instance) would still remain in the container.

# Docker ps

To get a list of all containers that are currently running, use

```
docker ps
```

You can use the -a flag to get a list of all containers that you've created, whether they're running or not. You should see a list that looks something like this (truncated to fit the page):

```
docker ps
> docker ps -a
CONTAINER ID  IMAGE     COMMAND     CREATED   STATUS  PORTS       NAMES
8f5d46c18633  nginx...  "nginx..."  38 min    Up      8080->80/tcp  myWebSite
```

You can also view this list by clicking the Docker icon in the task bar.

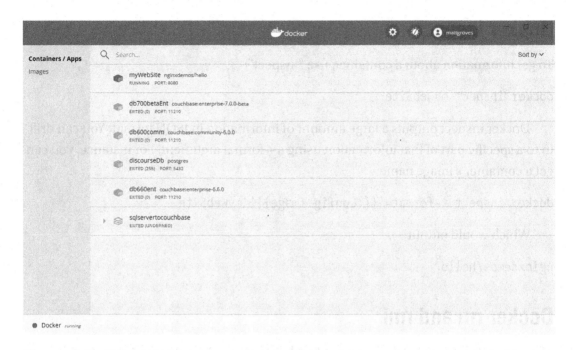

*Figure 8-7.* *Docker icon*

# Docker images

Images are the blueprints to create containers. Even when a container is removed, the image remains cached. You can get a list of these images:

```
docker images
```

This will output a list that looks like the following (truncated to fit on the page):

```
PS C:\> docker images
REPOSITORY          TAG               IMAGE ID        CREATED        SIZE
nginxdemos/hello    latest            aedf47d433f1    2 years ago    16.8MB
couchbase           enterprise-6.6.0  52d53315bb11    3 months ago   1.18GB
couchbase           enterprise-7.0.0  be0f9a8bda52    5 weeks ago    1.33GB
postgres            latest            c96f8b6bc0d9    2 months ago   314MB
chriseaton/adv...   oltp              d4849fa31749    5 months ago   1.73GB
```

As with containers, this list can be viewed by clicking the Docker icon in the task bar and then clicking "Images."

# Docker inspect

To get information about a container, use "inspect":

```
docker inspect myWebSite
```

Docker inspect outputs a large amount of information in JSON format. You can drill in to a specific part of that information using a --format argument. For instance, you can get a container's image name:

```
docker inspect --format='{{.Config.Image}}' myWebSite
```

Which would output:

```
nginxdemos/hello
```

# Docker rm and rmi

To remove (delete) a container, it must first be stopped. Then, use docker rm:

```
docker rm myWebSite
```

To remove (delete) an image:

```
docker rmi nginxdemos/hello
```

There must not be any container that are currently referencing it. For instance, if I tried to remove the nginxdemos/hello image without first removing the myWebSite container, I would get an error message like "Error response from daemon: conflict: unable to remove repository reference "nginxdemos/hello" (must force) - container <id> is using its referenced image <id>."

Before proceeding further, make sure to remove the myWebSite container, as we won't be using it anymore.

# Microservices and Docker

As discussed earlier, using Docker to standardize your delivery can be very beneficial when building a system of microservices. We've already looked at pulling images from the Docker Hub repository in the last section. In this section, let's look at how to containerize the ASP.NET microservices that you've been building so far in this book.

This section will assume that you are working with Visual Studio 2019, but along the way I will point out some of the equivalent ways of accomplishing the same task with the Docker command line.

## Adding Docker Support

Let's start with an ASP.NET web application that uses SQL Server for persistence. If we containerize the web app and add Docker support, we will also need for SQL Server to be accessible to the web app. A Docker container would not necessarily have access to a database outside of the Docker host.

But thinking back to the "onboarding" and "it works on my machine" discussion from earlier, it would be helpful if we could compose the ASP.NET service and the corresponding SQL Server database together within the Docker host. This will be helpful at least for development purposes, even if the actual deployment of the database isn't via container.

## Create ASP.NET Image

Let's start by adding Docker support to the ASP.NET web application. In Visual Studio, right-click the ASP.NET project and click "Add" and then "Docker Support" (Figure 8-8).

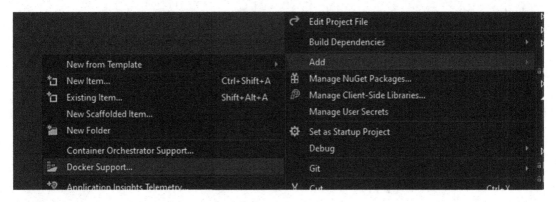

***Figure 8-8.*** *Docker Support*

Visual Studio will create a Dockerfile in this project's folder. This is a text file that Docker can use to build an image. What's in the Dockerfile will vary based on which version of ASP.NET/.NET you're using, but it should look something like

```
[examples/Dockerfile] (https://github.com/Apress/pro-microservices-in-
.net-6/blob/main/Chapter8/examples/Dockerfile)
```

With this Dockerfile, Visual Studio now knows how to create an image, create a container, deploy your latest changes to the container, and run your service in Docker (even when debugging). You should now see Docker as one of the execution options.

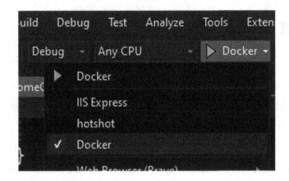

*Figure 8-9.*  *Docker as an execution options*

When you execute your ASP.NET service, Visual Studio will instruct Docker to create a new image (if necessary), create a new container (if necessary), and deploy the latest compilation of your service to that container. If you go back to the command line and try "docker ps" and "docker images," you'll see your container (with a :dev tag) and your image listed, respectively, something like

```
> docker ps
CONTAINER ID    IMAGE        ...     NAMES
74ce1db05c89    hotshot:dev  ...     hotshot

> docker images
REPOSITORY   TAG     IMAGE ID      CREATED   SIZE
hotshot      dev     31d38aadd403  ...       207MB
```

# Use Docker-Compose

Now the image for ASP.NET is created, but we still need a database for it to work with. Let's add "orchestration" support (the ability to manage more than one container in concert). Again, right-click the project in Visual Studio, click Add, and this time click "Container Orchestrator Support." Select "Docker Compose" for now. Even though we'll be using Kubernetes later in this chapter, Docker Compose provides a gentle introduction to orchestration that is still useful for the onboarding process.

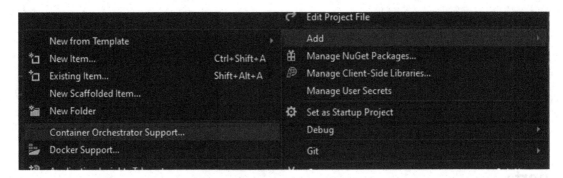

***Figure 8-10.*** *Container Orchestration*

Visual Studio will now create some new files in your solution, but we'll only be looking at docker-compose.yml today. YAML is a whitespace-sensitive superset of JSON that is often used for configuration and definition of containers and orchestration objects. The contents of the generated docker-compose.yml should look like

[docker-compose.3.yml] (https://github.com/Apress/pro-microservices-in-
.net-6/blob/main/Chapter8/examples/docker-compose.3.yml)

Only one service is defined here: the ASP.NET web service. Let's add another service to this YML (YAML) file to add SQL Server as a database. (If you have SQL Server already installed and running outside of Docker, you may want to turn it off to avoid any port conflicts from this point forward.)

At the same indention level as your service name (e.g., "hotshot" in the preceding example), add another service called "mssql":

[docker-compose.4.yml] (https://github.com/Apress/pro-microservices-in-
.net-6/blob/main/Chapter8/examples/docker-compose.4.yml)

Here is a short explanation of each line underneath "mssql":

## image

This is the name of the image that Docker will try to retrieve to build the mssql container. Microsoft publishes SQL Server images to Docker Hub, and we are going to use the latest SQL Server 2019 image.

## environment

Environment is an array of values that will be set as environment variables within the container. Environment variables can be used for many purposes, but in this case we're specifying two things: we agree to the EULA (End-User License Agreement) of SQL Server and we want to create a login with username SA (default System Administrator) with a password of "myStrongPassword1!"

## ports

This is another array containing a list of port mappings, similar to what we did earlier with "docker run." In this case, the port numbers are strictly optional: both services will be on the same "network" inside of the Docker host, and you do not need to open port numbers between them. However, as a developer, we may want to access SQL Server with a tool like SQL Server Management Studio or DataGrip from JetBrains. SQL Server's default port of 1433 mapped to 1433 will allow us to use those tools.

Upon making changes to docker-compose.yml, Visual Studio will notice and immediately execute the "docker-compose" command. Docker Compose will then download images (if necessary), build containers, and start those containers. Once again, you can use "docker ps" at the command line to see what has been created (truncated to fit on the page):

```
> docker ps
CONTAINER ID    IMAGE                       NAMES
5ec134336780    hotshot:dev                 hotshot
e03fc5ddc657    mcr.microsoft.com/mssql...   dockercompose71729...
```

Now you have both a web server and a database server running in Docker. How do you get your web server talking to your database? Remember back to the names in the docker-compose.yml file:

[examples/docker-compose.4.yml] (https://github.com/Apress/pro-microservices-in-.net-6/blob/main/Chapter8/examples/docker-compose.4.yml)

Docker has its own DNS service. The "mssql" name that you specified is now the hostname for SQL Server. So, a connection string in your ASP.NET service should look like

```
Server=mssql;Database=myDatabase;User=sa;Password=myStrongPassword1!
```

An important note: when you close your Solution in Visual Studio, these images will also be shut down *and* removed. Any state saved to the database will be swept away (unless you use Docker volumes, which will not be covered in this chapter).

One more important note: the SQL Server image used earlier does *not* come with any predefined databases, tables, or data in it. You can create these with other tooling, thanks to port 1433 being open. Alternatively, you can create your own custom SQL Server Docker image that will create a database for you.

## Push to Docker Hub

When you reach a point where you want to ship your container image (QA, staging, production, whatever), it's time to push your image to an image repository. For this chapter, we'll be using Docker Hub, since it's the default.

## Build an Image

First, we need to build an image. Docker Compose has been building images for development (notice "hotshot:dev" earlier), but we want to build an image that's suitable for deployment. From Visual Studio, you can do this by right-clicking "Dockerfile" and selecting "Build Docker Image."

***Figure 8-11.*** *Build Docker Image*

Another option is to use the command line. For instance, try

```
docker build -f "c:\path\to\hotshot\hotshot\Dockerfile" -t hotshot
"c:\path\to\hotshot"
```

This is telling Docker to build an image using the Dockerfile specified, name it "hotshot," and use the given path as the "current directory" for the instructions contained in Dockerfile. You may get an error message like "You are building a Docker image from Windows against a non-Windows Docker host." This is probably okay. It's just a warning that you're building a Linux image (assuming you choose Linux) and that file permissions work a little differently in Linux. Docker will be very permissive about the files in the image. This is just a reminder that if you want to reduce permissions, you will need to modify the Dockerfile.

Next, run "docker images" to see if the image you built is listed in your local repository of images. It should appear similar to this:

```
REPOSITORY    TAG        IMAGE ID        CREATED         SIZE
hotshot       latest     21eaa0802a9c    15 minutes ago  258MB
...
...
```

Notice that a "latest" tag has been applied to the image. This is fine for your local repository. But when you push out to Docker Hub, you'll most likely want to tag it differently.

## Docker push

Pushing to Docker Hub requires you to have a Docker Hub account.

Once you have an account with a Docker ID (the fictional "microservicemogul" in Figure 8-12), you are ready to start pushing images to Docker Hub.

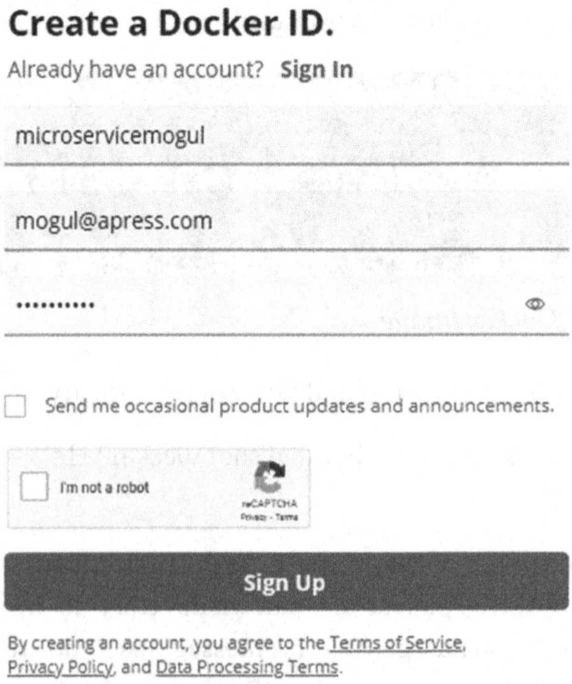

**Create a Docker ID.**

Already have an account?   **Sign In**

microservicemogul

mogul@apress.com

••••••••••

☐  Send me occasional product updates and announcements.

☐  I'm not a robot   reCAPTCHA
                     Privacy - Terms

**Sign Up**

By creating an account, you agree to the Terms of Service, Privacy Policy, and Data Processing Terms.

***Figure 8-12.***  *Create a Docker ID*

From the command line, let's first give our image a tag other than "latest." If this is the version 1 release, for instance, we can tag it "v1." I'm also going to use my Docker ID when I tag.

```
docker image tag hotshot:latest microservicemogul/hotshot:v1
```

Now your image is ready to push. Execute a push:

```
docker push microservicemogul/hotshot:v1
```

This may take a while, depending on how big your image is. You should see a progress screen that looks similar to

```
> docker push microservicemogul/hotshot:v1
The push refers to repository [docker.io/microservicemogul/hotshot]
f63f310c667d: Pushing
[==============>                      ]   14.68MB/50.71MB
1d2bedf89fe2: Pushed
33e20f752cf0: Pushing
[====================================>]   12.81MB/17.85MB
17c445eb92ad: Pushing
[===========>                         ]   18.15MB/76.77MB
b19f476f8dd3: Pushed
5128b7cb97a9: Pushing
[========>                            ]   7.238MB/41.33MB
87c8a1d8f54f: Pushing
[=>                                   ]   2.714MB/69.23MB
```

When the image is finished, you will be able to view it after logging in to your Docker Hub account (Figure 8-13).

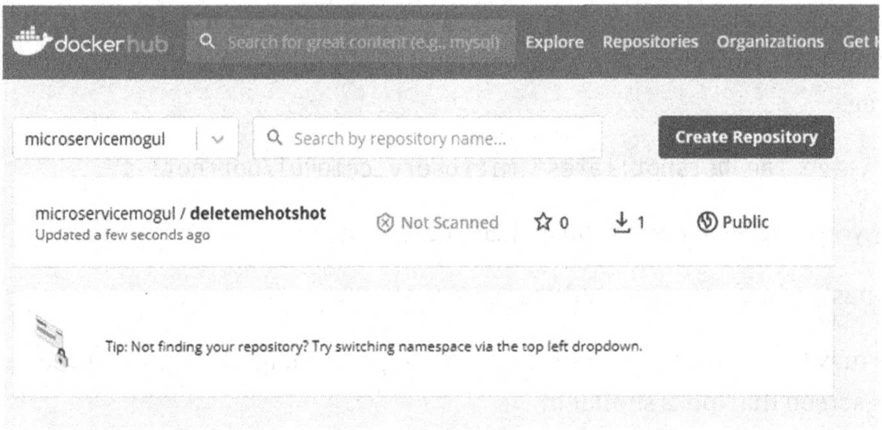

*Figure 8-13.* *Docker Hub*

So why add the v1 tag? Ultimately, the tagging strategy (if any) is up to you and your team. However, having a tag will come in very handy when actually deploying your image.

We've been using Docker, but now it's time to explore deployment with a container orchestrator. Docker has its own orchestrator known as Docker Swarm. However, Kubernetes has generally surpassed Docker Swarm (and other rivals such as Mesos) in popularity. This is why Kubernetes is used in this chapter.

# Kubernetes

Kubernetes is a container orchestration tool, sometimes abbreviated to "K8S," with the "8" taking the place of the letters between "K" and "S" in "Kubernetes." Like we saw with Docker Compose earlier, it allows you to declaratively define multiple services. Unlike Docker Compose, it can manage an entire *cluster* of machines (as opposed to Docker Compose running everything on a single machine).

If your application only consists of an ASP.NET web service, a database, and a small number of users, Kubernetes is probably overkill (for now). However, if you are deploying a system of microservices, databases, communication software, etc., employing a tool like Kubernetes can be very beneficial. Not only can you standardize your deployment, but now you can also manage scale and/or multiple instances of your deployment. For example, Kubernetes can handle your need to deploy multiple web servers (behind a load balancer) to handle an increase in traffic.

Kubernetes is a tool with many capabilities, but for this chapter, I'd like to boil it down to the simple mental model that I use (Figure 8-14). Kubernetes is a tool to which you provide machines (nodes) and YAML files, and it produces a deployment.

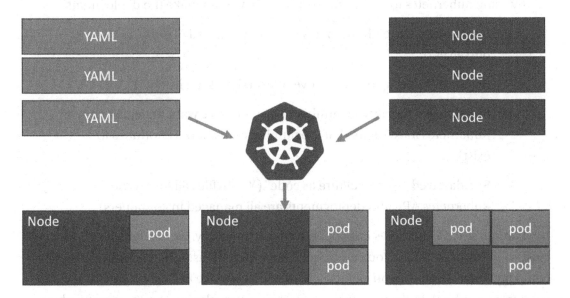

***Figure 8-14.*** *Kubernetes Objects*

In the preceding diagram, Kubernetes Objects are defined by YAML files. Kubernetes objects can be of various "kinds," such as Deployment, Service, etc. A deployment object, for instance, might say (to paraphrase in English), "I want two ASP.NET services running, and tag them with 'hotshot.'" A service object might say (again, to paraphrase in English), "I want a Load Balancer with a public IP, and it will pick a pod tagged with 'hotshot' to direct traffic to."

A "Node" is a machine where one or more containers can be deployed: each machine must be running a container runtime (most commonly Docker) and a suite of other Kubernetes components. A set of nodes make up a "cluster." Nodes can be added or removed from the cluster as more (or fewer) resources are needed.

Given a cluster and some YAML, Kubernetes will follow the instructions in the YAML and create "pods" on the nodes. Pods are typically running a single container. As seen in the preceding diagram, a given node may run a single pod, or multiple pods, depending on the resource requirements and limitations. Kubernetes plays a game of "Tetris," creating and fitting in pods where it makes sense to. And just like in Tetris, pods may disappear (if the software in the container crashed or closed down). But Kubernetes continually monitors the state of its cluster. If it sees that a pod is missing, it will create another one to take its place.

By using Kubernetes to orchestrate the system, we can make the deployment:

- Declarative (we tell Kubernetes what to do instead of doing it ourselves)

- Resilient (Kubernetes will recover crashed pods on its own)

- Scalable (we specify the number of instances we want to deploy and Kubernetes makes sure that the number of instances continues to exist)

- Standardized "infrastructure as code" (YAML files all follow the Kubernetes API, and deployments are all managed in containers)

Further, since Kubernetes is an open source technology, we can create a Kubernetes cluster wherever we'd like. You can create a Kubernetes cluster in your office, your company's data center, or you can use a Kubernetes service from your preferred cloud vendor (or vendors). In the next section, we'll look at deploying to a Kubernetes cluster on the Azure Kubernetes Service (AKS). However, most major public clouds have some equivalent implementation of Kubernetes.

# Kubernetes on Azure: AKS

If you haven't already, you may want to create a Microsoft Azure account (free accounts and getting started credits are available). However, once the AKS cluster is set up, the remaining instructions should be applicable to any Kubernetes cluster that is available to you.

You can create an AKS cluster through the Azure Portal website UI, the Azure Cloud Shell command line (in-browser on Azure Portal), or from your local command line by installing Azure CLI. I prefer the Azure CLI, since I also prefer to use the Kubernetes CLI (kubectl), and you will need Azure CLI later to connect to the cluster anyway. However, seeing the UI in action at least once may help familiarize you with the options available, even if you don't intend to use it in your day-to-day work.

# Azure Portal

First, sign in to the Azure Portal with your account at `https://portal.azure.com`. Next, click the "Create a resource" icon. From here, click or search for "Containers" and then "Kubernetes Service." You will be taken to a step-by-step wizard to create a cluster. For the "Basics" page, I've filled out the Project details and Cluster details (Figure 8-15).

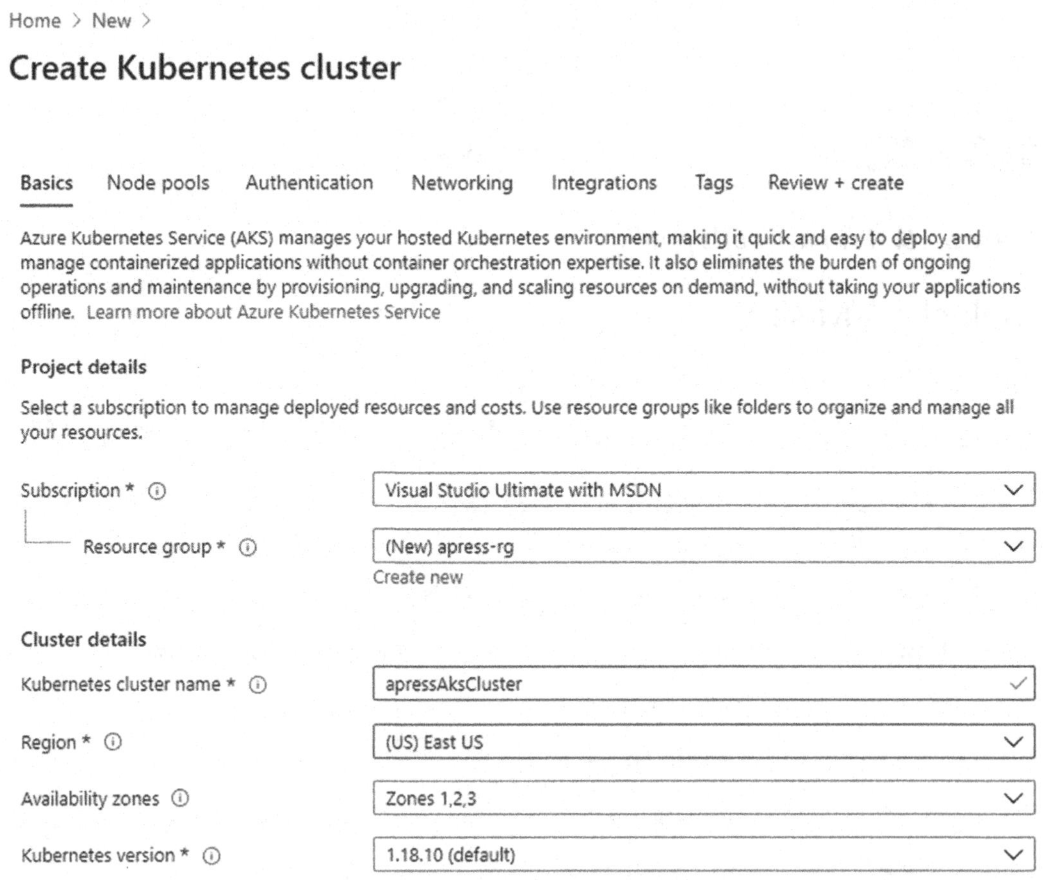

Home > New >

## Create Kubernetes cluster

| Basics | Node pools | Authentication | Networking | Integrations | Tags | Review + create |
|--------|-----------|----------------|-----------|--------------|------|-----------------|

Azure Kubernetes Service (AKS) manages your hosted Kubernetes environment, making it quick and easy to deploy and manage containerized applications without container orchestration expertise. It also eliminates the burden of ongoing operations and maintenance by provisioning, upgrading, and scaling resources on demand, without taking your applications offline.  Learn more about Azure Kubernetes Service

**Project details**

Select a subscription to manage deployed resources and costs. Use resource groups like folders to organize and manage all your resources.

Subscription * ⓘ

> Visual Studio Ultimate with MSDN ⌄

└──── Resource group * ⓘ

> (New) apress-rg ⌄
>
> Create new

**Cluster details**

Kubernetes cluster name * ⓘ

> apressAksCluster ✓

Region * ⓘ

> (US) East US ⌄

Availability zones ⓘ

> Zones 1,2,3 ⌄

Kubernetes version * ⓘ

> 1.18.10 (default) ⌄

***Figure 8-15.***  *Create Kubernetes cluster*

Under "Primary node pool," (Figure 8-16) you can select which type of Azure compute resources (Figure 8-17) you want to use as your nodes. If you are just evaluating AKS as a developer, you may want to select the less expensive, lower-performance machines (such as "Standard B2s" that I've selected) and leave the node count at 3.

**Primary node pool**

The number and size of nodes in the primary node pool in your cluster. For production workloads, at least 3 nodes are recommended for resiliency. For development or test workloads, only one node is required. If you would like to add additional node pools or to see additional configuration options for this node pool, go to the 'Node pools' tab above. You will be able to add additional node pools after creating your cluster.  Learn more about node pools in Azure Kubernetes Service

Node size *  ⓘ                                  **Standard B2s**
                                                2 vcpus, 4 GiB memory
                                                Change size

Node count *  ⓘ                     ◯────────────────────────────────    3

| Review + create |   | < Previous |   | Next : Node pools > |

*Figure 8-16.* *Primary node pool*

# Select a VM size

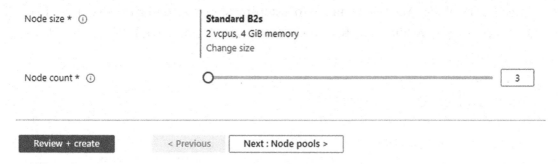

| VM Size ↑↓ | Family ↑↓ | vCPUs ↑↓ | RAM (GiB) ↑↓ |
|---|---|---|---|
| ⌄  Most used by Azure users↗ | | | The most used sizes by users in Azure |
| DS1_v2 ↗ | General purpose | 1 | 3.5 |
| D2s_v3 ↗ | General purpose | 2 | 8 |
| B2s ↗ | General purpose | 2 | 4 |
| B2ms ↗ | General purpose | 2 | 8 |
| DS2_v2 ↗ | General purpose | 2 | 7 |
| B4ms ↗ | General purpose | 4 | 16 |
| D4s_v3 ↗ | General purpose | 4 | 16 |
| DS3_v2 ↗ | General purpose | 4 | 14 |
| D8s_v3 ↗ | General purpose | 8 | 32 |

*Figure 8-17.* *VM Size*

However, depending on your needs, you may want to select more expensive machines and/or more of them to populate your node pool.

Later on, you can also set up "Autoscaling" (Figure 8-18) to meet demand automatically.

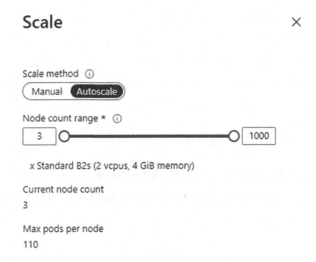

*Figure 8-18.* *Autoscaling*

This is a feature that requires careful thought and monitoring, as you may be surprised by a large bill (if you set your node count max too high) and/or a microservice system that fails under stress (if you set your node count max too low).

You are welcome to browse through the rest of the creating steps to learn more about possible configuration options you might need in the future. For now, if you're following along, you can leave the rest of the steps in the wizard at their default settings and click "Review + create." Click "Create" when the validation is completed. Provisioning the nodes and making them part of a Kubernetes cluster is not instantaneous. You will see "Deployment is in progress" (Figure 8-19).

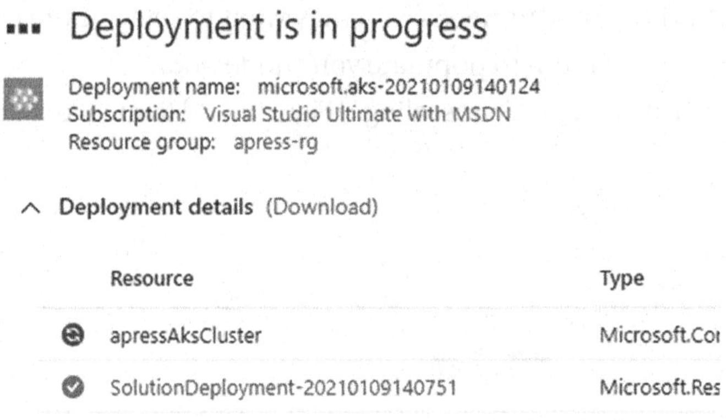

### ••• Deployment is in progress

Deployment name:  microsoft.aks-20210109140124
Subscription:  Visual Studio Ultimate with MSDN
Resource group:  apress-rg

∧  **Deployment details**  (Download)

| Resource | Type |
| --- | --- |
| ⊗ apressAksCluster | Microsoft.Cor |
| ✓ SolutionDeployment-20210109140751 | Microsoft.Res |

***Figure 8-19.***  *Deployment in progress*

When this has completed, you now have a Kubernetes cluster (called "apressAksCluster" in my example) inside of a resource group (called "apress-rg" in my example).

## Azure CLI

Before you proceed, install Azure CLI on your computer. Azure CLI is available for Windows, Mac, Linux, and even in a Docker image. You can also run the Azure Cloud Shell (Figure 8-20) right in your browser (click the "Cloud Shell" icon at the top right on the Portal website).

***Figure 8-20.***  *Azure CLI*

Once Azure CLI is ready, run "az –version" at a command line. You should see an output similar to

```
> az --version
azure-cli                    2.17.1
core                         2.17.1
telemetry                    1.0.6
```

```
Python location 'C:\Program Files (x86)\Microsoft SDKs\Azure\CLI2\python.exe'
Extensions directory 'C:\Users\mgroves\.azure\cliextensions'
```

```
Python (Windows) 3.6.8 (tags/v3.6.8:3c6b436a57, Dec 23 2018, 23:31:17) [MSC
v.1916 32 bit (Intel)]
```

Legal docs and information: aka.ms/AzureCliLegal

Your CLI is up-to-date.

The first step is to log in with the CLI to your Azure account. Execute "az login," which should open a browser. Follow the instructions.

Next, we will create an Azure Resource Group and AKS Cluster, just as we did in the UI. Again, you may want to use "az help" and especially "az aks –help" to see the full range of configuration options available to you. But provisioning a cluster as we did in the UI can be done with two commands:

```
> az group create --name apress-rg --location eastus
```

```
> az aks create --resource-group apress-rg --name apressAks
Cluster --generate-ssh-keys --node-vm-size "Standard_B2s"
```

Just like with the UI, Azure will take some time to provision the nodes. When it is finished, you will see a huge JSON readout on the command line.

## Connect to the Cluster

Before proceeding, you will need to install the Kubernetes CLI. This tool is available for Linux, Windows, and Mac. Once it's installed, run "kubectl version –client" at you command line. You should see response similar to

```
> kubectl version --client
Client Version: version.Info{Major:"1", Minor:"13", GitVersion:"v1.13.3",
GitCommit:"721bfa751924da8d1680787490c54b9179b1fed0", GitTreeState:"clean",
BuildDate:"2019-02-01T20:08:12Z", GoVersion:"go1.11.5", Compiler:"gc",
Platform:"windows/386"}
```

Now that you've created an AKS Kubernetes cluster, you need to connect your kubectl client to it. There is one more Azure-specific step to do this:

```
> az aks get-credentials --resource-group apress-rg --name apressAksCluster
Merged "apressAksCluster" as current context in C:\Users\myusername\.kube\
config
```

From this point on, you will be doing nothing that's Azure specific. You'll just be using the kubectl command-line tool to interact with the Kubernetes cluster that you've created. The same commands can be used with other Kubernetes clusters, no matter if they're on Azure, AWS, Google, etc.

# Define Kubernetes Objects

Let's create some simple YAML files to define a web service and a load balancer for it. First, create a file called "app.yaml":

```
apiVersion: apps/v1
kind: Deployment
metadata:
  name: mywebservicedeployment
spec:
  selector:
    matchLabels:
      app: mywebservice
  replicas: 3
  template:
    metadata:
      labels:
        app: mywebservice
    spec:
      containers:
      - image: "nginxdemos/hello"
        resources:
          limits:
            memory: 128Mi
            cpu: 500m
```

```
    imagePullPolicy: Always
    name: mywebservice
    ports:
      - containerPort: 80
```

There's a lot to cover here, but after a careful reading, it should start to make sense as a declarative set of instructions for Kubernetes.

## apiVersion

This is to specify the Kubernetes API version. It is currently version 1.

## kind

This is the kind of resource you want to create. A Deployment will result in one or more pods being created. The rest of the contents of the YAML will depend largely on the kind you select.

## metadata

This defines information about the deployment itself. We just need a name for now.

## spec

Under spec (specification) is where the deployment is truly defined. The instructions for the pods are here.

## spec.replicas

This specifies how many pods that this deployment is to create and maintain. Let's start with 3. We can easily add or remove by changing this number later. Literally, all you need to do is change the number and update the object and Kubernetes will handle the rest.

## spec.template

Another nested level, this area defines what specification that each pod should follow.

## spec.template.metadata

This metadata will be applied to each pod. This will become important when creating the load balancer object next.

## spec.template.containers

This is an array (each element of an array in YAML starts with a "-") that defines which containers should be deployed within the pod. You may want to create multi-container pods in the future, but for now we'll keep it to one container.

## spec.template.containers[0].image

This is the name of the Docker image to use in this pod. By default this will look to Docker Hub. Using a private repository requires additional configuration. In the preceding example, I'm again using the nginxdemos/hello image (this will come in handy for a demonstration later). As I stated earlier, it's a good idea to use a tag here; otherwise, Kubernetes will assume "latest," which may not be what you want.

## spec.template.containers[0].resources

Ideally, whatever container we select will behave and not take up too many resources. However, it's a good idea to specify resource constraints.

## spec.template.containers[0].imagePullPolicy

During development, testing, and staging, you may continue to update a Docker image without creating a new tag. If you do this, make sure this is set to Always; otherwise, the pod will continue to use the older cached version.

## spec.template.containers[0].name

A name to give each pod that is created.

## spec.template.containers[0].ports

Much like with Docker, you can specify ports to open in this array.

Kubernetes will create these pods, but now we need a way for a client's browser to make requests to them. The point of having replicas is to spread the load around (this is sometimes known as *horizontal scaling*). Since these are stateless, HTTP applications, we can simply use a load balancer to manage incoming requests and divide them up between the replicas. Create another YAML file called loadbalancer.yaml:

```
apiVersion: v1
kind: Service
metadata:
  name: myweb
spec:
  type: LoadBalancer
  ports:
  - port: 80
  selector:
    app: mywebservice
```

There's not as much to see here. Notice that the "kind" is now "Service." The type in the spec is LoadBalancer. The last important thing to point out is the selector: this tells the Kubernetes load balancer *which* pods that requests will be forwarded on to: anything that's tagged with "mywebservice."

# Deploy to the Cluster

This is a lot to take in, and there are plenty more options and settings to explore, but for now, we're basically telling Kubernetes that we want 3 pods (servers) of the "hello" image to run, and a load balancer to sit in front of them and broker HTTP traffic. To actually create this deployment on your AKS cluster, run these commands:

```
> kubectl apply -f app.yaml
deployment.apps/mywebservicedeployment created
> kubectl apply -f loadbalancer.yaml
service/myweb created
```

Kubernetes will immediately go to work for you, creating the pods and services that you specified. It's worth repeating that if any of those pods crash, Kubernetes will create and start new pods to take their place. Also, if you want to make a change (say, change replicas from 3 to 4), save the change to your YAML file and use "kubectl apply" or "kubectl replace" to let Kubernetes know about your changes.

Let's get a listing of all the pods:

```
> kubectl get pods
NAME                                         READY   STATUS    RESTARTS   AGE
mywebservicedeployment-6f78569c6c-cbndf      1/1     Running   0          108s
mywebservicedeployment-6f78569c6c-d8ct5      1/1     Running   0          108s
mywebservicedeployment-6f78569c6c-x2bjx      1/1     Running   0          108s
```

Make a note of the pod names. They have a randomly generated element (e.g., "d8ct5") at the end of each of their names that we will see again in a minute.

And we can get a listing of all the services:

```
> kubectl get services
NAME         TYPE           CLUSTER-IP     EXTERNAL-IP    PORT(S)        AGE
kubernetes   ClusterIP      10.0.0.1       <none>         443/TCP        9m13s
myweb        LoadBalancer   10.0.219.161   40.88.210.19   80:31679/TCP   2m5s
```

Notice that the LoadBalancer called "myweb" has an external IP address. Open this IP in a web browser (the IP you get will look different than mine). You should see a page very similar to Figure 8-21.

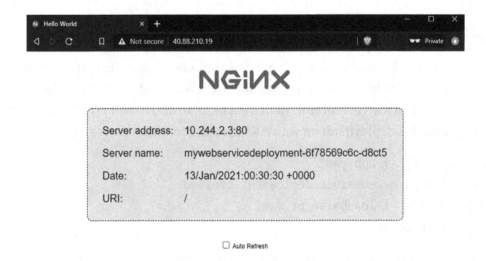

**Figure 8-21.**  *External IP address*

This should look familiar. Take special note of the Server name displayed. It should match one of the pod names from earlier. Try accessing this website from other browsers and devices. You will likely be directed to a different pod. This tells us that the load balancer is doing its job.

# Deploying Databases

For stateless applications like a web server, we're off to a very good start. However, for a stateful application like a database, message queue, etc., taking this same approach is going to be difficult for at least two reasons: pods that crash are replaced automatically, and horizontal scaling databases are more challenging. There are two tools that Kubernetes offers that can help: StatefulSets and Operators.

## Pod Replacement

The first problem is pod replacement. A stateless web application can be destroyed and created again and continue to function as designed with no interruption. However, when a pod crashes, the Kubernetes deployment we've defined earlier will not have any data saved to memory or disk. It will create a pod with a database image, for instance, but it will be a blank slate.

## Horizontal Scaling

The second problem is horizontal scaling. If you intend to use a distributed database that spans multiple machines (a database cluster within a Kubernetes cluster), then each of those machines must be able to find each other, set up communications, and coordinate. If one of them crashes, a naive Kubernetes replacement will not only have lost its state but also lost communications with its database siblings. Unlike the stateless web app, a simple load balancer will not do the job of replicating data.

## StatefulSets

Kubernetes provides another API to manage stateful applications: StatefulSets. Unlike a deployment, each pod in a StatefulSet maintains its own identity. This identity can be used to attach a Persistent Volume. Upon restart, this volume can be mounted by the new pod and it will basically pick up where the old, destroyed pod left off.

## The Operator Pattern

There are so many stateful applications that you may use in your microservice architecture (database and queueing systems being the most common). Kubernetes provides a rich API, but oftentimes it can be inelegant or inefficient to manage software (stateful or otherwise) with just the baseline API. Kubernetes allows the creation of custom resources that provide application-specific APIs. For instance, if I wanted to deploy Couchbase Server to my AKS cluster, I could use the Couchbase Autonomous Operator. After installing the operator in my cluster, I can now create objects of type CouchbaseCluster, CouchbaseBucket, etc., with their own flavor of YAML.

The Kubernetes Operator ecosystem is expanding all the time, with operators available for Kafka, Spark, and numerous databases (Cassandra, Cockroach, PostgreSQL, Redis, and the aforementioned Couchbase). When available, I highly recommend using the operator pattern when you can.

# Summary

This chapter has merely scratched the surface of containerization and orchestration. There's a lot to learn. The community and tooling are still growing and improving. This very high-level overview is not the end of your journey, just the beginning.

To start with, it's important to know *why* you are pursuing containers and orchestration. When you first start, it may seem like a lot of extra steps. And if you aren't building a complex system of microservices, it may not be worth committing to just yet. However, even as a developer, knowledge of Docker can help you be more productive in your day-to-day.

In this chapter, you built an image and started a container. Visual Studio can help you do much of this work, but knowing the basics of how to navigate around with the command line will help you to understand what's going on behind the scenes. Much like git, even if you rarely use the command line, it's helpful to be able to use it when you need to.

Finally, you created Kubernetes objects with YAML and deployed them to an Azure AKS cluster. Kubernetes and Docker can work together to standardize your onboarding, deployment, and dependencies. Declarative YAML, used for Docker Compose, or Kubernetes, or both, allows you to create your infrastructure from code. This code can be shared with your team, reviewed, and checked into source control. You can ship your machine to the customer with Docker, and you can ship your entire data center to any cloud provider you want with Kubernetes.

# CHAPTER 9

# Healthy Microservices

What do you think about when you think of keeping microservices healthy? Probably about failure. If it's healthy, you probably don't think about it at all. There's a lot of work to monitor, alert, validate, and correct services to ensure they stay healthy. This chapter looks at monitoring systems within containers and how to add health monitoring to our microservices.

Kathy, the developer at Code Whiz, is enjoying the new microservices for harvesting distance and building invoices. These services are melding with the monolithic application. But now, she's tasked with ensuring the system is running well.

Let's look at harvesting tracing, logging, and metrics, exposing health checks from our services, and collecting them with OpenTelemetry.

## Is It Healthy?

When we look at a microservice, how do we know if it's running well? As you look at a service, if it's running correctly, you probably didn't notice. But if it's running poorly, you probably noticed a lot.

Let's begin by enumerating what could go wrong with a microservice:

- Not responding to web traffic.

- Processing data incorrectly.

- Using too much RAM.

- Running slowly.

- Threw an exception.

- The system crashed.

© Sean Whitesell, Rob Richardson, Matthew D. Groves 2022
S. Whitesell et al., *Pro Microservices in .NET 6*, https://doi.org/10.1007/978-1-4842-7833-8_9

- Another process is behaving badly and choking the resources.

- Running system updates.

- The hardware failed.

How do we compensate for services that behave this way? The naive approach – often our first attempt – is to throw stuff at it. Is it running slowly? Let's buy a bigger processor. Is it taking too much RAM? Let's add more RAM to the machine. Is another process interfering? Let's move it to its own machine. Is the hardware flakey? Let's run multiple copies. This can often buy us time, but it's a really costly endeavor.

As we reach for high availability, we need both redundancy and well-functioning systems. Let's look deeper at how to handle the problem correctly.

# Where Do We Look?

We need a methodical approach to system diagnostics. We could definitely throw money at the problem, but that isn't a solid approach. Rather, we need to learn how the system functions and act methodically to correct the system when it fails.

When looking at a system, we can enumerate questions we'd like to know about the system:

- How many requests is it processing?

- How much RAM is it using?

- What percentage of requests are failing?

- What caused the exception?

As we enumerate these questions, groups start to form. Francisco Beltrao, a software engineer at Microsoft,[1] nicely enumerates three main groups of insights as he introduces these concepts to .NET developers: we need logging, tracing, and metrics.

**Logging** – Logs show us about events at a point in time. For example, the system started, or an exception was thrown. These logs may hold additional details like a stack trace, the date and time of the event, the currently processing URL, and the authenticated user if logged in. What distinguishes these from the other groups is they're a point in time – there's no duration.

---

[1] Source: https://devblogs.microsoft.com/aspnet/observability-asp-net-core-apps/

**Tracing** – A trace helps us put together the user's journey (the sequence of events). In addition to the details in a log, each trace ties to previous and successive events through a correlation id or a request id. We can follow a user's journey from the browser app to the API Gateway through the microservices to the data store with trace logs. Though logs can tell us if the database timed out, traces can tell us if this led them to abandon their cart or if they tried again. Traces could tell us their journey through the sales funnel.

**Metrics** – Metrics add a time component to the investigation. Logs mark a point in time, an event. By comparison, metrics don't need an initiation point; metrics are ongoing statistics about the system. How many requests per second are we processing? What percentage of requests are failing with an HTTP status that isn't 200? Is the CPU usage higher than normal?

As we're investigating a system, we need all three groups of insights. Let's log when an exception happened and when a new release is deployed. Let's trace requests going between systems to understand user usage patterns and give context and reproducibility to exceptions. And let's harvest system and application metrics to understand if the system is constrained or behaving badly.

# Logging

## Logging with ASP.NET Core and Serilog

In Chapter 4, we built a microservice to get distance given two addresses. Let's add logging to this service. As we add logging, we'll be able to track event details and diagnose unusual failures with the detail from these logs.

Open microservice-map-info.sln from Chapter 4, and in the Services folder, open `DistanceInfoService.cs`. Let's look at the `GetMapDistanceAsync()` method. In this method, we can find a few things that could go wrong:

a. What if the `originCity` or `destinationCity` were blank or invalid?

b. What if the `googleDistanceApiKey` expired or wasn't set?

c. What if `client.SendAsync()` threw an exception because the connection couldn't be made?

    d.   What if the response didn't get a success status code and caused `response.EnsureSuccessStatusCode()` to throw an exception?

    e.   What if we called the service too frequently and the API told us we had exceeded our limits?

    f.   What if something else happened that we didn't anticipate, like an out-of-memory error, a closed socket, or a machine reboot yielding a `ThreadAbortException`, or any of a number of other things?

We want to capture these exceptions and ensure that we have the necessary details to diagnose the problem and repair the error if the request fails. What information will we need to gain this context?

    a.   The origin city and the destination city.

    b.   The response status code and response body.

    c.   The client order making the request – sadly, we don't have this information in the service.

Though it's tempting to log the API key, this would lead to leaked secrets. If we find that all requests fail and don't see a pattern across the requests, we could check these secrets.

It's also tempting to log the request URL. This might speed diagnosis as we could easily reproduce the concern. However, this data can easily be derived from the origin and destination cities, and the URL contains the secret we're specifically not logging. Let's not log this data either.

We now have a decision to make. Do we want to log inside this method or in the calling method? If we log in this method, we need a way to signal the caller of the failure. If we log in the controller, we might lose the context of the response. In this case, let's arbitrarily decide to log in the controller.

In the Controllers folder, open `MapInfoController.cs`.

In the constructor, take in an additional parameter, `ILogger<MapInfoController>`, and set it to a private field. Also, add the using statement as directed:

```
private readonly ILogger<MapInfoController> _logger;
```

```
public MapInfoController(DistanceInfoService distanceInfoService,
ILogger<MapInfoController> logger)
{
  _distanceInfoService = distanceInfoService;
  _logger = logger ?? throw new ArgumentNullException(nameof(logger));
}
```

Why do we take in an ILogger<T> where T is the current class? Because we can filter the logs based on the source of the error. In appsettings.json, in the Logging section, we have different log levels for various namespaces.

In the action, wrap the call to the service in try/catch:

```
[HttpGet]
public async Task<GoogleDistanceData> GetDistance(string originCity, string destinationCity)
{
  try
  {
    return await _distanceInfoService.GetMapDistanceAsync(
      originCity, destinationCity);
  }
  catch (Exception ex)
  {
    _logger.LogError(ex);
  }
}
```

When we log, we choose the log level appropriate to the data we're logging. In this case, this is an error, so we choose LogError(). In order of severity from least to most severe, we have Trace, Debug, Information, Warning, Error, and Critical.[2]

Now we're logging the exception. Let's modify this method to grab additional context that'll help us diagnose the error. Change the logger line from

```
_logger.LogError(ex);
```

---

[2] https://docs.microsoft.com/en-us/dotnet/api/microsoft.extensions.logging.loglevel

to this:

```
_logger.LogError(ex, $"Error getting address details from Google:
{originCity} to {destinationCity}");
```

Now we have the input parameters, but we don't have the response status code or body. Probably these come as part of an HttpRequestException.[3] Let's add another catch blog for the HttpRequestException:

```
try
{
  return await _distanceInfoService.GetMapDistanceAsync(
    originCity, destinationCity);
}
catch (HttpRequestException ex)
{
  _logger.LogError(ex,
    $"Error getting map distance: ${originCity} to ${destinationCity},
    status code: {ex.StatusCode}");
}
catch (Exception ex)
{
  _logger.LogError(ex, $"Error getting address details from Google:
  {originCity} to {destinationCity}");
}
```

The last piece is to ensure we return an error HTTP status code to the caller. Change the return type of the method, and return a status code of 500. Here is the completed method:

```
[HttpGet]
public async Task<ActionResult<GoogleDistanceData>> GetDistance(string
originCity, string destinationCity)
{
```

---

[3] https://docs.microsoft.com/en-us/dotnet/api/system.net.http.httpclient.sendasync,
https://docs.microsoft.com/en-us/dotnet/api/system.net.http.httpresponsemessage.
ensuresuccessstatuscode

```
try
{
  return await _distanceInfoService.GetMapDistanceAsync(
    originCity, destinationCity);
}
catch (HttpRequestException ex)
{
  _logger.LogError(ex,
    $"Error getting map distance: ${originCity} to ${destinationCity},
    status code: {ex.StatusCode}");
  return StatusCode(500);
}
catch (Exception ex)
{
  _logger.LogError(ex,
    $"Error getting map distance: ${originCity} to ${destinationCity}");
  return StatusCode(500);
}
}
```

In this example, we rely on the `HttpRequestException` generated from `response.EnsureSuccessStatusCode`. As David Fowler points out,[4] the response body was removed from this exception to avoid exceptions as control flow. It is probably more effective to grab the response body and return a specific reply object that includes the HTTP status code and the success or failure object. John Thiriet has a great code sample[5] of this technique.

How do we test the error handling? We could run the application and fire bad data at it. Even better, we could create a unit test that mocks `HttpClient` and returns error codes. You can learn more about testing microservices in Chapter 7.

What if we want to log less? In `appsettings.json` it lists the default log level:

```
{
  "Logging": {
    "LogLevel": {
```

---

[4] https://github.com/aspnet/Mvc/issues/4311#issuecomment-198324107
[5] https://johnthiriet.com/efficient-api-calls/#custom-exception

```
      "Default": "Information",
      "Microsoft": "Warning",
      "Microsoft.Hosting.Lifetime": "Information"
    }
  }
}
```

Currently, the default LogLevel is set to "Information". This means that Trace and Debug messages are not logged. If we change this to "Error", then Information messages will also be ignored. If we set this to "None", then nothing will be logged to the console.

We can tune these for particular namespaces. In the default configuration, any code in a namespace that starts with Microsoft (such as Microsoft.AspNetCore.Mvc) will only log if the message is "Warning" or above. We won't get Microsoft's debug messages in our logs. Kestrel's request/response messages are logged from a class in Microsoft. Hosting.Lifetime namespace, so by default, this log is turned up to Information. This is a good way to exclude logs for chatty libraries so we can focus on the log content that matters.

Where do the error logs go? With this default configuration, the errors will go to the console. If we're running in containers, we can route the console output together with container metrics to our chosen log collector. If running inside IIS, we can tell IIS to log these details to a file.

What if we want more control over where the logs will go? For this, we can use Serilog. Serilog is not included with ASP.NET, but it has become the standard way for collecting and routing log messages in .NET. Let's add Serilog to route our microservice's logs to a file.

Open the NuGet Package Manager, switch to the Browse tab, and type Serilog.

Install the Serilog.AspNetCore package, the Serilog.Sinks.File package, and the Serilog.Settings.Configuration package as shown in Figure 9-1. The first wires up to ASP.NET. The second allows us to log to a file. The third can read the configuration from the standard configuration locations, including appsettings.json, environment variables, and command-line parameters.

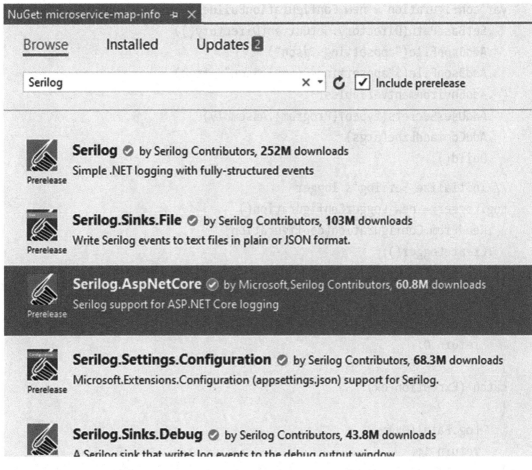

***Figure 9-1.*** *Select the Serilog.\* NuGet packages, but not Serilog itself*

Replace `Program.cs` to initialize the logger in `Main()` and to set up Serilog in `CreateHostBuilder()`:

```
public class Program
{
  public static int Main(string[] args)
  {
    // Mimic the configuration options in Host.CreateDefaultBuilder()
    var env = Environment.GetEnvironmentVariable("ASPNETCORE_ENVIRONMENT")
      ?? "Production";
```

```
    var configuration = new ConfigurationBuilder()
      .SetBasePath(Directory.GetCurrentDirectory())
      .AddJsonFile("appsettings.json")
      .AddJsonFile($"appsettings.{env}.json", true)
      .AddEnvironmentVariables()
      .AddUserSecrets(typeof(Program).Assembly)
      .AddCommandLine(args)
      .Build();

    // Initialize Serilog's logger
    Log.Logger = new LoggerConfiguration()
      .ReadFrom.Configuration(configuration)
      .CreateLogger();

    try
    {
        CreateHostBuilder(args).Build().Run();
        return 0;
    }
    catch (Exception ex)
    {
        Log.Fatal(ex);
        return 1;
    }
    finally
    {
        Log.CloseAndFlush();
    }
  }

  public static IHostBuilder CreateHostBuilder(string[] args) =>
    Host.CreateDefaultBuilder(args)
      .UseSerilog() // <-- Replace Microsoft's logging with Serilog
      .ConfigureWebHostDefaults(webBuilder =>
      {
        webBuilder.UseStartup<Startup>();
      });
}
```

That was a long walk to get the configuration details. Inside
`Host.CreateDefaultBuilder()` is a similar path of collecting configuration sources.
But we need to create the logger before we call `CreateHostBuilder()`, so we must also
do it here.

Now that we have all the Serilog code in place to read from the configuration, open
appsettings.json, and let's replace the "Logging" section with the "Serilog" section:

```json
{
  "Serilog": {
    "Using": [ "Serilog.Sinks.File" ],
    "MinimumLevel": "Information",
    "Override": {
      "Microsoft": "Warning",
      "Microsoft.Hosting.Lifetime": "Information"
    },
    "WriteTo": [
      {
        "Name": "File",
        "Args": {
          "path": "logs/log.txt",
          "rollingInterval": "Day",
          "rollOnFileSizeLimit": true
        }
      }
    ],
    "Enrich": [ "FromLogContext", "WithMachineName", "WithThreadId" ],
    "Properties": {
      "Application": "MapInfo"
    }
  },
  "AllowedHosts": "*",
  "googleDistanceApi": {
    "...snip..."
  }
}
```

We now have Serilog installed, and all logs will go not to the console but to the log file. We could have moved all this configuration to code inside `Program.cs`, but by setting it here in `appsettings.json`, we can easily override pieces with environment variables injected into the container. If it were hard-coded into our app, this reconfiguration per environment wouldn't be possible.

We've configured the system to roll the log file daily to avoid getting too big. Though we didn't set it here, we can also configure how many of these files to keep, automatically deleting the oldest ones. This is a best practice when logging to files. Without this, it would be easy to get a file so big that we could no longer efficiently read it or so big that it fills up the disk and crashes the system. It could also be easy to get so many files that it fills up the disk or makes it inefficient to read files in the folder. Carefully understand how big the log files typically get, how valuable older logs are to the organization, and how much space is available to log. If the logs need to last longer or more space is needed for the logs, consider sending them to another location or system.

In this case, we choose to send logs to a file. Instead, we could choose to send logs to another service such as a Splunk instance, an Elastic cluster, a cloud logger like AWS Cloud Watch, or a 3rd party service such as NewRelic or PagerDuty. Take a moment to add other Serilog Sync packages and adjust the configuration file to get data to your chosen logging platform.

# Avoiding "God" Classes

As Kathy, the Code Whiz developer, looks at this logging code, she can see some common patterns emerge. We're enumerating exception details; we're avoiding the log if there's no content. Kathy is eager to centralize this logic, so we don't need to duplicate it in each project.

In most cases, we lean on the DRY principle: Don't Repeat Yourself. Kathy is tempted to build a central logging class that all the projects could inherit from. This is an anti-pattern, and we should avoid it. But still, in the back of our minds, the DRY principle persists: we want to avoid repeated code. Why would we change course here? Why should we not copy this shared code into a central base library?

It's easy for these shared concerns to collect and reproduce. Today it's logging. Tomorrow it's enumerating enum values. Next week we're centralizing collection sorting. Pretty soon, we have a really large library: the god class.

All the decisions thus far made sense. We carefully walked this path, making the best choices we could at the time. But here we are with a monolith that every service must inherit. We have become the thing we sought to avoid. We're trying to refactor from monolith to microservices, not the other way.

The god class is this collection of sometimes related libraries. The client, Hyp-Log, had a previous employee that created a god-class library that included the logging library, a URL parsing library, some LINQ helper methods, an ADO.NET query helper when using Dapper, a forked version of an Entity Framework helper method, and a library that helps rectify drift between machine clock times.

Does this microservice-map-info service need all that functionality? Probably not. Kathy sure wishes she could just pull in the NuGet package that adds logging without having to make `Program.cs` inherit from the corporate god class to initialize it. Kathy also wants to be able to upgrade Serilog quickly without having to wait for Hyp-Log to upgrade the god-class library.

When constructing these utility libraries, you should prefer composition over inheritance and small pieces over large utility libraries. In Kathy's case, yes, there are a few lines of Serilog config we must copy, and there are a few lines we must add into `Program.cs`. But it's likely not worth the effort to abstract this away. The abstraction would become too opinionated. In this case, better to copy these lines into place and leave the simplicity of Serilog and .NET Logging.

With logging underway, we also need to understand the health of our microservices in an additional way: metrics.

# Metrics

We've added logging to track singular events. Now let's look at metrics to accumulate and aggregate events. This aggregated metadata is interesting for understanding items like how quickly the service responds on average, what percentage of requests fail, and other broader events than a single request/response or even a single exception.

In microservices, tracking metrics have historically been captured with Prometheus, and visualizing events has been done with Grafana. Both are open source products that can easily be incorporated into architectures big and small.

Unlike most logging systems where the software pushes content into them, Prometheus reaches out to each package, usually an HTTP endpoint, and asks for metrics. The advantage to this approach is Prometheus doesn't need to make assumptions: Did the service's data get lost in transit? Did the target system go offline? Are the metrics lost? Instead, Prometheus will query the service at configurable intervals and pull in all the metrics.

Grafana isn't the only dashboard for visualizing metrics, but it is a great choice as it plugs in seamlessly with Prometheus. Kathy can easily craft dashboards that directly query the Prometheus data or import prebuilt dashboards from a large collection of community-contributed solutions.

Together, Prometheus and Grafana have become the de facto standard for collecting metrics from disparate systems. Let's get both Prometheus and Grafana spun up. Then we'll add the code necessary to collect metrics from ASP.NET. Data Whiz developers can further extend this solution to monitor other new or legacy services whether written in .NET, .NET Core, or .NET Framework. Many other infrastructure components will likely expose Prometheus sinks that allow collecting metrics from these hardware and software systems as well.

# Prometheus and Grafana

The easiest way to spin up software is through containers, and Prometheus and Grafana are no exception. If you haven't already, head to `https://docker.com/` and install Docker Desktop. Once it's running, we'll be able to launch all the containers we need.

We'll need to craft a data file for both Prometheus and Grafana, and we'll launch both containers from a `docker-compose.yaml` file. Though Prometheus is great for alerting, we'll skip the alerting set up here for the sake of brevity.

## Prometheus

Let's start with a new folder for metrics. Create a new folder named metrics. Inside this folder, we'll create a docker-compose file, a `prometheus` folder, and a `grafana` folder.

Our first stop is the `docker-compose.yaml` file. Inside the metrics folder, create a new file named `docker-compose.yaml` and include this content:

```
version: '3'

services:
  prometheus:
    image: prom/prometheus
```

```
  ports:
    - 9090:9090
  volumes:
    - ./prometheus:/etc/prometheus
    - prometheus-data:/prometheus
  command: --web.enable-lifecycle --config.file=/etc/prometheus/
prometheus.yaml

volumes:
  prometheus-data:
```

The `docker-compose.yaml` file is a YAML file, so indenting is done with two spaces. Like Python, if you mix spaces and tabs or use more or less than two spaces, it'll error. Let's quickly tour through the details in this compose file.

The file defines the `prometheus` container based on the image from Docker Hub at `https://hub.docker.com/r/prom/prometheus`. It exposes port 9090, so we'll be able to hit Prometheus from `http://localhost:9090/`. It also tells Prometheus to use the `prometheus.yaml` file for configuration details. Let's build this next.

Create a new folder inside metrics named `prometheus`. Inside the `prometheus` folder, create a file named `prometheus.yaml` and include these contents:

```
global:
  scrape_interval: 15s
  evaluation_interval: 15s

scrape_configs:
  - job_name: prometheus
    static_configs:
    - targets:
      - 'prometheus:9090'

  - job_name: doesnotexist
    static_configs:
    - targets:
      - 'doesnotexist:567'
```

Here in `prometheus/prometheus.yaml`, we start off defining the timings. By default, Prometheus will look to each target once per minute. To speed our journey to success, we'll do it much more often: every 15 seconds.

Next, we define the systems from which we want to gather data. The first job gathers data from Prometheus itself. By default, Prometheus uses HTTP and hits the URL / metrics, so the full URL for the Prometheus job is `http://prometheus:9090/metrics`. This will work great because the container is named `prometheus` in the docker-compose file above.

The next job is a system that doesn't exist. We'll hit `http://doenotexist:567/metrics`, it'll fail, and we'll get to see both success and failure metrics.

With Docker installed, and both of these files, we're ready to start Prometheus. Launch a terminal or command prompt inside the metrics folder, and run this command:

```
docker-compose up
```

We'll see lots of console output as Docker downloads the image and Prometheus spins to life. Once it's running, open a browser to `http://localhost:9090`, and we've got Prometheus!

Wait, why is the URL inside Docker `http://prometheus:9090`, and we're launching `http://localhost:9090/`? Docker automatically forwards traffic across its router to the container's exposed port. We can think of this much like the Wi-Fi router in our home or the router in our office. If we want to host many websites from our home, they'll all come into our public IP. From the router's configuration screens, we'll forward specific public ports to our chosen machine. The docker-compose file lists this mapping: `9090:9090` says, "connect the public IP (localhost in our case) on port 9090 to the 'machine' (container) `prometheus` on port 9090."

Now that we have the Prometheus website loaded on `http://localhost:9090`, let's take a look around. In the Status menu, choose Targets. We can see both targets we defined: `prometheus` is running, and `doesnotexist` is offline.

Click the Prometheus name on the top left, and you'll be back at the Prometheus home page. From here, we can run queries to see the metrics Prometheus is gathering. In the box, type

```
up
```

This query shows both systems, shows that one is online, and one is offline. Next, type this query:

```
prometheus_http_requests_total
```

This query shows the unique web addresses Prometheus has served and the number of times it served each.

Now that we've launched Prometheus, let's also launch Grafana.

## Grafana

We need to stop the Prometheus container so we can add the Grafana container. In the terminal, hit Ctrl+C, and then run

```
docker-compose down
```

This command will stop and remove all the containers in the docker-compose file. Once complete, Prometheus and Grafana are no longer running.

Now let's add the Grafana details. Inside the metrics folder, open `docker-compose.yaml` and add the `grafana` content. Here's the new file:

```
version: '3'

services:
  prometheus:
    image: prom/prometheus
    // ... omitted for brevity ...

  grafana:
    image: grafana/grafana
    ports:
      - 3000:3000
    volumes:
      - ./grafana:/etc/grafana/provisioning/datasources
      - grafana-data:/var/lib/grafana
    environment:
      - GF_SECURITY_ADMIN_PASSWORD=admin

volumes:
  prometheus-data:
  grafana-data:
```

Here we've added the Grafana container, pulled from Docker Hub at `https://hub.docker.com/r/grafana/grafana`. We're passing in the configuration file we'll build next and exposing port 3000. We're also setting the password to admin, making it easy to log into.

Next, inside the metrics folder, create a folder named `grafana`, and add a new file named `prometheus_ds.yaml` inside. Here's the contents of `grafana/prometheus_ds.yaml`:

```
datasources:
- name: Prometheus
  access: proxy
  type: prometheus
  url: http://prometheus:9090
  isDefault: true
```

In the `grafana/prometheus_ds.yaml` file, we've configured our path to Prometheus. Though we could definitely do this inside the UI, it's much simpler to do it here. The URL from the Grafana container to the Prometheus container is `http://prometheus:9090/`.

Back in the terminal, still inside the metrics folder, we're ready to launch both containers. Type this in the terminal:

```
docker-compose up
```

Now both Prometheus and Grafana are launching. You can refresh `http://localhost:9090` to see Prometheus. Then browse to `http://localhost:3000` to see Grafana. The username is admin, and we set the password to admin as well.

We can see the dashboard is quite empty. Let's add a new graph. Click the plus menu on the top left, and choose Dashboard, as shown in Figure 9-2.

*Figure 9-2. Add new Dashboard: Click "+" then click Dashboard*

Click Add Empty Panel, and we can configure this new metric. We see a sample graph on the top left, the data source details on the bottom left, and other configuration details on the right.

On the bottom left, let's configure the graph. In the Data Source, switch from "--Grafana--" to "Prometheus," and then in the Prom Query window, type this:

```
rate(prometheus_http_request_duration_seconds_count[5m])
```

On the top right, change the title from "Panel Title" to "Prometheus Requests," and click Apply on the very top right.

Now we can see the new graph, but we're looking at the last 6 hours. In the top right, click 6 hours, and change it to the last 5 minutes.

On the top right, click the plus button to add another panel. Select the data source as before, and enter this query:

```
process_cpu_seconds_total
```

Set the panel title, and click apply. On the top right, click the Save icon to give this new dashboard a name and save it.

We created a new dashboard, but this takes a bit of work to dial in all the metrics just right. Let's pull in a prebuilt dashboard from the community.

On the top left, click the plus button, and choose import. In the box prompting for URL or id, enter id 1229. At the bottom, choose the Prometheus data source, and click import.

We can look through the gallery of community-contributed dashboards at `https://grafana.com/grafana/dashboards`, and specifically look at this dashboard at `https://grafana.com/grafana/dashboards/1229`. Right now, this dashboard is pretty sparse because this will show details about Docker. Let's get Prometheus to monitor Docker Desktop.

## Monitoring Docker

In the terminal, hit Ctrl+C, and then run

```
docker-compose down
```

This stops both Grafana and Prometheus, but because we've saved their data into Docker volumes, when we start it back up, the metrics and dashboards will still be there.

Open up the Docker settings by clicking the whale icon (bottom right task bar for Windows, top right menu bar for Mac) and choosing settings. Inside the Docker Settings section, add these lines if they don't exist already:

```
"metrics-addr": "127.0.0.1:9323",
"experimental": "true"
```

Ensure that all lines in the JSON file end in a comma except the last line. These lines tell Docker Desktop to expose a Prometheus sink. Click Apply & Restart.

Why didn't we use port 9090 to match other Prometheus work? We used port 9090 as part of the docker-compose file, so we'd get a port conflict on the public side of the Docker router. The Docker docs[6] use port 9323 for metrics, so it seems a good random choice.

Now that Docker Desktop is exposing Prometheus metrics, browse to `http://localhost:9323/` and take a look. Yeah, that's a big pile of metrics.

Open `prometheus/prometheus.yaml`, and let's add the Docker target. The file now looks like this:

---

[6] `https://docs.docker.com/config/daemon/prometheus/`

```
global:
  scrape_interval: 15s
  evaluation_interval: 15s

scrape_configs:
  - job_name: prometheus
    static_configs:
    - targets:
      - 'prometheus:9090'

  - job_name: idonotexists
    static_configs:
    - targets:
      - 'idonotexists:567'

  - job_name: docker
    scrape_interval: 5s
    static_configs:
    - targets:
      - 'host.docker.internal:9323'
```

Why did we use `host.docker.internal` rather than localhost? Localhost from our local machine will work just fine because of the magic of the Docker router in Docker Desktop. But localhost from the Prometheus container is itself. This magic word works great on Docker Desktop for Windows and Mac to get from a container inside Docker's virtual network back to the host computer.

Now that we have the Docker target configured, let's fire up Prometheus and Grafana and take a look. From the terminal running in the metrics folder, run

```
docker-compose up
```

Once it's running, browse to `http://localhost:3000`. Log in with the username admin and password admin, and from the list of dashboards, click Docker Engine Metrics. That looks much better. We can now see a lot of metrics about our Docker Desktop engine. When finished browsing, in the terminal, hit Ctrl+C, and close it down by running

```
docker-compose down
```

Prometheus and Grafana are great for monitoring systems. Now let's add Prometheus monitoring to the Google Location service.

# ASP.NET Prometheus Sink

In Chapter 4, we built a microservice to get distance given two addresses. Let's add Prometheus metrics exporting to this service. With the Prometheus sink in place, we'll be able to visualize the health of the microservice, understand how normal processing works, and identify then alert on unusual activity. We'll start by harvesting all the usual ASP.NET metrics, and then we'll add some custom metrics.

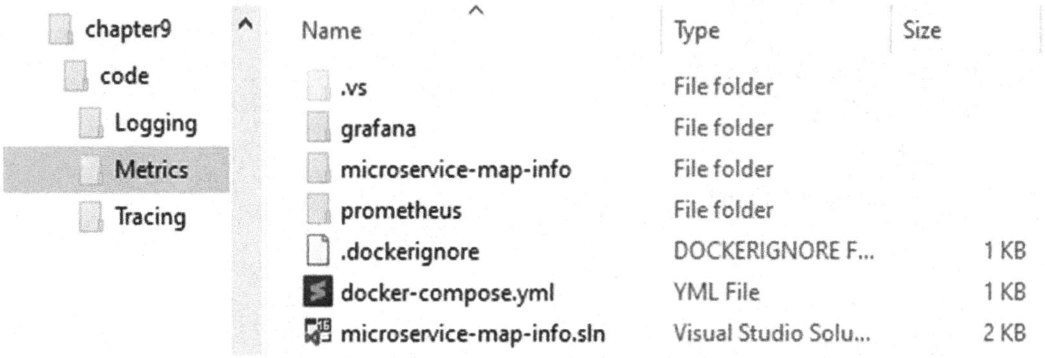

| | Name | Type | Size |
|---|---|---|---|
| chapter9 | .vs | File folder | |
| code | grafana | File folder | |
| Logging | microservice-map-info | File folder | |
| Metrics | prometheus | File folder | |
| Tracing | .dockerignore | DOCKERIGNORE F... | 1 KB |
| | docker-compose.yml | YML File | 1 KB |
| | microservice-map-info.sln | Visual Studio Solu... | 2 KB |

***Figure 9-3.*** *the new microservice-map-info folder copied from Chapter 4*

Copy microservice-map-info.sln and the microservice-map-info folder from Chapter 4 and set them inside the metrics folder, as shown in Figure 9-3. Then open microservice-map-info.sln in Visual Studio. In the Solution Explorer, right-click the microservice-map-info project, and choose Manage NuGet Packages. Click the Browse tab, search for `prometheus-net.AspNetCore` and install it.

Next, we'll configure the Prometheus sink.[7] Open `Startup.cs`. In the Configure method at the bottom, add these two lines:

```
public void Configure(IApplicationBuilder app, ...)
{
  // ...
  app.UseRouting();
  app.UseHttpMetrics(); // <-- add this line
  // ...
  app.UseEndpoints(endpoints =>
```

---

[7] https://github.com/prometheus-net/prometheus-net

```
  {
    // ...
    endpoints.MapControllers();
    endpoints.MapMetrics(); // <-- add this line
  });
}
```

The first line we add captures all the ASP.NET metrics, and it's important that it's after `UseRouting()` so it can capture the controller details. The second line we add exposes the /metrics endpoint so Prometheus can consume the metrics.

Next, we'll capture the metrics from `HttpClient` in the `ConfigureServices` method:

```
public void ConfigureServices(IServiceCollection services)
{
  // ...
  services.AddHttpClient("googleApi", client =>
  {
    // ...
  }).UseHttpClientMetrics(); // <-- add this line
  // ...
}
```

With all these in place, start debugging the API in Visual Studio or VS Code and browse to `https://localhost:5001/metrics`. That's great to see all the metrics there. Browse to `https://localhost:5001/swagger`, click Try it out, and run the service a few times. Then return to `https://localhost:5001/metrics`, and you can see the new details in place. When finished, stop the debugger.

Next, we need to containerize this service, add it to the docker-compose file, and launch all the pieces together.

Let's add a `Dockerfile`. In the Solution Explorer, right-click the microservice-map-info project, choose Add, and from the next menu, choose Docker Support. We're using Linux containers, so choose Linux in the OS selection box. This adds a `Dockerfile` and a `.dockerignore` file. We could trim these files down to make them more efficient and less confusing, but they'll work as is for now.

The next stop is the `docker-compose.yaml` file, where we'll add the details necessary to build this container and run it alongside Prometheus and Grafana. Add the microservice-map-info content into `docker-compose.yaml`:

```
version: '3'

services:
  prometheus:
    # ... omitted for brevity ...

  grafana:
    # ... omitted for brevity ...

  microservice-map-info:
    build: microservice-map-info
    ports:
      - 80:80

volumes:
  # ... omitted for brevity ...
```

The last stop is to tell Prometheus how to monitor this site. Because we named the container microservice-map-info in the docker-compose file, the URL to the metrics from the Prometheus container's perspective is `http://microservice-map-info:80/metrics`. Open `prometheus/prometheus.yaml` and add the content for microservice-map-info:

```
global:
  # ...
scrape_configs:
  - job_name: prometheus
    # ... omitted for brevity ...

  - job_name: idonotexists
    # ... omitted for brevity ...

  - job_name: docker
    # ... omitted for brevity ...
```

```
  - job_name: microservice-map-info
    static_configs:
    - targets:
      - 'microservice-map-info:80'
```

We've added a Prometheus sink to the ASP.NET service, we've added the ASP.NET project to the docker-compose.yaml file, and we've told Prometheus how to query it for details. Let's fire it all up and take it for a spin.

From a terminal in the metrics folder, start it all by running

```
docker-compose up
```

Once it's all running, head to http://localhost:80/swagger, click Try it out and execute the service a few times to build up some interesting metrics. Then head to http://localhost:9090/. See any new metrics in the list? How does the Targets list look?

Now let's head to Grafana on http://localhost:3000/ and graph these metrics. Once logged into Grafana, click the plus on the top left and choose import. Add dashboard id 10427, choose Prometheus at the bottom, and choose import. Add another dashboard and choose id 10915. Then look through other community dashboards at https://grafana.com/grafana/dashboards and import a few more interesting dashboards.

When finished, stop the containers from the terminal:

```
docker-compose down
```

## Custom Metrics

Now that we've got all the standard metrics collected, let's look at the business value of these metrics. Looking at the microservice-map-info, it consumes the Google Maps Geolocation API. Google throttles the use of this service per API key, so it would be helpful to know how many times we call the API to ensure we're not abusing this limited resource.

Load microservice-map-info.sln in Visual Studio, open the Services folder, and open DistanceInfoService.cs. Let's add a Prometheus metric to count the number of API calls.

At the top of the service, define and initialize the counter

```
public class DistanceInfoService : DistanceInfo.DistanceInfoBase
{
  private static readonly Counter googleApiCount = Metrics.CreateCounter(
    "google_api_calls_total",
    "Number of times Google geolocation api is called.");
  // ...
```

Why is this counter static? Open up Startup.cs, and in ConfigureServices, we note that this service is defined as Scoped. A scoped service means a new instance will be created for each request, and at the end of the request, the instance is garbage collected. We don't want our Prometheus metrics to only last for a single request. By defining this counter as static, we'll have one metric for the entire application regardless of which request calls it.

Inside the GetMapDistanceAsync method, increment the counter right before the call to execute the request:

```
public async Task<GoogleDistanceData> GetMapDistanceAsync(...)
{
  // ...

  googleApiCount.Inc(); // <-- add this line
  var response = await client.SendAsync(request);

  // ...
}
```

Now let's fire it back up with the new metric in place. From the terminal:

```
docker-compose build && docker-compose up
```

We need to rebuild the container because up will only validate the container is present, not that it's up-to-date.

Log in to Grafana at http://localhost:3000/ and create a new panel, capturing the metric we just added:

```
increment(google_api_calls_total)
```

It could be interesting to extend this further to capture histograms of request durations, counts of request successes, and failure reasons, both HTTP status codes and Google API result statuses. See if you can add these additional metrics to the microservice and display the details in the Grafana dashboard.

We've captured metrics, and so we now know how many times it happens. But what led up to this? And what happened next? For that, we dig into tracing with OpenTelemetry.

# Tracing

Distributed tracing is the process of gathering the user's path through various services. Kathy, the Code Whiz developer, has been tasked with adding visibility into the call chains of various services. We'd like to know when the monolith calls into the Google Maps API microservice, what parameters are passed, and the system results. For this, we'll leverage OpenTelemetry.

How does it work? How do we keep track of the user's progress as it traverses between functions in our app and between services in our software? A correlation id. A correlation id is a unique id tied to this request that we can use to tie all the elements of this request together. We can grab all the traces that have the same correlation id, and we know they're part of the same request. We can ignore all the traces that have a different correlation id, knowing they're part of a different request. We may choose to pass this correlation id between services as an additional HTTP header.

What happens if we run two tasks in parallel? How do we keep the correlation ids separate if they originated with the same original request? That's where we upgrade to trace ids. A trace span represents the current work being done. This span has a unique id, and it optionally has a parent trace id. As we traverse the system, each piece of work we'd like to track will start a new span, inheriting the previous trace as its parent trace id, and building a new unique trace id for this piece of work.

This creates a nested tree of spans where each links back to the parent based on matching the parent trace id. We can imagine this tree looks a lot like a Git history tree or a histogram's dataset.

OpenTelemetry's instrumenters keep track of the spans and automatically grabs the parent trace id as it begins a new span to track the new work. OpenTelemetry uses the `traceparent` HTTP header[8] to pass data between services. Much like the HTTP header that sets the Content-Type, telling the target system we'll send JSON or XML, the `traceparent` header tells the new microservice the current trace id. The target system can then create a new span and correctly set the parent trace id.

---

[8] https://www.w3.org/TR/trace-context/

# About OpenTelemetry

OpenTelemetry has emerged as an industry-standard mechanism for logging, tracing, and metrics. .NET 6 builds support for OpenTelemetry into pre-existing .NET base class libraries. We can use OpenTelemetry to add tracing to our application.

OpenTelemetry began as an effort to unify OpenTrace and Google's OpenCensus. It has since grown to a CNCF[9]-backed project to include metrics, tracing, and logging. There are implementations for Spring, ASP.NET Core, Express, Rust, Java, Ruby, Python, and more. OpenTelemetry provides options for logging, metrics, and tracing. Unlike Prometheus, in OpenTelemetry, all data is pushed to the provider.

As of this writing, OpenTelemetry's .NET implementation focuses almost exclusively on tracing. The .NET implementation adapts .NET concepts into OpenTelemetry concepts, providing incredible backward compatibility and system visibility for this new technology. The system still functions the same, but concepts are renamed. For example, in OpenTelemetry, a "span" identifies work being done, including start and end times, attributes or tags describing the activity, and the parent activity that spawned it. In .NET, Span<T>[10] means something completely different. Therefore the .NET OpenTelemetry implementation calls this an Activity.[11]

# Add OpenTelemetry to .NET

We'll begin with the microservice we created in Chapter 4 to get the distance given two addresses. In our examples, we'll push the data both to the console and to Jaeger, an open source tracing visualizer. We'll leverage Docker to host both the service and the visualization dashboard.

Tracing maps calls between services, so we'll create a console application that'll call the web endpoint every few seconds. This will allow us to visualize the calls between services. After we experiment with this technique, we could easily apply OpenTelemetry both to the monolith and to all the microservices so we can harvest the full call stack throughout the application.

---

[9] CNCF is the Cloud Native Computing Foundation. See also https://www.cncf.io/

[10] https://docs.microsoft.com/en-us/dotnet/api/system.span-1

[11] https://github.com/open-telemetry/opentelemetry-dotnet/blob/main/src/
OpenTelemetry.Api/README.md#introduction-to-opentelemetry-net-tracing-api

Navigate to the microservice-map-info.sln from Chapter 4 and open it in Visual Studio.

Add a new console application to this solution, and name it microservice-map-tester. We did this a few times in Chapter 4, so refer to this chapter for detailed instructions.

Inside the new project, open `Program.cs` and replace the Main method with this code:

```
public static async Task Main(string[] args)
{
  HttpClient httpClient = new HttpClient();
  string mapInfoUrl = configuration.GetValue<string>("mapInfoUrl");
  httpClient.BaseAddress = new Uri(mapInfoUrl);

  while (true)
  {

    Thread.Sleep(5000);

    try
    {
      string originCity = "Topeka,KS";
      string destinationCity = "Los Angeles,CA";
      var res = await httpClient.GetAsync($"/MapInfo/GetDistance?" +
        "originCity={originCity}" +
        "&destinationCity={destinationCity}");
      string data = await res.Content.ReadAsStringAsync();

      Console.WriteLine($"Response: {data}");

    }
    catch (Exception ex)
    {
      Console.WriteLine($"{ex.Message}\n{ex.StackTrace}");
    }
  }

}
```

This code will call into the mapping service every 5 seconds.

Right now, this code doesn't run correctly because we're reading the mapping service URL from the configuration. We need to pull the setting from the configuration because it'll change between our local environment, our docker-compose setup, and the production server. If we were in a web project or a worker service, we'd have a HostBuilder that would automatically add configuration details from each source. In this case, we need to build this up ourselves.

At the top of the Main method, add this configuration initialization:

```
public static async Task Main(string[] args)
{
  var envName = Environment.GetEnvironmentVariable("ASPNETCORE_ENVIRONMENT")
    ?? "Production";
  var configuration = new ConfigurationBuilder()
    .SetBasePath(Directory.GetCurrentDirectory())
    .AddJsonFile("appsettings.json")
    .AddJsonFile($"appsettings.{envName}.json", optional: true)
    .AddEnvironmentVariables()
    .AddUserSecrets(typeof(Program).Assembly, optional: true)
    .AddCommandLine(args)
    .Build();

  // ... code omitted for brevity ...
}
```

This configuration initialization will grab data from many places, including the appsettings.json file, appsettings.Developmment.json, or appsettings. Production.json file, environment variables, user secrets, and the command-line arguments. In a web project, this logic is all contained in the Host. CreateDefaultBuilder(args) method call.

To make this configuration work as expected, we need to add the NuGet packages that include these. Right-click the microservice-map-info project, choose Manage NuGet Packages, and install these packages:

- Microsoft.Extensions.Configuration.CommandLine

- Microsoft.Extensions.Configuration.EnvironmentVariables

- Microsoft.Extensions.Configuration.Json

- Microsoft.Extensions.Configuration.UserSecrets

Copy the `appsettings.json` file from the microservice-map-info project and paste it into the microservice-map-tester project. You could also copy the `appsettings.Development.json` file if you choose.

Inside `appsettings.json`, delete `googleMapsApi` section, and add a new string for the `mapInfoUrl`. The final file looks like this:

```
{
  "Logging": {
    "LogLevel": {
      "Default": "Information",
      "Microsoft": "Warning",
      "Microsoft.Hosting.Lifetime": "Information"
    }
  },
  "mapInfoUrl": "https://localhost:5001"
}
```

Now that we have a console app to call our microservice, let's run it and make sure everything works.

Right-click the solution and choose Set Startup Projects. In the list, set both projects to Start and click OK.

Start debugging the solution by choosing Debug menu ➤ Start Debugging or pushing the green play button.

From the console output, we can see we're calling into the map info microservice. It calls Google Maps and returns the results. Now let's add OpenTelemetry to both projects so we can watch the calls flow between the services.

Right-click the microservice-map-info project, choose Manage NuGet Packages, and install these NuGet packages:

- OpenTelemetry.Exporter.Console

- OpenTelemetry.Exporter.Jaeger

- OpenTelemetry.Extensions.Hosting

- OpenTelemetry.Instrumentation.AspNetCore

- OpenTelemetry.Instrumentation.Http

We don't need to install the OpenTelemetry package itself because each of these packages depends on it.

The first two packages are exporters. OpenTelemetry pushes the data to any location that we configure. In this case, we'll configure it to push both to Jaeger, the open source tracing dashboard, and to the console. We could also push the trace details to other systems like Zipkin or Prometheus or cloud platforms like NewRelic or Azure App Insights.

The other three packages include functions to harvest trace details from various sources. The Hosting and AspNetCore packages grab details from the web server while Http grabs details from the HttpClient class that makes a request out to Google Maps.

With these five packages installed, we're ready to add the code to use them.

All of the main trace harvestings are configured inside Startup.cs. Open Startup.cs, and let's add code to harvest traces.

At the top of ConfigureServices, add this code:

```
public void ConfigureServices(IServiceCollection services)
{
  var jaegerHost = Configuration.GetValue<string>("openTelemetry:jaegerHost");
  services.AddOpenTelemetryTracing(builder =>
  {
    builder
      .SetResourceBuilder(ResourceBuilder
        .CreateDefault()
        .AddService(_env.ApplicationName))
      .AddAspNetCoreInstrumentation()
      .AddHttpClientInstrumentation()
      .AddJaegerExporter(options =>
      {
        options.AgentHost = jaegerHost;
      })
```

```
    .AddConsoleExporter();
  });

  // ... code omitted for brevity ...
}
```

Use Visual Studio's lightbulb to add these two using statements: `using OpenTelemetry.Resources;` and `using OpenTelemetry.Trace;`

The first line pulls the URL of Jaeger from the configuration.

Next, we rig up OpenTelemetry. We start by creating a `ResourceBuilder`. By default, OpenTelemetry shows the application as "unknown_service." Here we're setting the application name from the environment. We could also hard-code it or set it from config.

Next, we add a bunch of trace instrumenters. We'll hook up to ASP.NET's middleware pipeline to get the URL, controller, and action for each request. We hook up to `HttpClient` to catch the URL, headers, and return status code of outbound requests.

Next, we configure the exporters – where will it send the metrics? In this case, we export both to Jaeger and the console. We probably only need one destination in a production scenario, but while debugging, it can be handy to export the data twice. If we were to be a bit more robust, we'd likely only add the Jaeger exporter if the `jaegerHost` config value was set.

This code doesn't quite compile yet because we're reading from _env, but this is currently injected into the `Configure()` method. Move this dependency from the configure method to the constructor, and set a private property. The new constructor now looks like this:

```
public class Startup
{
  private readonly IWebHostEnvironment _env;

  public Startup(IConfiguration configuration, IWebHostEnvironment env)
  {
    Configuration = configuration;
    _env = env;
  }

  public IConfiguration Configuration { get; }

  // ... code omitted for brevity ...
```

Now that we have OpenTelemetry installed into the microservice, let's add the Jaeger URL's configuration value. Open `appsettings.json` and add these lines at the bottom:

```
"openTelemetry": {
  "jaegerHost": "localhost"
}
```

Add a comma after the `googleDistanceApi` section to make it valid JSON.

This microservice is done. Let's rig up OpenTelemetry to our tester project too.

Like we did for the map-info project, we'll start with NuGet Packages. Right-click the microservice-map-tester project, choose Manage NuGet Packages, and install these NuGet packages to power the tester. This list of packages is slightly different from the other list because we're not in an ASP.NET project:

- OpenTelemetry.Exporter.Console

- OpenTelemetry.Exporter.Jaeger

- OpenTelemetry.Instrumentation.Http

Inside `Program.cs` in this tester project, add this code after the configuration section:

```
public static class Program
{
  public static async Task Main(string[] args)
  {
    var envName = Environment.GetEnvironmentVariable("ASPNETCORE_ENVIRONMENT")
      ?? "Production";
    var configuration = new ConfigurationBuilder()
    // ... code omitted for brevity ...

    // Add these lines:
    var jaegerHost = configuration.GetValue<string>("openTelemetry:jaegerHost");
    using var tracerProvider = Sdk.CreateTracerProviderBuilder()
      .SetResourceBuilder(ResourceBuilder
        .CreateDefault()
        .AddService(typeof(Program).Assembly.GetName().Name))
      .AddHttpClientInstrumentation()
```

```
  .AddJaegerExporter(options =>
  {
    options.AgentHost = jaegerHost;
  })
  .AddConsoleExporter()
  .Build();

HttpClient httpClient = new HttpClient();
// ... code omitted for brevity ...
```

In the same way, we defined the OpenTelemetry tracing configuration in the ASP. NET project, and we defined both the exporters and instrumentation details. We're overriding the default service name of "unknown_service" with the assembly's name.

Next, we need to add the settings into `appsettings.json`. Open up the test project's `appsettings.json` and add the `openTelemetry` section:

```
"openTelemetry": {
  "jaegerHost": "localhost"
}
```

We now have OpenTelemetry in place. Let's run it and see how it looks.

In the Solution Explorer, right-click the solution file, choose Set Startup Projects, choose Multiple Projects, and verify both projects are selected.

Then start debugging the solution.

In the console output we see activity messages like this:

```
Activity.Id:              00-8343d3a08cd8276108939d4a50b2309f-2af1291d92810529-01
Activity.ParentId:        00-8343d3a08cd8276108939d4a50b2309f-7818926375a69b3d-01
Activity.ActivitySourceName: OpenTelemetry.Instrumentation.AspNetCore
Activity.DisplayName: MapInfo/GetDistance
Activity.Kind:            Server
Activity.StartTime:       2021-10-01T20:01:33.6323228Z
Activity.Duration:        00:00:00.1768398
Activity.TagObjects:
    http.host: localhost:5001
    http.method: GET
```

```
http.path: /MapInfo/GetDistance
http.url: https://localhost:5001/MapInfo/GetDistance?originCity=...
http.route: MapInfo/GetDistance
http.status_code: 200
otel.status_code: UNSET
```
Resource associated with Activity:
```
service.name: microservice-map-info
service.instance.id: c4d9abf3-1590-4be0-b904-f33ff27d5a01
```

This is the OpenTelemetry metrics coming from the system. In this example, we see the message from microservice-map-info noting that the microservice received an HTTP web request. It routed it to the controller `MapInfo`, method `GetDistance`, and returned an HTTP status code of 200 after 0.17 seconds.

Of particular interest is the `Activity.ParentId`. This is the id logged by the microservice-map-tester service as it started the HTTP call. This correlation id allows us to link the two traces together. When we get to Jaeger, we'll see how we can use this to build a tree of network calls and system functions.

Let's add Jaeger, the tool for visualizing tracing trees.

## Visualize Tracing Trees in Jaeger

Jaeger is an open source tool for visualizing trace information. Jaeger not only can show the trace details, but we can also use it to visualize system dependencies. The easiest way to start Jaeger is via containers. Let's add Docker details to each microservice, add Jaeger to the mix, and start it all in Docker Desktop. If you haven't already, head to `https://docker.com/` and install Docker Desktop. Once it's running, we'll be able to launch all the containers we need.

Inside Visual Studio, right-click the microservice-map-info project, choose Add, and then choose Docker Support. In the dialog, choose Linux containers. This will generate a `Dockerfile` and `.dockerignore` file. We could definitely trim these files down to make them more efficient and less confusing, but they'll work as is for now.

Again right-click the microservice-map-info project, choose Add, and choose Container Orchestrator support; see Figure 9-4.

**Figure 9-4.** *Adding Docker support*

In the dialog, choose Docker Compose, and choose Linux containers; see Figure 9-5. This generates the `docker-compose.yml` file as well as a docker-compose pseudo-project.

**Figure 9-5.** *Choosing Linux container type*

Repeat these processes for the microservice-map-tester project: add Docker Support and add Docker Compose.

If we were to launch this right now, it would use HTTPS. Certificates are necessary for modern businesses, but we typically terminate the HTTPS connection at the Kubernetes ingress, and microservice containers communicate across HTTP.

In the Solution Explorer, click the triangle next to `docker-compose.yml`, and open the `docker-compose.override.yml` file.

Delete the line that says - "443."

Adjust the ASPNETCORE_URLS line only to include the HTTP line.

Here's the adjusted file:

```
version: '3.4'

services:
  microservice-map-info:
    environment:
      - ASPNETCORE_ENVIRONMENT=Development
```

```
    - ASPNETCORE_URLS=http://+:80
  ports:
    - "80"
  volumes:
    - ${APPDATA}/Microsoft/UserSecrets:/root/.microsoft/usersecrets:ro
    - ${APPDATA}/ASP.NET/Https:/root/.aspnet/https:ro
microservice-map-tester: {}
```

Next, let's add the Jaeger container into the docker-compose file.

Open up docker-compose.yml, and add these details for the Jaeger container at the bottom:

```
jaeger:
  image: jaegertracing/all-in-one
  environment:
  - BADGER_EPHEMERAL=false
  - SPAN_STORAGE_TYPE=badger
  - BADGER_DIRECTORY_VALUE=/badger/data
  - BADGER_DIRECTORY_KEY=/badger/key
  - BADGER_SPAN_STORE_TTL=8h
  - COLLECTOR_ZIPKIN_HTTP_PORT=19411
  volumes:
  - badger_data:/badger/data
  - badger_key:/badger/key
  ports:
  - 6831:6831/udp # Microservices publish events here
  - 16686:16686 # Browse to http://localhost:16686/

volumes:
  badger_data:
  badger_key:
```

This is YAML where whitespace is significant, so ensure the first jaeger line is indented two spaces to line up with microservice-map-tester a few lines above it and ensure volumes is not indented at all. The subsequent lines for each section are indented two more spaces. It will fail if the file has a mix of tabs and spaces or the indentation isn't exactly two spaces.

We expose two ports for Jaeger: 6831, where microservices publish events,[12] and 16686, where we'll browse to see the dashboard.[13]

We also need to configure both microservices to override the Jaeger URL and the microservice-map-info URL. In both `appsettings.json` files, we assume all services are on localhost. Inside the docker network, the URL to Jaeger is `http://jaeger:9831/` because the service name is jaeger.

Inside `docker-compose.yml`, add this environment section to both services:

```
services:
  microservice-map-info:
    # ... code omitted for brevity ...
    environment:
    - openTelemetry__jaegerHost=jaeger
    depends_on:
    - jaeger

  microservice-map-tester:
    # ... code omitted for brevity ...
    environment:
    - mapInfoUrl=http://microservice-map-info
    - openTelemetry__jaegerHost=jaeger
    depends_on:
    - microservice-map-info
    - jaeger
```

The `depends_on` sections are helpful but not required. It tells docker-compose to wait for the other service to start before starting this service.

Why did we set the environment variable as `openTelemetry__jaegerHost` rather than `openTelemetry:jaegerHost` as specified when we read it? Environment variables don't generally like having weird ASCII characters in them. ASP.NET provides this handy "double-underscore"[14] trick to avoid the colon in the environment variable name.

Now with everything in place, let's start this project with Docker Compose.

---

[12] https://www.jaegertracing.io/docs/1.6/deployment/#agent

[13] https://www.jaegertracing.io/docs/1.6/deployment/#query-service--ui

[14] https://docs.microsoft.com/en-us/aspnet/core/fundamentals/
configuration/#environment-variables

Open a new terminal or command prompt in the directory with the docker-compose.yml and microservice-map-info.sln and run

```
docker-compose up
```

If everything starts correctly, we'll see Docker continuing to run, and the console output from each of the three containers will start flowing into the console.

Open a browser to http://localhost:16686/.

On the left, in the Service menu, choose one of the services and push search at the bottom.

On the right, we see a list of traces that are involved in this service.

Choose one of the traces and click it to get to the details.

You'll now see a similar screen, as shown in Figure 9-6.

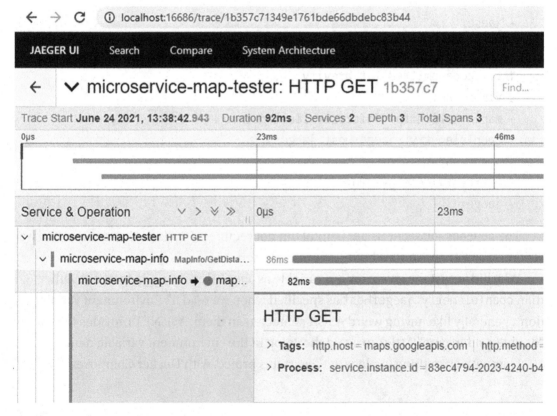

***Figure 9-6.*** *Jaeger dashboard trace detail shows the nested tree of spans*

In this picture, we can see that microservice-map-tester calls microservice-map-info and that microservice-map-info calls maps.google.com. Click each of the spans, and we can see the details associated with that work. Click the arrow next to Tags and Processes, and you can see specific labels showing details about the request, the response, the duration, etc.

When finished exploring, stop all the containers from the terminal. Hit Ctrl+C to stop the current process and then type

```
docker-compose down
```

We now have all the default trace details harvested in Jaeger. How do we add our own traces and spans?

## Custom Metrics

In the OpenTelemetry setup, we've hooked into the Jaeger and Console exporters and hooked up instrumenters to the standard behaviors. What if we want to capture our own metrics? Kathy, the Code Whiz developer, is tasked with adding specific details about the locations we ask for and the Google Maps response code. Let's add the custom trace and spans, or in .NET terms, the activity and tags.

In the microservice-map-info project, in the Services folder, open the DistanceInfoService.cs file.

At the top of the class, add a static ActivitySource:

```
public class DistanceInfoService : DistanceInfo.DistanceInfoBase
{
  private static readonly ActivitySource activitySource =
    new ActivitySource("microservice_map_info.DistanceInfoService");
```

This ActivitySource is static because we want exactly one for the entire lifetime of the application. If we were to create a new ActivitySource for each instance, we could easily overwhelm OpenTelemetry with trace instrumenters.

In the constructor, we pass a unique name. By convention, we can use the full namespace and class name. Optionally we can also pass a version as the second parameter.

In the body of the `GetMapDistanceAsync` method, add this call to get the activity:

```
public async Task<GoogleDistanceData> GetMapDistanceAsync(string
originCity, string destinationCity)
{
  // ... code omitted for brevity ...
  using var activity = activitySource.StartActivity("GoogleMapsAPI");
  var googleUrl = $"?units=imperial&origins={originCity}" +
  // ... code omitted for brevity ...
```

We want to put this at the beginning of the work we want to track. In this case, it makes sense to put it right before forming the URL and calling Google Maps. We add using here, so it'll automatically end as the method finishes.

The activity might be null here. As noted in the documentation, if there's no exporter listening for trace events, .NET can optimize the execution by not returning an object.[15] For this reason, we'll use the null coalescing operator introduced in C# 6.[16]

Add these two new lines to add the tags showing the source and destination of the call:

```
using var activity = activitySource.StartActivity("GoogleMapsAPI");

activity?.SetTag("google.originCity", originCity); // <-- add this line
activity?.SetTag("google.destinationCity", originCity); // <-- and this line

var googleUrl = $"?units=imperial&origins={originCity}" +
```

These tags are free-form values. We can add tags for any interesting behaviors we'd like. In this case, we want to capture origin and destination cities, but we really don't want to log the API key in the trace details.

Let's add one more tag for the results:

```
var distanceInfo = await JsonSerializer.DeserializeAsync<GoogleDistanceData> ...
activity?.SetTag("google.status", distanceInfo?.status); // <-- add this line
```

---

[15] https://docs.microsoft.com/en-us/dotnet/core/diagnostics/
distributed-tracing-instrumentation-walkthroughs#activity

[16] https://docs.microsoft.com/en-us/dotnet/csharp/language-reference/operators/
member-access-operators#null-conditional-operators--and-

That's it! We've created a new Activity (span) and added custom tags to it.

In the terminal, rebuild the containers:

```
docker-compose build
```

Then run the new setup:

```
docker-compose up
```

Browse to Jaeger at `http://localhost:16686`, pick a new trace, and you can see the new span and tags.

Tracing can be an effective tool for discovering and auditing the relationships between components. In this section, we used OpenTelemetry to gather trace details and send them to Jaeger, an open source tracing visualizer. Unlike other OpenTelemetry implementations, .NET's implementation uses existing .NET classes with slightly different names from the official OpenTelemetry concepts. Hooking into the existing tracing system allows OpenTelemetry visibility into much older content than would be possible with a brand-new library.

# Effective Monitoring

Understanding the health of a system of interrelated microservices is more than merely collecting all the system's logs, metrics, and traces. We also need to balance the frequency and detail of content with the usefulness of this data.

When gathering health data, it's easy to log too much, spam the logs, and make them useless. For example, a message with hard-coded values such as "here" or "executed this line" may be really helpful when writing the code but is really unhelpful when trying to diagnose a failure. If the content only includes hard-coded values like this, it's likely not a good message, and this code should be removed.

What is valuable data to save in logs, metrics, and traces? Save contextual data. Include the clues you'll need to understand how you got here, what options the user chose, and the operation results. Include extra detail in exceptional cases like stack traces and inner exceptions.

When writing logs, metrics, and traces, you may consider capturing:

- In the data tier, log SQL queries, query parameters, runtime duration, and any errors returned by the database.

- For REST queries, grab the URL, HTTP method, relevant headers, and the return HTTP status code and deserialized status message.

- For long-running tasks, log the start and end time and the number of items to process.

- In all logs, metrics, and traces, capture the currently authenticated user, the date and time of the event, the duration, the environment name, the current application name and version, and other system context. For example, the line number in the stack trace isn't that helpful without the product version number, release date, or Git hash to help find the correct version of the file.

- When capturing exceptions, grab the exception message, possibly the exception type, the stack trace (or at least the top file and line number), and loop through inner exceptions doing the same.

- For unique exceptions, grab additional details. For example, for an `AggregateException`, grab all the exceptions in the `InnerExceptions` list.[17] For `HttpRequestException`, harvest the `StatusCode`. For `DbUpdateException` coming from Entity Framework, grab details from the `Entities` list.

What data should we avoid saving? We shouldn't save anything that's hard-coded, redundant, or sensitive.

Avoid writing logs, metrics, and traces that include:

- Don't capture messages like "Here," "Did the work," or other hard-coded messages that don't include context.

- Don't include sensitive data, including API keys or passwords, social security or credit card numbers, personally identifiable information, or other sensitive data. Logging this data may increase the scope of a system audit to include the security of the logging platform.

---

[17] `https://docs.microsoft.com/en-us/dotnet/api/system.aggregateexception.` `innerexceptions#System_AggregateException_InnerExceptions`

- Don't include the list of items searched. For example, if looking through a list of offices or countries, we only need the item we searched for and the fact it wasn't found. If we also log all the options, we'll get a lot of unhelpful matches when searching the logs for these office addresses or country names.

- Filter out noisy messages from underlying systems. For example, it can be helpful to grab the current URL passing through ASP.NET, but it isn't helpful to log each middleware function's input and output parameters. It's helpful to know what parameters we passed to the PDF generation library, but it isn't helpful to get all the state changes inside the library if we treat the library as a black box.

As our health monitoring strategy matures, it can be helpful to publish deployment dates and versions, together with the Git hash of the software that produced this version. For example, if we notice that all system metrics are slower after the deployment, we can deduce there's a performance regression in this version. If we notice fewer failed requests, we know that we've correctly solved the issue. If we notice the volume of logs dramatically increases with a new version, we know there's likely a problem to address.

Finding the correct balance of message detail and helpfulness is a continuous process of refinement. We likely won't get it right the first time, but we can continue to refine our logging, metrics gathering, and tracing systems to ensure these systems are valuable debugging tools.

# Debugging with Logs

How do we diagnose a system failure if we can't hook up a debugger? What if the cause of the failure has since disappeared? The messages we have captured from our system health monitors can be useful debugging tools if we've configured them correctly. Let's walk through a scenario where we can use logs to debug a failure.

Kathy, the Code Whiz developer, notices a problem with the system. In the Grafana dashboard, she finds an increase in HTTP 500 errors indicating the maps microservice is failing in some cases. She's tasked with diagnosing and correcting the failure. With the test data she used to build the service on her local machine, the system works just fine. Now what?

Inside Grafana, Kathy creates a custom graph from the Prometheus data. She graphs the HTTP 500 errors over time and notices a correlation: the failures always seem to happen at 4 pm on Thursdays. Now what?

Do we add additional "it got here" messages and deploy a new version to production before next Thursday? This is hardly a robust and deterministic solution. Let's find a different solution instead.

Kathy pivots over to the Serilog files and looks through the error messages from last Thursday. Unfortunately, 80% of the logs are identical stack traces. These logs aren't very helpful. Kathy adds a new task in Jira to better handle these errors, possibly avoiding logging the stack trace and instead a unique message pointing to this section of code. Sadly, she concludes that the Serilog logs aren't helpful in their current state. The only piece that's helpful is Serilog recorded the inbound URL of the message that began this work. From the query string parameters, she now has the source and destination cities.

In the code, Kathy fires up the mapping microservice in Visual Studio, browses the Swagger test page, and plugs in both cities. "Still works on my machine." That wasn't it.

Kathy pivots over to Jaeger to look at tracing information. She zooms into last Thursday and identifies a trace that matches the inbound URL. From the nested trace tree, Kathy can see that Bob from accounting launched the request. He often catches up on the week's orders on Thursday afternoon. Could this be relevant?

As Kathy traverses up and down the trace spans in Jaeger, the innermost span has a tag that clues her in. Adding the Google results as a custom tag to the OpenTelemetry setup is really paying off. In this case, the results returned from the Google Maps API are OVER_QUERY_LIMIT. Here's the cause.

It appears our business is doing so well that we've exceeded the API limits of Google Maps. That's a good problem to have. So how do we monitor this limited resource? We could add specific metrics to count usage of this limited resource that could flow into Prometheus and get graphed in Grafana. We could add caching to the maps-info microservice. After all, the distance between two addresses won't change, given the same road conditions and closures. Kathy creates a few more tasks in Jira to address these changing business requirements. In the meantime, Kathy suggests that Bob complete the orders each day until the developers can add these new changes.

The scenario we explored here used the system health metrics to diagnose a system failure. Each of the components is helpful in painting a picture of the system's health and in diagnosing its failures.

Metrics are really helpful for learning about current or impending failures. These measurements over time can help us understand what normal looks like and help us discover when the system is not functioning normally. Over time, we'll learn what metrics are helpful, and we can add or remove metrics to get the proper visibility into the system.

Traces are really helpful for learning about the impact of interrelated systems. We can follow a single user's journey through each of the microservices and dependencies in the system. We can understand how the authentication state can impact web requests and how parameter validation failures can lead to system instability in downstream systems.

Logs are really helpful in digging into the specifics of a failure. The stack traces, system state variables, and other contextual information give us enough detail to recreate the problem – even if we can only do so in our minds. We can return to the code, write a failing unit test, and prepare a proper correction with this information.

Using all these systems to help us "debug with logs" is a really helpful and powerful technique. When systems are designed to expose the correct level of detail, it can be easy and joyful to diagnose system failures. By comparison, if we fill the health monitors with lots of noise, they can be burdensome to use.

In each development sprint, it's often helpful to find the noisiest, unhelpful message in the logs or traces and remove this message. After we've done this a half-dozen times, the logs will likely be much more valuable.

Sometimes we need more details from the systems to diagnose a specific issue. We can turn up the log level for a time to capture additional detail. We saw how we could configure Serilog to ignore content in some namespaces and to default to Information-level messages and greater in other namespaces. In some scenarios, it may be helpful to identify a specific namespace and turn up those logs to Debug. But be diligent in turning them back down when finished, or else the next time you're using the logs, they'll be overrun by irrelevant noise.

# Summary

In this chapter, we looked at ensuring services are healthy. We learned about logging for capturing events, tracing for capturing the relation between events, and metrics for capturing system state over time. Each of these data sources can tell different parts of the story, allowing us to easily monitor the services and debug error failures. We saw how the built-in ILogger<T> can easily capture content and how Serilog can redirect this data to other systems. We saw how classic monitoring tools like Prometheus and Grafana could capture metrics. We also saw how new systems like OpenTelemetry allow us to level up our view of the system. We ensured the logs are useful by adding context and eliminating excess noise.

# Index

293

© Sean Whitesell, Rob Richardson, Matthew D. Groves 2022
S. Whitesell et al., *Pro Microservices in .NET 6*, https://doi.org/10.1007/978-1-4842-7833-8

Printed in the United States
by Baker & Taylor Publisher Services